GOSSY

THE AUTOBIOGRAPHY

GOSSY

THE AUTOBIOGRAPHY

JEREMY GOSS
with Edward Couzens-Lake

AMBERLEY

I dedicate this book to Maggie, Joseph and Jacob.
You are my love and my life.
Also to my mum and dad – Joy and Bob. My brothers,
Mike and Tim, and sisters, Jen and Jayne.
Thank you for creating the foundations
that I have always stood upon.

First published 2014

Amberley Publishing
The Hill, Stroud
Gloucestershire, GL5 4EP

www.amberley-books.com

British Library Cataloguing in Publication Data.
A catalogue record for this book is available from the British Library.

ISBN 978 1 4456 1901 9 (print)
ISBN 978 1 4456 1912 5 (ebook)

Typesetting and Origination by Amberley Publishing.
Printed in the UK.

CONTENTS

Foreword
by Mick Dennis

What happens next? It is the question about footballers that has always intrigued me. They spend their boyhoods fantasising about being professionals, they fill their adolescent years by working hard to make the most of their talents and opportunities and, finally, they 'make the grade'. They experience the full-on commitment of a career in the game – with its insecurities, its rewards, its extremes of joy and despair – and then, some time in their thirties, it's all over.

They probably have more than half their lives ahead of them. So what happens next? How do they cope with the abrupt change and the thought of those years stretching ahead? What do they do?

I once asked the question to an ex-player soon after he had retired from the game. He had captained and scored for his country at a World Cup and been adored by the supporters of the club where he spent most of his career.

He told me, 'When it all ends it is hard. It is very hard. In fact it is a scary time. I was thinking, "What am I going to do for the next twenty or twenty-five years?" I wasn't only thinking about what I would do for money. I was thinking "What am I going to do with every day?" There are a million good things about being a footballer, but the one downside is that it finishes so early.'

Another London-based footballer I knew well went on to have a very good spell as a coach of a top club; a good, but exceptionally brief spell. The manager was sacked, and my mate was dismissed too. He ended up with a window-cleaning business. He had contracts for a lot of big offices – and there's nothing wrong with cleaning windows – but it is a very different life from running out onto a pitch to do something you love with the roaring acclaim of tens of thousands of fans.

I still see him from time to time. And of course, we talk about his playing and coaching days. That's how it is for ex-footballers. They've provided memories for thousands of people, and years later, the memories are what folk want to talk about.

Life moves on for most of us. But footballers are always being prompted to relive events from their twenties and thirties. Down the decades, the same conversations and the same memories.

Now think about Gossy, the subject of this fond biography by my friend Ed Couzens-Lake. Gossy has had to cope with all that – the question about what to do with the rest of his life, the sudden adaption to very different day-to-day experiences and the constant reminders of his old life. But for Gossy, that last aspect has been even more marked, because we all remember one moment in his career – that goal. He did so much more in his playing career. He has done so much since it ended; I don't know any other ex-footballers who have become charity fundraisers. Yet he is defined forever by one moment – that goal.

It was a gloriously improbable goal, a spectacularly successful piece of impromptu football brilliance. It was the very kernel of the greatest night in the history of Norwich City FC. It is etched indelibly in the memory of all who saw it. It is part of the fabric of English and European football.

So it is not too shabby a moment for which to be remembered! But what happened next? What happened before it, come to that? What about Gossy, the England schoolboy international? What was that like? And what was it really like that night in Munich? And what about when Gossy was eking out the last days of his career at King's Lynn? There are so many questions.

I am profoundly glad that Ed is the guy who asked them, because that ensures the answers will be diligently reported and interpreted, by someone who is seeped to his core with affection for football and for Norwich City.

Ed is a student of the era in the club's history when Gossy's goal wrote such an extraordinary chapter. He has written fascinatingly about the era, describing how football was on the cusp of changing forever, because the new Premier League was beginning to reshape it entirely.

But Gossy's story isn't just a football tale. It is an engrossing human story, with universal truths about life. It's about toiling away for nearly thirty years to become an overnight success. And, of course, it's about what happened next.

Mick Dennis
Daily Express Football Correspondent and Broadcaster

Prologue
by Edward Couzens-Lake

I first met Jeremy in 2007 after I'd arranged with him to do an interview for *Backpass* magazine. It remains one of the most enjoyable I have ever done with anyone. He immediately came across as a genuinely modest and self-effacing man, one who was grateful of what he had in life and deeply appreciative of the things that we normally take for granted, like family, friends and being content with not only who he was, but what he had been and the journey that his life had so far taken.

Needless to say, I liked him immediately. It was refreshing to talk to someone who, for me, reached some great and hugely memorable heights in his football career and yet went to great lengths to emphasise how they were part of a team effort, the culmination of all the hard work he and his fellow professionals had put in at Norwich City over the years, and that he was just one of them. For him, it was a case of being in the right place at the right time and enjoying the rewards that all that hard work had brought them.

He described football as his passion, speaking fondly of it and the moments of fame and glory that it brought him, swift to lavish praise on the people he says did so much to help him achieve those heights. His mum and dad, his brothers and sisters and a teacher, who for many years sent him some money to put towards a new pair of football boots. Then people at Norwich City – Ronnie Brooks, Ken Brown, Dave Stringer and Mike Walker, the man who he says 'had total faith in me'. Teammates as well, notably Bryan Gunn, Mark Walton and Rob Newman.

And most of all his wife, Margaret, who, along with their twin boys, Joseph and Jacob, are the epicentre of Jeremy's life today, tomorrow and for always. His love and devotion to them is total, they are the most precious things in his life, not the great goals he has scored or matches he has played in, nor the souvenirs he has collected as part of his time in the game. His idea of heaven is a Saturday afternoon spent with his family. It could be anywhere. Walking on the beach, perhaps, or just exploring somewhere new. Just him, Margaret and the boys.

A little over two decades ago, my idea of heaven, together with many thousands of other Norwich City supporters, was watching our side complete the very first season of the Premier League, playing football that had a certain *joie de vivre* about it, and with freedom of spirit and expression, daring, as the saying goes, to win. At the end of that 1992/93 season, we dared to finish in third place in the Premier League. If we were to do that today there would probably be a public enquiry about it.

Jeremy played a full part in that memorable season, plus the campaign that followed, one which included memorable goals at Leeds and Liverpool, as well as the three he scored in the UEFA Cup. So rapid was his elevation to star performer and BBC 'Goal of the Month' winner that people thought he must have dramatically risen from the Norwich ranks, a young tyro elevated to the first team and taking his chance, one for the future if ever there was one. Chelsea and Benfica certainly seemed to think so as, following Jeremy's goalscoring exploits against Bayern Munich, both were reported to be preparing multi-million-pound offers to Norwich for his services.

Yet the truth of the matter is that Jeremy scored that vital equaliser against Bayern at Carrow Road in November 1993 nine and a half years after he had made his first team debut for the Canaries. He was twenty-eight years old and had previously made, in the nine seasons prior to that opening Premier League campaign, just sixty-eight first-team starts for the club – an average of just over seven a season.

And that, just as much as all the goals and the glory we are all a lot more familiar with, was the story I wanted to tell. It was the motivation for my constantly asking him to sit down with me and tell it. The Premier League exploits, the UEFA Cup nights, the internationals with Wales are all included, of course they are. But so is this lesser known part of Jeremy's stories – the early rejections, the transfer requests, the time spent in the reserves, all of the frustrations, the anger and, at times, the loneliness and near despair. All of that is as important a part in his life as the goals and glory. We've tried to tell it as it is here. We hope you enjoy it.

Edward Couzens-Lake

1

The Rejects Club

It was absolutely the last time I'd walk back, defeated, into a manky, stinking changing room to the accompaniment of a bored coach going through the motions, queuing for a cold shower whilst he banged on about our performance, on autopilot as usual. 'You were crap today lads.' It meant nothing, I'd heard it all before. But I was never going to hear it again. Because, with the end of that game had also come the end of my career as a professional footballer. I was done in. Knackered. Finished.

The referee finally, and oh-so-thankfully, raised the whistle to his frigid lips to bring an end to the game.

And with that signal I finally stopped running, put my hands upon my knees and stared down at the cut-up, muddy and sodden pitch, steam cascading from my tired and soaking body, physical proof of the effort and commitment I'd put into my game. Again.

Yet, as it dissipated into the crisp air, a little of my spirit, previously so indomitable, seemed to drift away with it. I stayed in that position for a few more moments than maybe I would have done normally, lost in my thoughts – or, rather, one single, overriding thought: that, with that final whistle, I realised I no longer cared. In fact, I was long beyond caring and probably had been for some time. It was only now, standing there, in my sweat-soaked, steaming shirt, staring at that mud, that I began to realise it. Mind and body were numb, fingers brittle with the cold, lungs aching with the effort of the last 90 minutes. Momentarily, I put my feelings to one side and focused on recovery, breathing heavily and deeply into my worn-out lungs, watching that sweat cascade from my head and drip down onto the tips of my boots, the boots which claimed they would make you play like Bryan Robson but which had, in harsh reality, cut like razors into my blistered feet for most of the second half.

As life steadily, painfully, began to creep back into me, I stood up straight and, legs aching, began to walk off the pitch, oblivious to the few players that were still around me, chatting, griping, groaning and bitching. The things all footballers do. Especially the bitching. And, as I trudged towards the tunnel, I vowed to never again be part of yet another crap and totally meaningless football match.

Never again would I have to bust my gut trying to impress anyone who might, by some miracle, have actually cared, by covering every blade of grass on every inch of a nothing pitch, in a nothing game, played out in front of a nothing crowd. This grim realisation was almost a triumph, a release. My pace quickened with the thought I could walk away from all this, that it was a pivotal moment in my life. It was absolutely the last time I'd walk back, defeated, into a manky, stinking changing room to the accompaniment of a bored coach going through the motions, queuing for a cold shower while he banged on about our performance, on autopilot as usual. 'You were crap today lads.' It meant nothing, I'd heard it all before. But I was never going to hear it again. Because, with the end of that game had also come the end of my career as a professional footballer. I was done in. Knackered. Finished.

This was what the constant grind of reserve team football did for you, or it had done, finally, for me. The Ressies. It's the graveyard of professional football, a vast and endless plain where thousands of dreams have been laid to rest. Now it was my turn. Except I was already there as I'd played in so many reserve team fixtures I felt as if I was 6 feet under. Buried and gone.

Here lies Jeremy Goss. The perpetual reserve. Well, so be it. I was packing it all in because, for all of my hopes and dreams, I was getting nowhere. In fact, at twenty-three years of age, I was going backwards, running away from the so-called 'beautiful game' that had been part of me since I was six years old. A football career seen out and finished on that horrible, sloping pitch at Manor Ground, the dilapidated home of Oxford United. Football and I had fallen out for good and, come the dawn (which would be a bright new one for me), I was going to see Ken Brown, my manager at Norwich City Football Club, and ask for my contract to be ripped up so I could walk away a free man. Then, I was going to become a professional ironman triathlete and run around the world. And to hell with the 'beautiful game'.

So what changed and what lured me back to all of that? What was it that dragged me, kicking and screaming, from those bleak days as a season-ticket holder in the Norwich City 'stiffs', to a first-team regular? What was the inspiration behind my being able to turn my professional life around from going absolutely nowhere to those glory nights in Munich and Milan, to unforgettable goals at Elland Road and Anfield, two of the mightiest stages in the game? How did I get from Manor Ground anonymity to Munich hero?

This book is my story about my time. It's about Jeremy Goss, an average lad, nothing out of the ordinary, but one who chased and harried his hopes and dreams armed with nothing more than an already fairly beaten-up old bucket full of passion and respect. It's about a young man who arrived in the far-away and mysterious county of Norfolk back in 1981, a shy and naive character, prepared, if not exactly equipped, to compete in grown-up life and the tough, and occasionally very cruel, world of professional football. To play with the 'grown-ups' and look to compete with them on their patch and pitch, to be accepted as a boy among men and to cope with not only being constantly put to test, but, more often than I care to remember, put to the sword as well. My book will explain how I coped with failure, constant rejection and the fear of being labelled as 'not good enough' – both as a man and as a professional. But it will also reveal how being stabbed in the back, badmouthed, occasionally ridiculed, and plenty more, drove me on. It taught me not to quit and walk away, but to push forward and achieve regardless. It will also reveal how my absolute and unconditional obsession with training and practice ultimately saved my career and helped me survive in the world of professional football, one that doesn't so much exist behind closed doors. Doors that are triple locked with secured solid-steel barriers, into which newcomers are treated with disdain, while those that don't meet the entry qualifications are met with damning ridicule. It's an industry that is perceived, more so today than it ever was, as one that is full of glamour and glory, of untold riches and opportunity, big houses, baby Bentleys and all the willing women you could ever want. But one that is, in truth, full of arrogance, sarcasm and selfishness. An industry that embraces the 'Billy big timers' who swagger with their overloaded ego and arrogance.

But you know what? Despite all I experienced, my love for life and the game burns ever brightly, and as strongly as ever. I look back at what I went through and achieved over the years, and I'm proud of what I did and how I coped. Maybe I didn't always make the right decisions, maybe if I had listened to what my dad used to say to me more than once, I'd have been another ex-footballer with a few trophies on the shelf and a few more quid in the bank.

But hey, it wouldn't have made half as good a story if it was purely about winning matches and trophies year after year after year, would it? It might even have been a bit dull. Now listen. This isn't a story about glamour and glory. Far from it. It's one about how sheer, bloody determination and enthusiasm got me through life and work then, just as it does today and every day. I have always been, and remain, a man with a high moral ethos, one who has built his life around a code of common and mutual courtesy and respect. Football has allowed me to experience many wonderful and sometimes completely euphoric emotions. It has also been the catalyst to some amazing lifelong friendships, some of those friends being people who have played alongside me in some of the world's best stadiums, alongside, or against, some of the world's best players. It sounds, in those few short lines, as if it has been nothing but a life of luxury, a bed of roses as some would dismissively say.

But it hasn't always been like that. Far from it.

2

Rejection

'Son, thanks for turning up today. But you will never be a professional footballer as long as you live. Get yourself off, get changed and off to the station, get yourself home and get yourself a real job.'

I remember wonderful sporting memories growing up, big moments that had an influential effect on my life and my future aspirations. One such moment was the FA Cup final of 1977. Manchester United (sorry but I was a fan back then) took on Liverpool at Wembley. My favourite United players – Gordon Hill, Stuart Pearson and the brilliant Steve Coppell – terrorised their arch rivals in front of 100,000 fans, going onto win the game 2-1. Immediately after the final whistle, my brother Tim and I proceeded to do the normal thing, jumping up and down on the settee for the next twenty minutes, singing at the top of our voices. I have to say, this was not the case for my other brother Mike. He was a Leeds fan so he left us to it. Needless to say, Mike has had very little to sing about, football wise, in recent years.

Another powerful visual moment for me was watching the 1978 World Cup finals in Argentina. I was thirteen years old and seemed to spend that whole summer staring at the living-room television in amazement at Mario Kempes, Karl-Heinz Rummenigge, Zico and Arie Haan burst into life, stamping their names into football history. I watched every kick of the ball during that competition, dreaming, as I did so, of playing in one myself one day alongside the best players in the world and the biggest stage the game has to offer.

Away from football and onto the athletics track, and my everlasting memories of that glorious sporting summer of 1981. Never mind the recent golden sporting summer of 2012, it was the personalities and moments of that time that matter to me. This was for good reason, primarily because of my all-time sporting hero, Sebastian Coe. He dealt in excellence and was the very best there was, in my opinion, at any time. There are, and there will be, athletes that run faster races, but at that time, for me, Coe was the best of then and now. He didn't mess about. The year was still young when he ran a new indoor world record at Cosford over 800 metres, with a time of 1 minute 46 seconds. In June, he went to Florence and added his own work of art to that very special city, with another phenomenal 800-metre time of 1 minute 41.73 seconds. At the time of researching and writing this book, it remains a British record, and is still the third-fastest time at that distance ever recorded.

I know this is my book but I could go on about Seb Coe for ages. I was a half-decent runner myself way back then, with a liking for both the 800- and 1500-metre distance races, as well as the more gruelling cross-country. In every instance, I tried to copy Seb's smooth and effortless running action, unfortunately without much success. He was my hero then and he remains so today. He, like I, was captivated, driven by the passion and desire he had for his sport. And he wanted to win. That is what I admired so much about him. Then and now.

Seb is a born winner, someone who knew only tough training would get him to the top. He worked hard, then harder, and he repeated the process constantly. In an interview he gave the *Daily Telegraph* only last year, he looked back on his training and said, '[I open a] training diary for any year between 1973 and 1990. I randomly select any day of the year, including Christmas Day, and survey the tortuous sessions set by my coaching team-and take comfort that I am not still doing it.'[1]

In other words, he devoted his whole life to training. Which is exactly what I did throughout my career. I knew what I wanted and I knew how I wanted to go about it. And it showed. Mike Walker saw it in me, he saw it so much that he said he wanted to build a team around me. He had that same attitude, he wanted to win and he wanted his teams to be full of winners. If he picked you out as someone who had that attitude, who had genuine honesty and could be trusted, someone who was prepared to run for him and to go above and beyond the minimum requirement, and someone who was desperate to succeed and be part of a successful team, then he would put all of his faith in you. He would let you know he was doing just that. When people place that sort of trust in you, more often than not, you'll do anything for them. Just ask Seb if you get the chance. I'm sure he'll agree.

Because of my love and obsession with sport, many of my memories growing up surround the sport events of any given year, rather than what I was doing myself. I think of the year, the sport, and then what I was doing, aside from watching it and idolising those who excelled at it. The sporting year I mentioned earlier for example, 1981, apart from Seb, there was Ian Botham, an easy scene-stealer at whatever he does. In the summer of '81, he seemed to win the Ashes for England almost single-handedly, ending the summer's Test series with 399 runs and 34 wickets. When he came in to bat, you knew he didn't hope he'd score a century. He knew he would. Just as he knew he'd take a wicket with every ball he bowled. If he didn't then he'd move on, knowing that he'd definitely get one with the next ball. And so on. What an all-rounder! He put fear into the Aussies by just having his name on the team sheet. And what confidence. He knew he was the best and it showed. The young Jeremy Goss, watching it all unfold on a little television in Folkestone, with his sporting-mad family, was very impressed.

Young Gossy was just as impressed with the achievements of Ricky Villa in that season's FA Cup final at Wembley. Remember it? It was between his team,

Tottenham Hotspur, and Manchester City, who were then managed by the former boss of Norwich City, John Bond. The first game had ended in a 1-1 draw, the abiding memory of that game being the sight of Villa, shoulders slumped and head down, trudging off the pitch in the middle of the second half to be replaced by Garry Brooke, someone who'd later go on to be a club mate of mine at Norwich.

You couldn't help but feel sorry for Villa. He was a makeweight in the deal that had brought Osvaldo Ardiles over to English football after the 1978 World Cup finals. Ossie was a superstar, a favourite throughout the English game, as well as at White Hart Lane – and rightly so, he was a class player. They even wrote their FA Cup final song about him. 'Ossie's going to Wembley' – it was awful! Mind you, they all are. But that was Ossie, big-name player, World Cup winner and one of the best in the world. He and his mate Ricky, 'the other one' who came along for the ride. Perhaps he'd played in that final in place of players as good as him, players who might have thought they were worth considering. And it looked as if he had blown it. I bet the likes of Brooke, as well as a few other players like Mike Hazard, or even someone who ended up a big mate of mine at Norwich, Ian Crook, were thinking 'hello, I might have a chance in the replay, maybe get on the bench'. Because it seemed clear that Villa had lost it, and that there would be no way Keith Burkinshaw, the Tottenham manager, would have picked him for the replay.

The fact that he did pick him shows just how effective it can be when someone has faith in you and your ability, making it very public that he believes in you 100 per cent. For me, this type of man-management will get a positive response every time. I've seen it myself. And that's exactly what Keith Burkinshaw did with Ricky Villa in that replay. Despite the fact he had a bad game in the original match and got pulled after just over an hour, despite the fact that he was seen trudging off that Wembley pitch with what looked like tears in his eyes; his manager believed in him, told him so, picked him for the replay. Now, you think of what an impact that would have had on Villa. He's feeling lower than a snake's belly, rock bottom, the worse day of his professional life in all probability. He thought he'd blown his Wembley chance and just wanted to take the first flight back to Buenos Aires – anything but be seen at the replay. But no, his gaffer has faith in him. 'You're playing Ricky because I believe in you. You're a great player. You've got the ability to go out and win us this match.' How can you not respond to that? Villa knew he was a good player – after all, he wouldn't have played in the World Cup and for Tottenham if he hadn't been. However, as good or great as you might be, you sometimes need that little 'pick me up', that little refresher course for the ego. The ability of a manager to motivate his players is crucial. Burkinshaw motivated him and gave him belief. And how was he rewarded? Two goals and a Man of the Match performance. His second goal at Wembley, the winner, is still one of the best you'll ever see. A great goal from a great player. And he knew it; he just needed reminding of the fact.

Some of the role models for the young Goss during those far-off sporting years were Coppell, Coe, Botham and Villa. The main features of what became a very significant few years for me; memories and achievements that are as fresh a part of my sporting memory now as they were then. Yes, I've got my own memories of moments that I played a part in. But I also remember those that were contributed by others as well. They became an extra motivation tool for me. I wanted to know what it was like to be the best. I wanted to feel, touch and taste sporting success like they had. They, and the great sporting memories that they created, acted as my inspiration to succeed in life, playing a very significant part in what drove me on to the next level in my footballing journey.

So, to the Manchester United class of 1977, to the great Brazil, and to Seb, Beefy and Ricky. Thanks for the memories lads, and thanks for the inspiration.

Despite all of that, there is one more powerful, abiding memory that I have of that time, one that is forever popping into my head, especially when I'm at the place itself. I bet you are thinking: Gossy, is this another of the world's great sporting venues, a stadium, an event, a venue where more of the great and good gathered to engage in sporting combat? Well no, it isn't. It's the humble surrounds of Norwich railway station. You may or may not know it. I've been there on countless occasions, many a journey of mine has started and ended there, many a friend met and picked up, else dropped off. It's part of my life; the way in and out of Norfolk for many people, part of their lives, and a place which always, even for a quiet city like Norwich, seems to be a hive of activity.

It was at that station, back in the summer of 1982, where that young and somewhat nervous Jeremy Goss alighted, having sat a few moments earlier, with his face fixed at the window as he caught sight of the four floodlights that marked Carrow Road for the first time, barely half a mile distant. This was a place that I desperately wanted to call my footballing home. It is a memory as clear and sweet to me as any of those sporting moments that had gone before. Yet, despite all of the determination I had, and the faith I'd put in myself to succeed here, it was a very raw and nervous young man who joined all the other passengers snaking their way towards the ticket barriers. I had left the friendly and comfortable confines of Folkestone around five hours earlier that day, so it was a fairly long trip. Yet, as I stood and took in the Norwich air and steadied myself for what was to come. It seemed, somehow, as if I had travelled across countless international borders and time zones. It was all very new, very strange, and, if you really want to know, a little bit scary. But it was exciting as well. Because I was setting out on what I hoped were the first steps of a career with the local football club, known to all in the game as the Canaries, a club that, like the brightly coloured bird, were small and humble in stature, yet more than capable of fighting above their weight. A bit like me really. I was yet another seventeen-year-old who had left the family nest for the first time and was now looking to make his own way in life. Yes, I was sad to be leaving home. But I felt I was coming to the right place, to a football club that I hoped would welcome me, embrace me and give me a chance.

A football club that, like me, wanted success despite the odds. I was positive that now I was finally here, I'd do well. Everything just felt right, the place and the circumstances that had led to me being here on this day, from meeting chief scout Ronnie Brooks for the first time, to how my first trip had led to another invitation, this time to come back for a further five days. This was the beginning of a six-month trial where I would eat, drink and sleep football. What a chance.

It wouldn't be easy of course. I had done well to get this far. But now the really hard work began. The club had committed to taking me on for that six month spell, and now I was expected to pay back that faith by delivering. I had to prove it to every single person at the club, starting with the first-team manager and his coaching staff. I had to prove it especially to Ronnie Brooks and all the people who would, over the coming weeks and months, decide on whether I was good enough for their club. Would I just be another young wannabe footballer with stars in his eyes, fit only for a return ticket home and an all too familiar sentence that started with the words 'Sorry, but we think...'?

You didn't want to hear the rest of it. The route to Norwich had not been an easy one. I'd already heard variations on the theme of rejection. And more than once. I'd love to be able to say that Norwich City were the first name on my list, the first club I contacted and the only one I wanted to play for. But no. The Canaries were just another port of call on my nationwide tour to find a club that would give me a chance to prove myself, and show that I had both the skill and self-belief to become a professional footballer, to nail down my dream. Because I had 'previous'. I'd already played in, oh, at least 10 minutes or so of a trial game at the training ground of Aston Villa. A big club with a history to be proud of, with great players, managers and achievements on the football pitch. One of only five English clubs to have won the Champions League – or European Cup as it was then known. One of the best places you could go to, as a young footballer, to prove yourself, to show you had what it takes to make a career in the game. I mulled over the day I spent in Birmingham as I found my way to my digs, a day that had pretty much started as this one had. I left Folkestone early in the morning to make my way to the station, from which I'd head off into the great unknown. Trial games back in the early 1980s were nothing like the long and drawn-out procedures they can be today. There were certainly no academies, just the football club in question and its teams, the firsts, reserves, 'A', youth and schoolboys. If you made it through their schoolboy schemes, you'd be offered youth terms when you turned sixteen and, if you were still good enough, you'd be offered a professional contract when you turned eighteen.

If you weren't up to standard, then there was little ceremony or consideration for your feelings. You'd be informed of the fact and released, out of the club and on your way. Back then, coaches, at all levels of the game, would be regimental and harsh in their communication techniques, and would show little sympathy to anyone who they believed wasn't pulling their weight, or just wasn't good enough. With trials, such as the one I had at Villa, it was a case of just get them in, look at them, and, if they're no good, get shot of them as quickly as possible. Which is exactly what happened to me.

The funny thing is, as that trial game started, I'd felt great and soon got involved. I impressed in the short-passing drills that we all started with, but I was in for a very sharp and blunt shock during the five-a-side game that followed. Again, I thought I was doing well. I'd got some nice touches, made a few tackles, got my passes away to teammates and generally put myself about, hungry for the ball and desperate to show what I could do. And, with all that, my confidence grew and I looked to express myself a little more, to really make an impact. Things were going well.

Until, completely without warning, one of the coaches stopped the game and walks onto the pitch. Bloody hell, what's going on here, someone's blown it, has something happened, has that big lad chinned someone? No, wait. He's approaching me. What have I done? Hell, maybe I've done enough already, or perhaps he wants me to put a bib on and play for the other side for a while. They did that a lot in these sorts of games; it was a way of seeing how you coped with any situation, in this case from playing in a strong side to a weaker one that might be struggling to compete. So, with some anticipation as to what I would be expected to do next, I waited as he strolled over to me, looking him up and down as he got closer. He looked as if he was one of their top coaches, initials on his tracksuit top and everything, a different class. All the Villa gear, pristine and brand new, even his shorts were initialled. Decent physique, fit and confident. He reminded me of some of Villa's first team players I'd seen on *Match of the Day*, people like Dennis Mortimer, Gordon Cowans (and what a player he was) or Peter Withe. All top-class players at the time and with the honours to prove it.

The sights and sounds of Norwich faded as I recalled that moment with pin-sharp clarity. I was back there at Bodymoor Heath, that vast training complex of Villa's, remembering the thoughts that went through my head as he approached. Here he comes now, head up Gossy, look him in the eye, what's he going to say to me? Well I know one thing already. He sees me as a mate. He puts his arm around me and leads me to the edge of the pitch while the other lads carry on with their game. Instructions maybe, else he wants me to do a specific job. Perhaps he wants to run a few set plays by me?'

We're still walking, moving over to another grassy area near the training pitch. To be honest, I was getting a bit scared by now. Then he stopped and looked at me, unblinking, calm, practiced.

'Son, thanks for turning up today. But you will never be a professional footballer as long as you live. Get yourself off, get changed and off to the station, get yourself home and get yourself a real job.' Then he turned away and was gone.

And that was the end of my footballing career at Aston Villa. It lasted for ten minutes! As far as that coach was concerned, it was the end of my footballing career, period. That's not how I felt about the matter, not by a long way. I said thank you for their time, how much I'd appreciated them giving me a chance, and walked back to the changing rooms – alone. I might have looked back once, caught out of the corner of my eye, that same coach walking up to my mate, escorting him off the pitch as well. At least he'd know what was coming to him. As for me ... well, as far as I was concerned, my chance at Villa was over. But I didn't let it affect me. I let his opinionated little speech bother me for around 20 seconds and then I did what my dad would have done, and was always proud to see me do, and that was lift my head high and go away to prove that coach wrong. So I got changed and headed back to the station. But with one thought in my mind ... which club should I write to next?

As soon as I got home, I found some time to talk to my family, letting them know what had happened and what my thoughts and plans were. Positive ones, naturally. Like who shall we contact next, Dad, what other clubs might be worth a call? Because if you were a young player at the time, getting a trial with a club wasn't that difficult, crazy as that might seem. Providing you played the game at a fairly high level, as schoolboy or junior then, in the eyes of many of the coaches at the league clubs, you'd certainly done enough to warrant having a look at – or a very quick look at – as turned out to be the case at the Villa. The one way, the only way to get a look in, was to write to the clubs and ask for a trial. That's what I'd done for Aston Villa. You write the letter, put in some bits and pieces about yourself, your position, what level you'd achieved and so on, and you waited for a reply. More often than not, you'd get a standard letter back telling you, not asking or inviting you, but literally ordering you to be at such and such a place, at such and such a time, on such and such a date. The end. No choice, no options, no negotiation. Be here when we tell you or forget it.

And that was the gist of the letter I got from Villa. They, like all the other clubs, would have held structured trial days right through the year. On each of those occasions, they'd maybe take a look at a hundred or so kids, all starry eyed, all sure they're the next Tony Morley or Gary Shaw, two of the club's leading players at the time. So off I went, confident as hell, expecting a nice welcome from the Aston Villa coaches at the station before, perhaps, getting the chance to meet the manager Ron Saunders. He was renowned as a bit of a hard man, one who demanded and expected a lot of his players. But I was sure I could do my best and deliver to Mr Saunders. So, imagine my surprise when, after I'd found my digs in the city and made my way to the training ground (perhaps they'd forgotten to meet me?), there were all these other kids, crammed into this tiny, sparse changing room, a blur of muddy boots and sweaty tops with one loo between all of us. Football, glamorous? Of course it is.

I guess that day was pretty much like your first day in the Army might have been. A load of young lads nervous and uncertain of themselves, some taking up more time in that single loo than they might have normally done. We were all numbers in the same kit, reporting to some bored-looking bloke with a clipboard and a brusque manner that I, used to the polite and respectful manner in which my family treated everyone, found a bit out of order. 'Get over there, get changed, get on that pitch.' There was no welcome, no preliminary talk, no tour of the ground offered, or even a few words said about the club; what a great one it was, the history, the players. There was none of that. Just, 'get over there'. Yes, nice one mate. That's what you call a decent welcome, one to really make us all feel at home. I suddenly felt I had a lot to learn.

Time and time again, orders and instructions were curt, swift and cutting. We were all out on a pitch before we knew it and split into two teams. As you now know, I got around ten minutes before I was sent on my way, my mate who came with me maybe getting a minute more. Great. The day was nowhere near ended and we'd arrived, changed, played, changed, headed back, packed before we were on our way home again. And yes, while I did hold my head high and vow to prove them wrong, it was a kick in the nuts. So, in a gloomy mood, I got to the station and headed back south again on the train, staring out of the window as I listened to the silky voice of Journey's Steve Perry via my Walkman, through a pair of massive, clunky headphones. All I did for the entire journey back was mull the same words and phrases over and over again in my head. 'What have I done wrong, I didn't even get a chance to kick the ball, what was it about me they didn't like?'

It was rejection, *X-Factor*-style decades before that programme got on the air. And the bloke who'd given me the old heave-ho was a track-suited version of Simon Cowell. But I would prove him wrong. I just knew it.

Looking back at it now they must, of course, have seen something they didn't like, something down the line. Maybe it wasn't about the football at all; maybe they thought I was too small, too lightweight, not as assertive or physical as some of the other lads who were there. After all, I was a runner and covered miles and miles every day to make myself as fit as I could possibly be. Around 10, maybe 15 miles most nights wasn't a problem for me. And I'm serious! Maybe I was *too* trim, too skinny, not strong-looking enough? For a while, after he'd told me I'd never make it as a footballer, I'd actually believed it, for about 20 seconds remember. Then, I saw sense. I had a think and thought, well, hang about Gossy. There are other clubs out there. I'd keep at it, sending out a load more letters, see what came from those. And at least I knew what the procedure was now, aware of what these days would be like, and how single minded you had to be to cope with them, to stand out, to be noticed. I decided I wouldn't worry or take any notice of any of the other lads who were attending. I would focus on myself, my appearance, my game, my focus and, most importantly of all, my attitude.

Ultimately, maybe that's what helped me? Don't forget, I was still only sixteen. And yes, maybe some of those lads were better players than me. Maybe they were bigger, more skilful or more technically able. After all, I was a big fish in a small pond back in Folkestone. Now I was looking at a bigger ocean, swimming alongside a lot of sharks from all over the country. But I knew that very few would be as fit as I was. And they certainly wouldn't have my attitude or approach. They wouldn't have my positivity, my determination. And also, they couldn't compete with the way I presented myself, which was, again, testament to my family.

I was smart, upright, had good posture and was polite. Anything that helped me to stand out and get noticed. Pride, in other words. I knew all of that would get me a long way, and anything extra that was needed would come, there was no doubt about that, especially when I was being coached by professionals and playing in and among them. I'd absorb it all, I'd be a sponge. So, I got myself settled again and started writing to a load of other clubs. As I saw it, it was a lesson learnt, and, with some regained confidence, I would start all over again. As for my mate, the lad who came to Villa with me and got exactly the same response from that bloke in the tracksuit, what did he do? He believed in what he was told and packed it up, there and then. He got a job and moved on. Maybe that was the easy thing to do. But it wasn't for me. I hated the coach that day, arrogant and horrible. I wanted to prove him wrong.

The next club I got a trial with was Southampton – but only because they were the first to reply. Like Villa, they were in Division One, a good club with some quality players at that time. Kevin Keegan was there, the only man in football with a barnet as curly as mine. I got stick about my hair everywhere I went, because people were convinced I'd permed it. It was all natural, I promise. Anyway, Southampton had Charlie George and Alan Ball, and I was a similar sort of player to Ball – a busy midfielder, hard working with a desire to get the ball, win it, and get it to someone who could do something with it. Bags of energy and desire. Much later on in my career, I heard him make a speech at a sporting dinner at Carrow Road. He was a different class. Honesty like I had never heard before. I remember him saying, 'my job on the pitch was simple, chase the ball all day, get it and give it to my mates who could play football'. Wow. That modesty, that sincerity, immediately won my total respect for him.

They also had one of the big characters in the game – Mike Channon. In fact, when you look at it, they were full of characters, and big-name players with personalities to match. Keegan, George, Ball, Channon. How could a young footballer not improve by being at a club like that, surrounded by that type of player? It wasn't as if they didn't have some good, young players at the time. Danny Wallace was at the club, he was only a year older than me while Steve Williams had joined the club straight from school and was now on the fringes of the England team. And if he and Danny Wallace could do it, if they could prove they were good enough at that tender age to mix it with some of the greats, well, why shouldn't I?

They also had one of the game's great young managers in Lawrie McMenemy. He'd won the FA Cup with them (I remember it well. They beat 'my' team, Manchester United to do so) when he was still only thirty-nine, a ridiculously young age for a manager at that time. Yes, all things considered, Southampton seemed to be the perfect fit for me. The city was also not that far away from home. In fact, compared to Birmingham, it was just a short hop from Folkestone and all of my friends and family. Now, don't get me wrong, I was willing to go anywhere to play, even, as you'll read later, out of the country if necessary. But the fact that

Southampton only seemed to be 'down the road' from all of those near and dear to me was a help. So yes, this was a great club to be on trial with. I saw these players regularly on television and was in awe of them. But to watch such stellar footballing names on *Match of the Day* was one thing, the prospect of getting up close to them on a training pitch was another matter altogether. Suddenly, therefore, the prospect of this trial became quite a daunting one. I felt apprehensive, even scared to a point. And the stupid thing is, I don't know why. The shy, young Gossy who got embarrassed in the company of top professional footballers was an unwanted character trait that I had to securely lock away somewhere fast. So I did, there was no choice in the matter. And, bit by bit, the positive attitude and confidence returned. Saint by name and Saints by nature. It had a nice ring to it. Thus, full of confidence, I got all of my kit ready and made my way along the coast.

The whole day was, as I'd expected, pretty much the same as that I went through at Villa. Loads of lads again – maybe some of them had been at Villa on the same day as me? It was the same routine, the same hurriedly organised arranged match, the same track-suited members of the coaching team watching us. It was the same conclusion about me. Thanks for coming bla, bla, bla, however, in my opinion you do not have the requisite skills and ability, bla, bla, bla, to make it as a professional footballer. Bla, bla, bloody bla.

It must have been the standard quote that they all came out with at the time! Maybe they all learnt it in the classroom when they were doing their coaching badges, all Charles Hughes and his 'POMO' at that time – that's if some of them even had a qualification in the first place.[2] Perhaps they all read it from a whiteboard in unison. 'Now lads, you'll all have to go through this with the bloody kids when they all turn up to spoil your day, this is what you tell them'. 'Repeat after me "thanks for coming, however, we do not think..."' etc. There was nothing nice in it, nothing personal or positive, and nothing that I, or any of the other lads, could take away with us and store as a little bit of hope for the future. I wonder how many potentially great players were put off ever having a career in the game because they were told they weren't good enough, believed it, and moved on regardless?

Norwich City let a few slip through themselves. They didn't think Dion Dublin was good enough, releasing him in 1988 without him ever getting close to the first team. He was barely out of his teens and might have thought about packing it in, but he didn't and look at the career he ended up having, playing for clubs like Manchester United, Coventry City and Aston Villa. In fact, he ended up back at Norwich and ended his professional career two decades after the Canaries had originally let him go for nothing. Maybe bucking the trend, when he was released by Norwich, they put in a good word for him and gave him self-confidence and a reference to go with it. Knowing the club as I do, I'm sure they did as Norwich have always tried to do things the right way. But what if they hadn't and Dion had packed it in, him and countless others. Not because they had been written off, more the way it was done, the way a club dismissed you, said you weren't good enough and showed you the door, period. But then, most clubs would have released players who they didn't think were good enough. Look at Anthony Pilkington, he's played for Norwich City in the Premier League and represented the Republic of Ireland – yet he was let go by Manchester United when he was a schoolboy.

Thankfully, it's all done differently today. Don't get me wrong, clubs still reject players. But they do so in a way that gives them hope. They'll say that maybe this isn't the right time for them, but suggest that what they need to get back into their local team, playing regularly and keeping fit. They might suggest one or two things that they can work on, such as speed, agility, ball distribution and physique. They advise them that this isn't a final rejection or the end of their football careers, but that they are good players and that they will still keep an eye on them. That sort of approach makes such a difference to the lads trying to make it. It gives them something to build on, work towards and hasn't really cost the club anything.

It was wrong that one man could make the decision so suddenly and with little to go on, watching you in a quickly-organised game for all of ten minutes or so before giving it, in so many words, the old 'hey you're crap son, go on, get lost!' line. And it was tough for me to digest those words. But, like I said, it only worried me for a few brief seconds. Because I'd then be thinking of what I could do next.

I suppose the other thing to remember is that this all happened in the early 80s. There was a mix of two messages, one being the 'cruel to be kind' mantra that was especially popular in that decade, together with a little dash of 'welcome to reality'. And it had to be. The fashions, trends and music of the time were seen by many as being an affront to masculinity. A lot of lads were into New Romantic music – disposable glitzy pop like Duran Duran, Spandau Ballet and Visage. I hated '80s music and this 'new look' in all honesty, I was a rock teenager still trapped in the '70s. Some lads were even experimenting with make-up! This was in stark contrast to the set ups and coaching ethics of a lot of the clubs, and the hardened, experienced former pros who ran their schoolboy and youth teams at that time. Men were treated like men and expected to behave like them.

The chap who ran the Aston Villa Youth Team, at around the time of my trial, was Keith Leonard. He was probably not the man who gave me the old 'heave-ho', as trial matches were more likely to be judged by the club's less senior coaches. But, whoever it was, he had earnt the right to work in coaching (probably through playing rather than a bunch of certificates). So yes, it was tough, but Leonard and all the other coaches at the time would have thought it justified. And I'm not having a whinge about it. That's just how it was. Football was, and is, a tough industry where we had to grow up quickly, there was no choice. You adapted or you dropped out of the game. It's different today of course. Yes, it's still tough and players still drop out of the game in their hoards when they are fifteen, sixteen and seventeen years old. But at least the communication skills and the techniques used by today's coaches have improved, as has the terminology. So, thankfully, has the music!

At the time of the trial, I was going through footballing mill myself now, I had 'form', a footballing CV if you like. Two trials, two rejections. I left Southampton's training ground, got to the station and went through a well-practiced routine. I would find a seat, settle down and get the Walkman on. What was I listening to? Mostly the sort of stuff I still listen to today. Bands like Dire Straits, Journey, Queen or REO Speedwagon. More likely than not, it would have been ELO. The Birmingham-based band was huge at the time and their great album from 1977, *Out Of The Blue,* was certainly doing it for me back then. In my mind's eye, I was scoring great goals in big stadiums as the train sped me back to Folkestone, accompanied by Jeff Lynne singing 'Mr Blue Sky'. I didn't realise it at the time but this sort of visualisation to music would go on to play a big part in my matchday preparations. That song and the beat used to give me a real buzz. It still does.

The music cheered me up a little bit, which was just as well, as the worse part of these trips was still to come. It wasn't the rejection or the being turned away that got to me, it was having to go home and tell my family, all expectant and wanting to know how I'd got on, that I hadn't made it, stating 'guess what, they sent me home'. I felt I'd let them down. They'd all done so much for me, not just my mum and dad but also my brothers and sisters. Always there for me, just as they always have been and always will be, just as I will be for them. But, right then, right at that time when I had to come home feeling defeated, I felt as if I couldn't look them in the eye.

All I wanted to do was get writing again, contact a load of new clubs, and get another trial, then another, then another. I wanted to make it as a professional footballer. The journey home after a successful trial, now, that would be done in style. The ELO would be belting out big time that day, no question. So, I consoled my disappointment with Southampton by visualising another journey home, that would follow with a club wanting to take me back and sign me on. The thought of it put a big smile on my face. Because my time would come, I just knew it. And the biggest pleasure and biggest thank you I could give then would be to my family, for their support and their faith in me. They were the best family anyone could have with the best upbringing you can hope for. So, amid the disappointment and rejection, how lucky was I?

---

1   Sebastian Coe in the *Daily Telegraph* (www.telegraph.co.uk), 'Watching Mo Farah training reminded me of what it takes to be a Champion', 16 August 2013.

2   'POMO' – Positions Of Maximum Opportunity. Hughes, the FA's Director of Coaching, asserted that players would score if the ball was played into the 'POMO' enough times. He particularly stressed the importance of set plays and crosses into the penalty area.

3

Young Gossy

I fell in love for the first time. I've never forgotten that moment – you never do. The feel, the touch, the soft texture, the scent. A smooth skin, slightly yielding to the touch but not so delicate that you were afraid to let your fingers dance over its surface, its mysteries. I held it close, savouring the feeling and the expectation of what was to come, giddy with anticipation at this unravelling of the young Gossy's senses, this amazing discovery of something new and exciting. Yep, you're absolutely right. I was six years old and this was my first football!

Now I've told the world just how special my family are to me, I'd better expand on it and explain hadn't I? And it's important that I do because if it hadn't been for them then this book wouldn't have been written, and none of the defining moments of my career – Elland Road, Munich, Anfield etc. – would have happened. Yes, they are that important and that special to me.

So what about that upbringing? Well, it wasn't all that long ago remember. We're not talking about young Gossy being sent up chimneys or pushing his bike up the hill over the cobbles like the lad in the bread advert. As a matter of fact, I was an army brat. A lot of people will know what this means, but for those that don't, let me briefly explain. My dad was a colour sergeant in the Army, C-Sgt Goss of the Gloucestershire Regiment to be exact. He remains proud of the now disbanded regiment, and his time spent serving, as upright and respectable a man now as he was then. He is as respected and admired by me today as he has always been, a giant of a man who, together with my mum and family, have played a huge part in shaping me into the person I am today.

We were a very close family. We still are today. I'm so very proud of my mum and dad for all of their life achievements. Bringing up five children couldn't have been easy and, being a dad of twin boys myself, I more than appreciate all the difficulties they must have faced and gone through. They are exceptional people made of strong stuff, and they've been so resilient, so loving and so very compassionate to all of us. The opportunities and experiences that we have all had in life are down to the personal sacrifices that my parents have made. We are, and will always be, grateful and I am so lucky that they, along with my sisters, Jennie and Jayne, and brothers, Mike and Tim, have always been right at my side, helping me live out my dreams of footballing glory. They all live down in Folkestone now but I try to get to see them as much as I can. It's a long drive from Norfolk down to Kent, but I enjoy it and the time we spend together. It's nice that they've been able to put down roots and settle down because, let's face it, if you want a quiet and settled home life, then the Army is hardly the best environment in which to practice it. Because dad was serving under the behest of Queen and country, he had to be ready to move quickly, and quite often, with no notice. No arguments, just 'this is where you're going next, end of'. It meant that, wherever he was posted, my mum, brothers, sisters and I had to follow. So it wasn't at all unknown to come home from school one day and to see the big wooden packing cases all stacked up outside the front door, some of them already full, others with a few bits and pieces and one for my things. All of them with GOSS stamped on them in big, black capital letters. Their arrival meant one of two things. We were off somewhere new or we'd just arrived there, with the boxes reaching that destination just before us.

My whistle-stop tour of places to call home started in Cyprus where I was born, Dad serving out there with his regiment at the time. I'd love to regale you with tales and memories of life in the sun-kissed eastern Mediterranean but they are, unfortunately, somewhat insubstantial. Soon after my birth, at the British Military Hospital in Dhekelia in May 1965, all of the packing cases came out again, and the entire family, now self-labelled as 'The Magnificent Seven', or the 'nomads', were off on another European adventure, familiar to all of those who have experienced life in the services. I won't go into great detail about the ins and outs, and the pros and cons of each posting, but I will list them here as and when they happened just so you can get an idea of all of the moving around that we all, my parents most of all, experienced over that period.

From Cyprus, we moved onto Bodelwyddan, near Rhyl in North Wales for a few months, before moving up to Chester in Cheshire. From there, we moved to Berlin (in what was then West Germany) from 1967 to 1969; Shorncliffe in Kent from 1969 to 1972; then back to West Germany and Minden from 1972 to 1974. Then, from 1974 to 1977, we spent six months back in Wales, Cardiff this time, before eighteen months in Crickhowell in Mid Wales – part of the beautiful Usk Valley. From there, it was onto Weeton Camp in Lancashire, then Ballykelly in Northern Ireland, another eighteen-month posting. Once that posting was up, it was back to West Germany for a third time, with stays at Senden and Munster from 1980 through to 1982, before finally, ending up in Folkestone from 1980 to 1982. Busy times. By the time I arrived in Norwich at seventeen in 1982, I had attended one primary and five comprehensive schools.

It's a unique and wonderful experience for anyone to go through, especially, in my case, when you are so young. Different countries, languages, accents and cultures. So many different houses lived in, bedrooms slept in and adjustments to make. It may sound exciting and a world away from the sort of 'ordinary' childhood that many people will have had, with little or no change at home, school or among their friends. And yes, of course it was interesting. But there were plenty of daunting, even downright unpleasant experiences in the midst of it all. I made new friends easily and some became good friends. Then, all of a sudden, it was time to say goodbye to them and start the whole cycle off again. You mean to stay in touch of course – hasn't everyone been in that situation? I certainly said and thought I would keep in touch with some of them. But you lose contact eventually.

One of the most difficult things about moving was starting a new school. I always found being the 'new boy' very intimidating and often a little scary. And, if I'm honest, I was subjected to a little bit of bullying at all of them. This was standard procedure among the local lads, the self-styled 'governors' of the school finding out how big and hard the new Army boy was, the one who lived apart from everyone and everything else on the Army camp. This was never easy or pleasant to have to deal with.

When I was at school in Northern Ireland, this happened quite a few times. I have, for example, vivid memories of walking down one of those endless school corridors to go to a science lesson where, before I got there, I was confronted by four or five of the local lads, all leaning on one or the other side of that corridor and dishing out various levels of abuse to me as I approached. On this occasion, however, I decided not to turn around and walk in the opposite direction, as that would mean admitting I was scared of them – and hey – maybe I was. But I didn't want them or the school hearing all about it. So, I carried on walking, head held high, before, seconds later, my legs were kicked away from me and I was on the floor. I got up immediately and sprang at the ringleader, grabbing him around the neck and pushing him down to the ground where we started to scrap. Luckily for him, or maybe me, the fight was stopped almost as quickly as it had began, when a teacher arrived from nowhere and broke us up amid dire warnings as to what might happen to us if such an event occurred again. It would, of course. Such instances were not uncommon, and I quickly found out that I had to stand up for myself and not let these groups of lads pick on me every day.

I wasn't, and I am not, the kind of person who goes around looking for trouble but, at the same time, I knew I had to take whatever steps were possible to stand up for myself. Mike and Tim, my brothers, were always there for their little brother in the event of a skirmish or some pending aggro, and that was great. It was reassuring that if I had to send in the big tanks to help win the war, I could; but I preferred to fight my own battles even if it meant getting a bloody nose now and again. But that was what we were like as a family, always sticking up for and fighting for one another. We were never against each other. But don't all families do the same? And that includes the 'family' at a football club. Maybe the drive I had to stand up for myself and my family at such a young age stuck with me, and led to the reputation I had in my playing days as being 'Gossy, the great team player'. But when your teammates are also your family, you stick up for them as well. Going from school to school was also made difficult in academic terms. What was quite advanced at one school would be regarded as something for beginners at another. More often than not, I'd join a class and think I was set to get on, only to find out that what I had been doing was what they had done, mastered, and moved on from some time before. So there was always a lot of catching up to do.

Eventually though, Dad left the Army after completing twenty-two years of service, and the family decided to put down roots where his last posting had been, which was, of course, the town that was my first 'real' home – Folkestone in Kent. It's an old-fashioned seaside resort with lovely partially wooded cliff-top walks down to the beach. It's a bit sleepy now after the sad decline of the shipping trade which used to bring in a lot of wealth and jobs. I like it, as my family must do, as they've lived there for over thirty years now. I've some great memories of training and playing football there.

The hills that make up Folkestone Downs were magnificent locations to run around, their steep inclines providing the perfect place for me to have some real hardcore 'killer' sessions, the harder the better. But there is some gentle beauty about the place as well. There are lots of woods and hills, and, on the other side of town, the glorious pebbled beach at Sandgate, which does its best to keep the English Channel at bay, with only around 30 miles of it between the town and France. I had some seriously hard runs along that beach, especially during the summer months. One particularly mad one always springs to mind. I was running against Mike and Tim, except I was doing it in trainers while my brothers were in the car. They were fully up for the game mind you, keeping a nice slow pace alongside me for a while, but, steadily, going a little bit faster, encouraging me to keep up with them. I ran against them at around three quarters pace to begin with, then, went up to just under flat out before giving it everything I had for a mile. This meant Mike had to press down on the accelerator just that little bit harder. That was a particularly mad session but there were compensations. However battered and beaten up I felt at the end of them, there was always a dip in the deliciously cool sea to finish off with, and a nice, long, relaxing swim.

Although Norfolk is very much my home now, I have such fond memories of living down in Kent, along with all the other places we've lived in. One very vivid and fond memory is when I fell in love for the very first time in my life. It was a moment frozen in time that I've never forgotten – you never do. That all-over sensation of joy. The feel, the touch, the soft texture, the scent. Smooth skin, slightly yielding to the touch but not so delicate that you were afraid to let your fingers dance over its surface, its mysteries. I held it close, savouring the feeling, the expectation of what was to come, giddy with anticipation at this unravelling of the young Gossy's senses, this amazing discovery of something new, mysterious and exciting. Yep, you're absolutely right. I was six years old and this was my first football!

I can picture that ball in my mind now. It was nothing like the modern ones you see the professionals play with now. It was made of that hard leather that absorbs moisture if you're playing in the rain, so much so that the ball becomes almost impossible to kick. As for heading the thing, forget it. You had to be particularly careful not to head it where the big old laces that held the thing together were sticking out on the ball's surface, else you'd not only end up with a lace-shaped imprint on your forehead, but a mighty headache that stuck around for days. That ball. We went everywhere together, It was more than just a football, a toy, plaything. Whatever else you would want to call it, it became part of my life, my routine. If I wasn't kicking the thing against a wall then I'd be thinking about getting outside and kicking it against a wall.

Or, I would be having a game with my brothers. The problem with that, of course, is that it was 'my' ball and I became attached to it. So although I wanted them to play, I didn't want them to have the ball. Not at all. Ideally, for me in any hastily-arranged game of football with jumpers for goalposts, I'd have the ball all of the time. Should one of my mates find themselves, by accident, having it themselves, they would have to give it back to me immediately. Because I wanted it back again. I wanted to feel the enjoyment I got from running with it at my feet and keeping it from others. Get, give, get, give. This is something that became quite a pattern for me, and the football, as I went through my life. But all started with that old leather ball with the sticking out laces. Brian Clough once said of one of my old teammates, Gary Megson, that he 'couldn't trap a bag of cement'. That statement has gone down in football as one of the most cutting ever made. Trap a bag of cement? When that old ball was wet, it was like kicking one.

I remember it so clearly. Probably because I spent so much time wearing it out. That old ball was played with in hundreds of different places and in all types of conditions you care to name. Pouring rain, howling gales, snow, frost and heatwaves. During the summer, I used to play out in the sunshine and always got burnt in the process, the skin peeling off my back in great swathes. The ball got sunburnt too, big patches of the leather lining the size of 50p pieces coming away, which peeled off the surface. It soon got into a hell of a state with these bare patches where all those bits had come off. But that didn't matter to me. We were both a bit burnt, a bit sore, but we were brothers in arms that ball and me. It was mine, and there was little more that I loved at that time than spending time with it, practicing and perfecting little tricks and techniques, trying out new ones and honing them until I got it right first time, every time. Then I'd want to do it five times in a row, then ten, and twenty. I wanted it done perfectly on every occasion and with no mistakes. If I did make one, I'd start again, get it right this time. And I did. It might have taken a little while on some occasions, but I made sure I did it properly and I did it well. Then, I thought of something else to do and off I'd go again.

From all of that practice, all of those lessons I gave myself, those little routines and tricks I learnt to do hour after hour, week after week, from relentless experimenting and exploring, I discovered exactly how it felt to strike a ball well, to connect with the sweet spot. Then, I would practice more and more until I got it right first time and every time. The goal I scored for Norwich in that game at Bayern Munich's Olympic stadium came out of all that practice, all those volleys against a wall with that knackered, old football.

Moments like that, from all those hours and hours of work, were one of the rewards for all that commitment growing up. It was because I had been determined to get it right, to master all of the skills needed. Trapping the ball with both feet, controlling it as it came back off a wall towards me, running with it at my feet either in a fast, controlled dribble, or in and out of some traffic cones. Then, maybe dribbling it through and around some trees, running with it on pavements, going from one slab to another and trying not to knock people over in the process. My brothers and I would play headers and volleys, where you can only score a goal if it was a header or a volley. Maybe it was just another game to them, but for me it was serious stuff and so much more than just a kick about. It all helped give me the grounding and the basics required, as far as skill sets are concerned, that are so essential for any young footballer to have.

As a youngster, I was about average with regard to the technical aspects of my game, but I had a stack of weaknesses. My left foot was purely for standing on, and I might not have been the cleverest footballer, one with the ability to 'ghost' past players with both pace and trickery, but I had what the teachers and coaches were looking for. I was half decent at those basics with good technique, balance and posture. However, I firmly believe that the one ingredient that I possessed, more than many around me, was my outstanding hunger for the game, exemplified by all of this practice I was putting in. I wanted it more than most. I wanted it more than all the better players around me. I played with honesty, a big heart and showed the attitude of a winner. It was those traits, more than any other, which lifted me up the ladder.

It was important that I mastered all of those other arts of the game as well. Having the right body shape and balance is crucial for any footballer. Look at Ian Crook, who I used to play alongside at Norwich. Chippy is, without doubt, one of the most naturally gifted players I have ever played with. Unbelievably so. You could watch him shape up to make a pass and know from the shape his body would make as he played that pass that it could be analysed in the same way people slow down and look at a top golfers swing now. Because, for a footballer, having the right shape, in the execution and the follow through of the move, is essential, critical even.

Chippy had all of that when I played in the same side as him, but then he would have had it when he was ten and maybe even when he was younger than that. He would have been a regular first-team player at Tottenham with no problem, none at all. The only reason he wasn't was people like Ossie Ardiles and Glenn Hoddle played a similar game and role to Chippy at Tottenham. How unlucky is that? If they hadn't been there, he'd have been 'top man' at the club for a long time. It would have been Chippy, not Glenn Hoddle, dictating play at White Hart Lane, and maybe even for England.

For all of the skills and ability he had, he was struggling to get a game at Tottenham. Ridiculous. He'd signed for them as a schoolboy and had made his first-team debut against Liverpool when he was just seventeen. You don't debut for a club like Tottenham, and you certainly don't start your senior career playing against a team like Liverpool if you don't have something about you, and he did in abundance.

But it wasn't just me putting in the hours and the effort at that time. As I have already mentioned, my family were brilliant. They encouraged me, backed and supported me, drove me around wherever I wanted to go. Into my dad's car we'd get and off we'd go to a game somewhere, a trial or training, anything to do with my football. My dad's a very strong man, a tough character. I guess the Army made him that, his was a hard and very responsible job and he did it very well. I idolise him. He's mentally tougher than me. Maybe I could have done with some of that professional nastiness, that aggression that he had, which was essential for him as a colour sergeant in the Army. Time and time again, he's said to me ,'Jezz, you need to be more of a bastard in the game. Nastier, more aggressive.' And he was right. Maybe if I hadn't been a 'decent lad', too honest in my makeup, and I had been a tougher character like my brother Mike in my early days as a player, then I might have achieved something sooner rather than scratching around in the Ressies at Norwich year after year, sat eternally on the bench every week, I'd have been somewhere else, playing in the first team regularly and making a name for myself. Who knows. But you can't change who you are. Each and every one of us can look back at our lives and say 'should have done that', 'could have done this' and 'had a chance to do that'. But what's the point? What's done is done, and I'm more than content with my achievements and all that I have ended up with.

Don't forget, when I really came to everyone's attention for the first time with that volleyed goal at Elland Road against Leeds United in August 1993, a goal that won the BBC's Goal of the Month award, I wasn't some exciting young thing that had suddenly burst onto the scene. I was already twenty-eight and had been at Norwich for well over a decade. If I'd listened to Dad, I might have been somewhere else, playing in European football on a regular basis and sat at home somewhere, watching my first club play in Europe on my massive television set and feeling really pleased for them. But no. As I have already said, I don't regret anything and there is little that I would change. What's done is done and that was yesterday, what I can achieve for me and my family tomorrow is far more important to me now. Dad certainly knew his sport so I always took onboard his advice and opinion. His sporting speciality was cricket, and he was certainly regarded as a 'top sportsman' in that game. He was a fast bowler. I say 'fast' – but, actually, with his 30-yard run up he wasn't merely that – he was a bloody fast bowler. He played for all the Army cricket teams and firmly believed in ruffling up a few batsmen with his own version of bodyline bowling. He was also regarded as a tough sportsman for his natural ability in being able to knock people out in the boxing ring as a member of the Army and combined forces boxing team.

When he couldn't play, he managed. He put together a youth football team who were beating any and all of the adult Army teams that they came up against. So yes, he was a good sportsman, a good manager and an excellent motivator. And, with my character, he needed to be. He knew that I had to be a bit meaner, a bit more of a 'bastard' as he put it. He was right. My sisters, Jen and Jane, were always very fit and excelled at many sports, including athletics and swimming. My mum was, and is, a very strong swimmer and has completed many miles of swimming in the English Channel. She's tough too, even today I can't beat her at an arm wrestle!

My brothers were both handy players as well. Mike was a centre-forward – big, strong, and uncompromising, a bit like ex-Villa, Wolves and Everton forward Andy Gray. I've never known anyone as physically strong as Mike. He had, and still has, this amazing strength. He'd throw me and Tim around for fun, just as he would any centre-half that happened to get in his way. Tim, on the other hand, could play in any position at the back. He read the game well. He had that awareness, the anticipation that you need to play in those positions. They were both so good that I have little doubt that they could both, had they wanted, made it in the professional game. Yet, out of the three of us, it was me who decided he wanted to get his head down and try to get somewhere in the game, not just for me but for my family as well. I wanted it to be a shared success. So I'm part of a happy, fit and healthy family who'd always buck me up whenever I got back from a trial, else received a disappointment of one type or the other. 'Come on', they'd all say, 'brush yourself down and give it another go.' Mum as well. She has such tough mental strength. Her glass is never half empty, or half full for that matter. It's always full to the brim and overflowing. I don't think I've ever seen her down, low or depressed – or even just solemn. Just happy and positive *all* of the time. She's an incredible lady who has given me so much comfort and encouragement and I love her dearly. Little did I know, as I was building my career and dreams, just how much of it she would share with me, and the media attention it would command during my moments of European footballing glory.

Luckily for me, my efforts hadn't gone completely unnoticed. I'd been working my way up through all of my school teams, right the way back to playing for Crickhowell Primary School back in the mid-1970s. I played for all the secondary schools I went to, including those in Northern Ireland, where I made the first, big step forward as far as my fledgling football career was concerned. I was invited for trials with Coleraine, one of the country's top sides, as well as the Northern Ireland schoolboys. Nothing more came from either of those two games as Dad was then given the posting in Kent, which meant I wouldn't be able to take those opportunities any further. But it was nice to get the recognition and the chance to prove myself while we were out there, and it gave me the confidence to push on once the family had relocated to Kent. This kept up the momentum I was creating for myself with selection for Kent Schoolboys, Kent County Youth and, finally, the England Under-19 squad.

Ambitious and determined as I was, this one did come a little out of the blue! I'd arrived home one day to find a letter waiting for me. It was an invitation from the FA to meet up at the Lilleshall National Sports Centre in Shropshire, and join a big group of other young players from around the country to attend a five-day trial. But it got better! From all of us attending, they'd be looking to select a squad to represent England at Under-19 level in three games against Scotland, Wales and the combined services. Brilliant. What an opportunity. I was on the ceiling – prise me down someone!

This was a great opportunity for me, but not only that, it was recognition for all the hard work I put in at junior level, what with playing for all of my schools as well as Kent Schools FA side.[1] This was the game that would have seen me noticed by the FA for the first time, and which led to the invitation. I'd no idea who'd seen me of course, no idea which one of the nameless faces at the games who'd made a note of my name and given a favourable report back to his colleagues, but, whoever you are, you helped me on my way with that vote of confidence and I'll always be grateful for that.

These trials at Lilleshall were intense. They'd watch everyone who was there, and, bit by bit, those lads who were 'not up to the required standard' were politely asked to pack their things and go home. Luckily for me, I wasn't one for them, and I remained part of a group that was getting smaller and smaller by the day, until, at the end of the trial period, I was selected for the squad that was set to play the three international games. As you can imagine, this was a huge confidence booster for me. I'd started out as one of hundreds of young hopefuls and had survived the cull to make the squad and, ultimately, the team itself. How, at that time, could it have been any better for me? My stepping-stone progress in the game and my goal to become a professional footballer was most definitely back on track again and heading in the right direction. It also meant, as far as progressing in my career at club level was concerned, that I was in the best possible shop window for young players at that time, young player who were keen, ambitious, hungry and looking for a club. It was a huge step forward for me. All the signs looked good and were pointing in the right direction for me. I'd played for my school football teams at county level and had started getting some games for Folkestone Town, and now, the icing on the cake – I had been selected for the England Under-19 team, an amazing personal achievement of which I remain very proud.

It was just as well that I was stepping up my training and fitness efforts because one thing that swiftly became very clear to me, as I stepped up each level of the game, was how much more difficult it became in terms of sheer physicality and pace. At school level, it's basically muck, blood-and-guts football, with players who had a decent first touch and could strike the ball well being the ones who stood out. Go to county standard and you need to have a bit more in your personal armoury. Awareness, vision, agility and a good technique were essential qualities needed to get in and stay in.

It was only when you were performing well consistently at county standard that you could look for that last elusive step up to national level. That's when your 'A' game had to kick in, big time and permanently. You needed to show a good and high-quality variety of first touches, crossing and shots. You also had to have the ability to keep the ball well in any given match situation. You had to pass well and, critically, not give the ball away. Physically, at this level, players would have better pace, power and endurance, as well as a host of other skills like vision, composure and leadership. It was not just the physical stuff they were looking for. It's a big step up and many lads just don't have what it takes, including those who were on the trial with me who, day by day, started to disappear. More importantly than all of that, however, you were expected to do everything at speed and without a second thought. You need to think quicker, move quicker and pass quicker. Pace and speed is everything, you only need to look at any Premier League game today to see that.

And, on top of all that, in addition to all these crucial individual requirements, you also had to understand and learn new, and more professional, variety of training drills, all of which were conducted by significantly better coaches than any you might have worked with before. Long gone were the days of listening to your teacher, the wannabe coach with a nasty tracksuit and a whistle around his neck that he couldn't stop blowing.

At that time, a lot of the coaching surrounded the mantra, for want of a better word, of Charles Hughes, the one-time director of coaching at the FA I mentioned earlier. He had some strong ideas on how the game should be played and was very fond of utilising statistical analysis when he was looking at games, teams and players – revolutionary then but now common throughout the game. He was very big on 'route one', set plays and crosses into the penalty area, both the crosses themselves and how they should be defended. A full-back, for example, wasn't regarded as doing his job properly if he let even one cross from an opposing winger get through. So everything was very precise and detailed. We'd all sit around and watch videos of players like Kevin Keegan, studying every aspect of their game. As far as the coaching itself was concerned, even the way the sessions were set out was exact.

There was no messing about, it wasn't like turning up after school or with your local club, doing a spot of running or just playing a game. The cones, for example, had to be the same distance apart and always in the same place. The drills and routines we went through were strict and regimented. If you didn't get it done right, you'd do it again. And again if necessary. Turn, control and pass. We'd learn it all. It was engrained in us so much that I'd lie in bed at night going through all the sessions in my head. Maybe some of it was, dare I say it, a little boring? But hey, hang on. Should I even go there? After all, repetition is a crucial aspect of improving. Its why I was out doing all the running, week in and week out. And, secondly, look at where I am, sat here with the three lions on my chest. I'm going to play for England. Me, Jeremy Goss. Of all the young players in the country, I'm one of the best, one of those deemed good enough for that honour. That felt, as you can imagine, unbelievably good, a real buzz, and just what I needed after the recent disappointments at Aston Villa and Southampton.

The FA also taught us a bit about how to play the game. The structure, formations, movement off the ball, offensive counter-attacks, defensive organisation and so much more. Their coaches were on a different level to anything I'd previously experienced. So professional in everything they did, it was brilliant. And, on top of all this, they made sure we engaged it, and were familiar with good sportsmanship. We were encouraged to play like gentlemen, have a little bit of that old Corinthian spirit about us. You tucked your shirt in and had your socks pulled up. If you fouled someone then you'd make sure you were there to offer them a hand, pick them up, apologise and see that they were alright. You were tough in the challenge and apologetic in the aftermath, showing respect for your opponent. And as for the referee – whatever he said was law, end of.

He could make the most ridiculous decision but you'd abide by it, no matter what. It was an exaggeration of the last of the 'old school' influence of the FA, a throwback to how things had been done in the 1940s and 1950s, and was most certainly not the way it was being done in the 1980s – after all, did anyone ever see Stuart Pearce or Terry Butcher apologise to an opponent for taking them out at knee height? Yet, for me my character and my mannerisms, it wasn't so difficult to fall into those ways on the football pitch, it was an extension of my personality. But it might have been a bit more difficult for others! The overall method in the madness was simple. You play with pride and respect, you win with dignity and you lose with dignity.

So, after a couple of knock-backs, I was happy. Being picked for England is as good as it gets. But it got better. Because I was named captain! How about that? Jeremy Goss, the Army brat, trialled and released by two of the biggest sides in the country after barely half a day at each, not even nearly good enough for them, yet good enough to play for England. I was alongside another lad in that team who, like me, went professional and had a good career in the game. I'm talking about Leroy Rosenior, whose clubs included Fulham, QPR and West Ham – a very decent footballing CV.

Leroy was a top man, a really good lad with a great sense of humour, I liked him a lot. Mind you, he probably didn't think much of me after the first of the games we played for the England U-19, which was against our counterparts from Scotland. Now, never mind the game or the result (it was a pretty dull draw as I recall), what stands out for me about that match was what happened beforehand. As I was the captain, it was my responsibility to introduce the England team to the local mayor before the match. He'd been invited along as the guest dignitary, and we had to go through all the ceremony that you see at any international or big game, the captain steering the guest down the line pre-match, letting him know who all my teammates were once the national anthems have played. So there I am, with the mayor, introducing him to all the lads, one by one. The only problem I've got is that we'd only been together for a short while and I couldn't remember anyone's name. Big problem! But, rather than say nothing or just mumble something incoherently, I made up every single name. Brilliant eh? I think I introduced Leroy to the mayor as Dave on the day. Hilarious. Well, I thought so. Poor old Dave. I mean Leroy. I guess it was my very own trigger moment, what a place to have one though. Funnily enough, or not, as the case may be, I was never asked to introduce the lads to a special guest again.

Despite all of the confusion before the game, I played well. We had a double incentive to do so after all. Not only were we playing for England, we also knew that there'd be representatives from some League clubs there. Hardly surprising of course. We were the perceived elite of England's young players. It wasn't going to do them any harm to send someone along, even if, at this stage, it wasn't one of the top managers. One person who was there was Ronnie Brooks, who was then in charge of the youth teams set up at Norwich City. Now, Ronnie was quite a character, both in the game and in life. In spotting and developing young talent he was outstanding, having a real knack for seeing what made a young player special. If even the lad in question was tearing up and down a muddy old pitch at his school or in a park, with twenty-one others, Ronnie would see what set him apart. He was one of the best people you could ever want to meet, and it's very sad that he's no longer with us. He certainly wouldn't have been in it for the money, but he would have been proud to have done the job for the prestige and he loved it. Among the players he spotted and brought to Norwich when they were still youngsters was Mark Barham, Justin Fashanu and Peter Mendham. Mark was capped by England, Fash was a £1 million player and a BBC Goal of the Season winner, and Pete won the Second Division championship and League Cup medal for Norwich during his decade at the club. Not bad going by any standards.

At Priestfield, the home of Gillingham FC, he took a liking to me, the curly-haired captain of the side, running his heart out in midfield. As a football scout you either like the look of someone, how he runs, or moves, tackles and passes, or you don't. There was no inbetween and there certainly wasn't with Ronnie. He liked what he saw and that was enough for him to want to give me a chance, for which I will always be grateful. Not that I knew who he was when he came walking up to me after the game. I just saw him as a friendly-looking bloke out for a quick word. I can remember the conversation that followed as clear as day.

'My name is Ronnie Brooks. I'm from Norwich City Football Club. I want you to come up to see us and play in some games, train with us and let us take a closer look at you. And you at us, of course.' What could I say? What do you think? 'Thank you very much Mr Brooks, I'd love to have the chance to do that Mr Brooks.' He smiled. I don't think any young lad had called him Mr Brooks before. Then, he let me know where and when, the time, date and what to expect. It was the third time I had been given all that information, yet this was different, this wasn't a response to a speculative letter, this was someone who has already seen me play. It felt good. After all, he wasn't responding to yet another query from another kid with stars in his eyes; he'd seen the person in question play for his national team. Big difference.

'Thanks again Mr Brooks. I'll see you then.' I ran off back to the dressing rooms with a massive smile on my face. Then it hits me. Oh shit! I stop dead in my tracks, looking around. Where is he, has he gone already? No, there he is, making his way to the exit. I ran back after him, only just catching up with him in time. 'Um, excuse me Mr Brooks. Where, erm, exactly *is* Norwich?'

Even as I'd said the words, I regretted it. Gossy, what are you saying? He's going to think you're brainless mate. Captain of the England Under-19 side and you don't even know where Norwich is. I've got to be honest, I didn't know much about Norwich then. I'd maybe seen them play on *Match of the Day* once or twice, and I knew Justin Fashanu played for them. I even had a faint recollection of an incident there where someone fell out of the directors' box down into the dugout as well. I think that was Kevin Bond, although I could be wrong. Funny how you remember the sort of little details that are useless in times such as this. I didn't, for example, know that their manager was Ken Brown and, well, I'm sorry folks, but, at that time, I really didn't have a clue where Norwich was. I was never the best at geography at school. Still, I won't have been the first, or the last young player to have that problem. Ronnie Brooks gave an even bigger smile. 'Don't worry about that son. Ask your Dad, I'm sure he'll buy a map.'

Naturally enough, I told Dad as soon as I could. 'Dad, Dad, I've got another trial, this chap, Ronnie Brooks is his name, came up to me after the game and invited me along for a few days at Norwich. Trouble is, isn't Norwich miles away, middle of nowhere? I'm worried about just how...' Dad interrupted me. 'Don't you worry about that, we'll take you there.' Which he did. It's a fair old haul up from Folkestone to Norwich. A four- or five-hour trip. I do it myself now of course, whenever I drive down to see Mum and Dad with my twin boys, and yes, it's a long old drive. Little did I know, way back then, as my dad drove me up to Norwich that, one day, it would be a trip I'd be doing time and time again, only with my lads coming with me to see my parents, their grandparents. All because of what Ronnie Brooks said to me at the end of that game.

Ronnie passed away in 2010. I owe him a lot, as do many lads, including all of those he brought to Norwich. He was an active and busy worker in and around Norwich and Norfolk, doing whatever he could to help people out. As well as working for the football club, he'd also worked for the old electricity board, so he met a lot of people that way. He helped form the Norwich City Roller Hockey Club, was the chair of the governing body at the Hewitt School in Norwich and was both a Norwich City councillor and the Sheriff of Norwich. He was, among other things, a lovely bloke. You can ask anyone who knew him or came into contact with him.

So, on the day, Dad came with me and drove all the way to Norwich. I ended up at Trowse where the club used to have their training ground. The remit was, as before, to take part in a practice match. It was on that day that I met a man who was to become a great friend, and a person who would have a huge impact on my career at Norwich City, the then youth-team coach, Dave Stringer. I played in that game, and believe me, it was great to finish it and not get hauled off after ten minutes, and, better than that, straight afterwards I was asked to come up for an entire week so they could have a better look at me. For me, this was amazing! A whole week to prove myself. At Aston Villa and Southampton I'd had no more than ten minutes or so to impress, whereas, at Norwich City I now had five whole days. Five days to play, train, learn and show both Dave and Ronnie that I was good enough.

Dave, as I swiftly learnt, was already a Norwich City legend. He'd made around 500 appearances for the first team as a player, and was now garnishing quite a reputation as a coach of some quality, one who didn't, admittedly, suffer young fools gladly, but also one who would look out, and after his players, ones who would treat him and the game with the respect, honesty and passion he'd always had for it. Because of this, because of his professionalism and enthusiasm, I took an instant liking to him, and very much wanted to be a player who met his exceptionally high standards. He and the feel of the whole place was brilliant, so welcoming and friendly, I just wanted to be part of it, to make it with them and to play for this club forever. Another love affair had most definitely begun, this time with a football club known as the Canaries.

I duly came back for the five day trial and did well enough for Norwich to want to take me into their ranks a bit more permanently, and initially for a period of six months. Thrilled? You bet. And so proud. They took me on under the old work experience scheme. In fact, I was the first player that Norwich ever signed under that system, with £25 a week paid to me as a wage by the government and £25 a week paid by the football club for my digs. And I did well enough at that trial for Norwich to want me to sign me on a full-time basis for the start of the 1982/83 season.

This brings us full circle and back to that place that I referred to earlier, one that holds as many fond memories for me as any of the great stadiums or cities I have played in. Norwich railway station, which is where I ended up one sunny day in August 1982, taking that long walk down the platform, was where I started my career as a professional footballer. I had the opportunity and now it was time to grasp hold of it and make the very best of what I had been offered. I had no intention of doing anything less.

---

1 The Kent SFA haven't done badly with their pick of players from the schoolboy ranks. As well as myself, the likes of Tony Cascarino, Andy Townsend, John Salako and Jimmy Bullard, as well as my old mate at Norwich, Mark Barham, have all 'graduated' from the KFSA to a successful career in the senior game.

4

Becoming a Footballer

Knocking on that dressing room door was a nightmare. You'd knock and no one would answer. So you knocked again, harder. Still no reply. By now, my heart would be in my mouth – what should I do? Try for a third time or walk away? Yet I couldn't do that. Say Mick was after a change of studs or something, he had to have them. I had to go in, there was no choice in the matter. Ever stood outside the headmaster's office when you were at school, frightened to go in? As far as I was concerned, this was worse than twenty or so headmasters in that room. So I would knock again, harder. By now, my heart would have been beating almost as quickly and loudly as the knocks. Then you'd hear a voice from inside. Oh shit, it's Channon and he doesn't sound happy.

So then. It's been a long journey but here I am. On Platform One at Norwich station. It's a warm summer's afternoon in Norfolk and I've arrived at my destination, away from friends and family down in Kent to begin a new chapter in my life, one that has already seen a lot of moving around from place to place. Except I'm now more than ready to put down roots. Every journey, as the saying goes, starts with a few short steps. And, right now, mine are short ones as I try to stroll, or stagger, down the platform, oblivious to the people around me. I carry two heavy suitcases, a large rucksack and, most importantly of all, a Walkman by my side, to which is attached a pair of headphones, which are almost permanently connected to my ears. You think it's the modern-day footballer who hides behind his 'cans' as he chills out to his favourite sounds? Think again. I started it back in the eighties; they've all been copying me. No doubt the soundtrack that accompanied my arrival in Norwich was something of a rock persuasion. I've already mentioned ELO, so it might have been them. Rainbow, Journey, Foreigner, Boston – something like that, tasteful and contemporary. The sort of stuff I still have on today in the car, my twin boys giving me stick for it, as you can imagine.

They'd certainly have given me some if they'd have seen what I was wearing. I had on an old-fashioned three-piece suit, waistcoat included. The whole ensemble was coloured in tasteful light beige, with bell-bottomed trousers and the standard 8-inch zip, plus a shirt with an extra wide collar, that was finished off with a thick, dark-brown tie with an enormous knot in it. To complete the look, I sported a pair of platform shoes and a Kevin Keegan style hairstyle – very blonde, very curly. There was no doubt about it, I looked ridiculous. There I was, a young lad of seventeen all alone, lost in his own little world and his music, dreaming of becoming a professional footballer with Norwich City. To be perfectly honestly, looking as I did strangely out of place, lost and lonely, vulnerable even, what chance did I have?

Feeling sorry for me? There's no need. I might have looked a bit overdressed, but there was a conviction in what I was doing and where I wanted to go. Sure, I stood out. But that was down to respect. Remember, my dad was a colour sergeant in the British Army. So looking well turned out, smart, immaculate came as second nature to him. He would have expected me to go off to my first job looking the part. Never mind how the other lads might have been dressed, or what they might have thought of me, I wanted to set a standard for myself so I made the effort. If you're going to do anything in life, do it in the very best way you can, however you can. In my case, well, I looked good, if a bit dated. I was someone who might have got a passing glance or smart comment from my fellow youngsters as I passed them by, all resplendent in their trendy Next gear and pixie boots. I laugh about it now of course. The look might not have been the best. But my intentions were honourable and they, at least, set a habit in motion that I have kept with me to the day. If you look the part then you'll act the part. From that, of course, you'll get the impression that I wander around Norwich in a Versace suit and iron my pyjamas every night before I go to bed. All I can say to that is, I draw a line in the sand somewhere.

One of my first ports of call upon arriving in Norwich was to head to my lodgings, a place that played a huge role in those early months at Norwich and one, I'm glad to say, which is still there and thriving to this day. It was the Stracey Hotel which was to become my little home from home over the weeks and months to come, courtesy of the football club. Now, I am sure that you've all heard some of the horror stories regarding the type of digs that young footballers were expected to survive in when they started in the game. Stories like young players being locked in their rooms or being fed food you wouldn't normally give to the dog, or even minding out that they weren't eaten by the dog themselves. Naturally, I'd like to furnish this chapter with tales of my own terrible experiences in my new lodgings but, truth be told, I can't. They were great and just what I needed at the time. For, as much as I was confident of my ability and sure that I was going to succeed in what I was doing, you have to remember that, underneath all of that, I was still a young lad who'd just left home for the first time to live on his own, in a strange city that he didn't know. Nor did he know anyone, in a profession that wasn't exactly renowned for its twin values of nurturing and tolerance. Carl and Diane, the owners of the Stracey, were my new landlords and looked after me from the off, which was just what I needed. Because, however bullish I might have been on the outside, there was still the little lad deep down who was going to miss his family and feel a bit lonely.

Life there was great. When I moved in there was already a Norwich player who made it a little easier for me. His name was Dennis van Wijk, a Dutch lad who'd recently joined the club himself from Ajax, one of the leading teams in Holland and Europe. He'd come through their youth system but, finding it difficult to break into the first team there, opted to come over to England to play for Norwich after he impressed the club's coaching staff at a youth tournament they played in with Ajax in France. He came back for a trial and, like me, never looked back, being signed up almost immediately. He was a good lad, Dennis. Friendly, intelligent, sociable. And one hell of a footballer. He had been brought up at Ajax and there are few better places to learn the trade anywhere.

Dennis and I got on well from the off, both at the Stacey and the club. He was a little bit older than me but, for goodness sake, he'd travelled to a different country in order to play the game and needed to master a new language and everything. Yet there I was, just up from Folkestone, thinking I'd come a long way. Although, to be fair, Amsterdam is closer to Norwich than Folkestone, and Dennis could fly home to Amsterdam from Norwich airport in about an hour! Regardless of that though, he'd done that little bit extra to play and prove himself, something which, in the end, I did myself when the chance to play abroad came later on in my career.

Dennis and I spent much of our time in the Stacey improving our snooker in one of the upstairs rooms, and I eventually got quite good at it. Life was good. I had his company as well as a nice room of my own, plus good food on the table every night. It was the right type of food as well, as Carl and Diane would have been advised by the club on what to feed us. And I had free time. I used to spend that wandering around Norwich, getting to know my new home and enjoying the fact I had £25 in my pocket. I used to do my little walks thinking, 'I wonder if any of these people know I play for Norwich?' Replica kits weren't such a big thing then as they are now, but plenty of people would wear a Norwich scarf, especially those that worked in the market.

I never saw myself as big time. Hell, no way. I've known players who think they are and act the part accordingly, but it was never how I was going to be. It was enough for me to be doing what I had always dreamt of doing, enjoying it, and, if I wanted to, just being able to buy myself a can of Coke with my own money as and when I wanted. I certainly wasn't one to go around all the pubs and clubs or anything like that. So I kept my head down, enjoyed the new life and my time at the Stacey and, most importantly of all, I cracked on with the real job in hand, that of becoming a professional footballer.

And what a place, what an opportunity to learn. Norwich might have been regarded as a bit of a footballing backwater then. Indeed, some people see the club and area like that today. But take it from me, they did everything properly. The playing and coaching set-up there was superb, even if the facilities weren't quite as top of the range as they are today. I thoroughly enjoyed it. We played properly organised games against other sides in the Southern Counties East League, playing against teams like

Chelsea, Tottenham and West Ham, our best against their best and a high standard of game and opposition. You could only improve your game playing against some of the players we came up against. Players like Tony Adams and David Rocastle at Arsenal. You spent some time on the pitch playing against them and you just thought, 'Wow, quality'. It shone through. It only made you want to do better yourself.

So we played, we competed and we trained. And did we run? Oh yes. We ran and ran and ran. And, when we could run no more, we did a bit of running. Then, finally, after we'd gone through all of that and were bringing our breakfasts up at the end of it all, the coaches took pity on us and gave us a little warm down exercise to do. Which was a little run – only a little one mind.

Dave Stringer was, as I've already said, in charge of the youth team. He was a good man and a hard one at times, as befitted his image as a player. But one who wanted the game played in the right way. He reported to Ken Brown, the first-team manager, and his assistant, Mel Machin. Most people will have heard or know about Ken, but maybe not so many about Mel. He was, like Dave, an ex-Norwich player, and a very neat and tidy one, a defender who joined the club from Bournemouth soon after John Bond became manager at Norwich.

Mel was, having played under Bond, very much for playing the game 'the Norwich way'. He'd been preached it all of his playing life under Bond, so there was only one way he wanted to coach. This was the same with the gaffer, Ken Brown. He was another disciple of Bond. They'd both come from West Ham, a club that, like Norwich, had a way about them on the pitch. A passing game, lots of movement on and off the ball with an emphasis on working it forward rather than booting it from one penalty area to another. Ken was a lovely bloke, always with a smile on his face and time for you. Mel, on the other hand, was a real hard nut, a tough guy. It was good cop, bad cop with him and Ken. One story about Mel always comes to mind when I think about those early days. It features another young hopeful who was at the club with me then, called Paul Kinnaird.

He came down from Glasgow and would have been about seventeen/eighteen at the time, joining us a short time after I had. We were all at the club's then training centre, Trowse: the first team, the reserves, the youth team plus all the management and coaching team – a full house. Paul was, as was the responsibility of the younger players at the time, doing one of his tasks. In this case, it was mopping the floor of the big foyer at the entrance to Trowse. Now, as he's doing that, the phone rings. It's also the apprentice's job to answer the phone, except that Mel Machin is sat right next to the phone reading a newspaper while Paul is away at the other side of the room, a nice clean floor between him and the phone. He's doing that and, everywhere else, other young players are working away, washing, cleaning, scrubbing. Anyway, the phone keeps on ringing. After a while, Mel, without looking up, shouts, 'Oi, Kinnaird, are you going to answer the phone?'

Normally, you'd go 'yes Mel' and do just that. The 'if he says "jump", you say "how high?"' sort of thing. Mel has spoken. Don't mess with Mel. Mel is tough, you know what. You do as he says, it's his way or – well, you don't want to find out what the alternative might be. But wait ... Paul is carrying on with his mopping, hasn't he heard Mel? But he has heard, and, as he works, he looks towards Mel and says, 'What, me, get the phone?' Now you've got to appreciate what is happening here, someone is threatening Mel's authority in his kingdom. So there's a quiet little buzz about the place all of a sudden, the lads are waiting to see what Mel will say or do next. It's a scary moment. But no, it's Paul who speaks next, calm as you like and in that deep Glasgow brogue of his, calmly saying 'Mel. Get it yourself. You're sat right on top of the f*****g thing.' Cue sharp intakes of breath all round. Some of the lads want to run. Others are frozen in mid-motion, daring not move or breathe. And with good reason because Mel went mad. He went absolutely nuts, like you wouldn't believe. This was one of the four horsemen of the apocalypse, saddling up and getting ready to ride down his enemy in downtown Trowse.

However, right at the end of his tirade, one which had featured words and expressions that would have been new to some young ears and required further explanation at a later date, Mel looked Paul straight in the eye and concluded with a smile, saying, 'You've got a bit of spunk about you, son. I like that.' The phone, needless to say, was never answered. Paul had cleaned that floor up a treat, however, and lived to tell the tale.

So that was the hierarchy. Ken Brown in charge, the fearsome Mel at his side. Dave Stringer, who could be just as volatile himself, was in charge of us with the physio, Tim Sheppard, another really lovely bloke, was charged with looking after all of the youthful strains and pulls, of which there were usually a few to go around. Tim served the club for twenty-one years as physiotherapist. He is a man who I have great faith and respect for and he's treated me so many times, he probably knows my body better than I do.

Finally, there were the players. Lots of big characters and a good mixture of experience and youth. Players like Mark Barham, Keith Bertschin, John Deehan, Mick McGuire, Peter Mendham, Martin O'Neill, Steve Walford, Dave Watson and Chris Woods, to name a few. And then there was Mike Channon. Mike had done a lot in the game. He'd played for England on nearly fifty occasions and won the FA Cup with Southampton, his first and greatest footballing love. Like Matt Le Tissier many years later, Mike could see no good reason to leave the Saints. He was a West Country lad who maybe didn't see the need for the bright lights and the big city. He didn't leave Southampton until he was nearly thirty, doing that to join Manchester City. He then came back to the Saints before playing for anyone who'd give him a game. He was counting down the days at Bristol Rovers when Norwich signed him. At thirty-four, he probably thought top flight football had passed him by, but Ken Brown thought differently. Norwich had always been on the lookout for players coming towards the end of their careers; players, who, when they were at their peak, would never have considered playing for them, but as age took its toll, saw it as a good move. John Bond signed Martin Peters, a move which, even today, most Norwich fans will say is one of the best the club ever made.

So Ken was just carrying on with the long tradition when Mick turned up at Trowse for the first time. Unfortunately for me, I ended up being his apprentice and let me say, for the lovely, cuddly, friendly image he cultivates, he made my life as an apprentice hell. He'd leave his kit all over the place, or throw a pair of socks or shorts up into a tree and expect me to climb up and get them. Then he'd want them all cleaned and back again, before I even had a chance to get started. As we all know, he loved the horses. Indeed, it wouldn't be unknown for the team to be getting ready to go out onto the pitch at a little before three on a Saturday afternoon, only for the call of 'where's Mick?'

He'd appear right at the last moment, having nearly missed the kick-off and Ken Brown's prematch talk, all because he'd be in the boardroom alongside Greg Downs, watching the 2.45 at Haydock Park on the TV. But that was Mick, there'd been no one like him in the game and there certainly hasn't since. He could certainly still play and he proved that over and over again during his time at Norwich.

Mick pretty much had the run of the place when he was at the club. He'd stroll into the dressing room after placing his bets, look Ken in the eye and say, 'Sorry, just putting a bet on.' Nothing would be said. Mick did as he pleased. He'd do that, go out and play, invariably perform brilliantly, come back, clear off and do his own thing. One of a kind.

It was a great opportunity for me, and the downsides weren't so bad. They were irritations at most, especially when you consider everything that I did have going for me. I'd be in for training every day, cycling from the Stracey Hotel in order to arrive at the Trowse training ground for 8.30 a.m. sharp. But then it was down to some serious training, time to get the balls and the cones out and learn how to be professional footballers? You're joking, right? We had to earn the right to play a bit of football and we did that by getting down to some hard work – cleaning!

This meant doing all the jobs that needed doing in and around Trowse. Even if they didn't need doing. See the army comparison again? It meant scrubbing the floors, washing down the walls and making sure everything, including the fixtures and fittings, were spotless. Don't forget, Mel Machin was around and he gave Paul Kinnaird a right bollocking for answering him back that time. Mel had seen tougher blokes off than us, hardened footballers with hearts and minds of ice. Players, for example, like Willie Young. Willie had come to us from Nottingham Forest but he'd also played for Tottenham and Arsenal. He was coming to the end of his career, but was a big name in the game with a big reputation to live up to. On one of his first training sessions with us, Mel wanted us to run. He wanted a long, hard run, for us to get a sweat on and make some effort. Willie wasn't having that and growled to Mel, 'I came here to play football, not to bloody run.' Oh no! Maybe not the best thing to say to Mel. It was like a red rag to a bull, and a few of us who were witness to this held our breaths, waiting for Mel to let Willie have it, a double-barrelled reply that would take no prisoners. We weren't disappointed but we were shocked at both its severity and the outcome. Mel screamed at him before telling Willie to get in, get changed and 'f**k off home'. Brilliant! When you're on the receiving end of these rebuttals then it's a nightmare, but, if you're in the background listening to it happen to someone else then you turn into a silly little schoolboy, giggling under your breath and whispering to your mates, just as I did that day. I don't recall seeing much of Willie around the club after that.

Mel's hardline approach to everyone, no matter who they were, meant we were as committed to keeping the training ground clean and tidy as we were to our football. I've already mentioned looking after Mike Channon's kit, or, at least trying to given the circumstances and his, shall we say, occasionally awkward attitude to his young apprentice? But then we had to look after all the kit for all the players. And, as one of the senior pros and one of the most respected professionals in the game, Mick had earnt the right to demand the best and to give you a bollocking if you didn't come up to standard. Which would have been the same attitude and expectation of any member of the senior squad. We had to get it right. They didn't expect to have to check to see if their kit was clean, pressed and correctly put together. They assumed it was. So there'd be trouble if you got it wrong. We all worked together to make sure that wasn't the case. See how teamwork comes into play at a football club off the pitch as well as on it? That's what I am talking about here. Only the repercussions of not getting it right would be a lot worse than a misplaced pass or badly-timed tackle. You couldn't be thrown out on your ear for that. But, irritate one of the senior pros or coaching staff by doing something wrong, or, even worse, not doing it at all? Then you were in trouble.

The jobs we had to do at Trowse were the worst of the worst. I've read about how Paul Kent, one of the apprentices at Norwich back in the 1970s when Ron Saunders was in charge, had to clean out the players' baths, peeling away old bandages and plasters from its side as he did so. Horrible. But Paul will, even now, tell you that was part of the learning process. It was for us as well. The more gritty, dirty, horrible and filthy the job was, the more likely it would be that we had to do it. We couldn't even speak to the senior players unless they spoke to us first, and that would never be to ask us how we were or how life was going. It would have been an order: 'do this, fetch that, why hasn't this been done?' On occasion, they wouldn't even look at us as they spoke, thinking the fact that one of the kids was in the room was enough, that he'd do. It didn't matter which one. Luckily for us as far as the kit was concerned, we had Betty the cleaning lady on our side. She knew what was what, was pretty organised and knew what went where at Trowse. I'm sure she saved a young lad going over on more than one occasion.

On a regular basis I'd be asked to run down to the bakery in Trowse to get the players their snacks; sandwiches, rolls, pasties, that sort of thing. Players weren't so conscious of health and dietary requirements at that time. Think that might have been easy and one of the lighter duties? Think again. A dozen or so professional footballers, all knackered, stinking and swearing after training, some of them will have a cob on into the bargain, all giving you their order and throwing banknotes and coins at you. They only asked once. You had to get it right, and if you didn't, or if you got their change wrong, then they'd have a go and you'd get a right bollocking. That wasn't a job any of us liked. You could almost see them sidling up to the gaffer Ken Brown, at the time, and saying 'hey Gaffer, that young lad with the blond curls, what's he all about, why is he here – he's effing useless'. It might have been because I gave someone a cheese roll and they asked for tuna and tomato, but Ken might have thought they'd been watching me in training and were commenting on my ability as a player.

Knocking on that dressing room door was a nightmare. You'd knock and no one would answer. So you knocked again, harder. Still no reply. By now my heart would be in my mouth – what should I do? Try for a third time or walk away? I couldn't do that. Say Mick was after a change of studs or something, he had to have them, I had to go in, there was no choice in the matter. Ever stood outside the headmaster's office when you were at school, frightened to go in? As far as I was concerned, this was worse than twenty or so headmasters in that room. So I would knock again, harder. By now my heart would have been beating almost as quickly and loudly as the knocks. Then you'd hear a voice from inside. Oh shit, it's Channon and he doesn't sound happy.

'Get in here.' I walk in, head down. Someone's already delivered all the sandwiches and rolls, they're on the side with cans of Coke and the like. One of the players is effing and blinding, claiming whoever got the order in has cocked his request up again. Without even looking at me he says 'did you get these in today?' It's only Dave Watson, not someone I, or anyone, wants to wind up. He's captain and one of the big names and personalities at the club. 'No Dave, I didn't go down the bakers today.' 'Well who was it then, because they've f****d up my cheese and ham roll.'

Of course, I knew who it was. Like all the other apprentices, I'd had heaved a big sigh of relief earlier in the day when I saw who'd got the job, but I wasn't going to grass up on my teammate, so I played it all innocent. 'Don't know Dave. I was getting Mick Channon's change of studs so didn't notice who it was. I'm sorry, do you want me to go and get you something else?'

Thank God he doesn't. And I'm lucky. Big Dave Watson stands up and lobs the offending roll into a nearby bin, shaking his head. He towers over me, towers over most of us to be fair. A giant of a man, even though he's 'only' 6 feet tops. You don't always need to be tall to be big and physically imposing, if you see what I mean, and Dave Watson is a good example. But he's a good player. Most people at the club were certain he'd get England caps, the only question was whether he would still be at Norwich when he did. It looks like Liverpool had made a rare mistake in letting him go so cheaply.

I look over to where Channon is sitting. Typically, he's got his head in the *Racing Post*. He knows I'm there though, and without even looking up from his selections, holds out one hand. I drop the studs into them and go to leave, grateful that this particular trial is over. But wait, there's some whispering going on in the far corner of the room. It's John Deehan and someone, Chris Woods I think. And they're looking right at me. This is not good news. As I said earlier, you didn't look the first-team players in the face. Catch their eye and they might order you to do something, or, simply take the piss out of you, embarrass you or just test you out to see how you respond. Even if they wanted something they'd look at the floor, the opposing wall, their newspaper as they did so. Looking at you? That could mean trouble. They all knew I was a relatively new face still. A bit unfamiliar, a bit fresh. And it wasn't as if I could melt into the shadows, what with my mop of curly blonde hair. There' was a game afoot and some of the senior players could sense a bit of fun. Some of them could smell it like a shark scents blood.

'Get him over here; he's one of the new lads.' 'What, is he a new lad? I've seen him before, scrubbing out the bogs I think. He didn't do that very well so he must be a bloody awful footballer.' Channon looms up from his paper and that West Country burr comes out. 'He is a bloody awful footballer. And he can't clean boots properly either.' Shit shit shit shit shit. This is not good. 'Get him over here. Is the gaffer about? Shut the door. Get over here you, what's your name? Never mind. Stay there. You're going to sing us some songs. And we're going to enjoy it. And if we don't enjoy it, we're going to throw things at you. Heavy things.' Channon remarked 'We'll give you a good ol' kick up the backside an' all lad.'

This sort of thing really did happen at football clubs. It was all about character building. You can look at it and say that they were just bullying of course, but they weren't. In truth, they will look out for you because, regardless of the fact that you are, in their eyes, the gofer, you're still one of them, you still wear the same shirt. And in a year or so, you might be sharing that first-team dressing room at Trowse with them. That, or you'll end up at another club and they'll join it one day. Football is a small world sometimes. But it's also a tough one. And they wanted me to know that. So they were testing my character, reminding me that they were in charge and ensuring that, if I wanted to join them, then I had to toughen up and stick it out just as they have. I've got to be prepared to take the bollockings, to develop that thick skin.

So there was method in their madness. They were testing me out, waiting to see how I would react. Some youngsters would burst into tears, others would head for the door and run for a mile or two, and that could be the end of them in the game before they're even eighteen. But I wasn't going to do that. I wanted this, I wanted their world. It was important that I didn't give them any cheek back. Mouthing off at Channon, for example, would be like the young squaddie having a pop at the RSM on his first day. It's not something you do. And I didn't. I stood there and got ready to sing. And then Watson, the captain, fizzes open a can of Coke and motions for me to go. 'Clear off. And make sure you get my bloody roll order right next time.' I was out of the door like you know what off a stick.

Funnily enough, I had lucky escapes like that one all the time. Indeed, I never really went through the whole initiation process, which I was very pleased about.

I lived in terror of Channon getting bored one lunchtime and coming after me, cornering me somewhere, saying 'I know you Gossy, you're going to be a good player. I've watched you and I've seen you score some good goals as well, but right now you're going to get back to those changing rooms and strip naked before you sing us a few songs.'

It was horrendous at times. It just wasn't something I was used to, or liked. I was the quiet lad from a nice family in Kent. We didn't like to party or have a wild time. My dad? I don't think so. I kept my head down, kept away from the big nights out and team get-togethers, even when I started to get near the first team. Once they were in the party mood it didn't take them long if they saw me. 'Look at Gossy. Look at his barnet, look at his shoes, look at his...' Yeah lads, have a good evening. I'm washing my hair tonight so it's nice and clean when you take the piss out of it again tomorrow.

And I'd go off and have a nice quiet night somewhere, assuming that, one day, it would all quieten down. If I was out with some of them I'd sit quietly, head down, laugh at their jokes, make all the right noises. Try to fit in but not really enjoying it. Like I've already said, you could easily mistake it for bullying. But I never saw or heard of anything that might have been considered that bad. No one ever constantly picked on one person, there was certainly no physical stuff and no one was hated. We were tolerated, just as they would have been at one time, and, how we would eventually tolerate the young lads coming into the club when we were established in the team. But, because I wasn't the big drinker, the party animal, I still had to gain their respect and their acceptance, only I had to do it another way.

The best possible way to do that was out on the training pitch. I'd stand up for myself when we were playing games, get stuck in, make some big tackles and come away with the ball. Likewise, if someone crunched me, I'd get up and carry on without saying a thing. I'd look to get them back as well. Nothing gains you respect in the game like proving you've got what it takes out there on the pitch. Thus, I won their respect at the training ground and the players started to look at me when they spoke to me. It wouldn't be 'Oi, you', or similar, it would be 'morning Gossy son, you alright?' Little things. Maybe some people wouldn't even notice. But I did. And it made a hell of a difference.

Aside from all of that running around, cleaning, scrubbing and polishing and general everyday aggro, we were, of course, allowed to play football every now and again. It was as if the management suddenly remembered you weren't there to do all the odd jobs but to learn your footballing trade, rather than that of a cleaner or butler. And when they did let us out to play it was fantastic. It reminded you of why you were there, what you wanted to achieve and why you put up with all the shitty jobs and dealing with being wound up by people like Mike Channon. And the club's coaching staff knew exactly what they wanted from me. I was lucky enough, alongside Mick, to have Peter Mendham as one of the senior players I had to look after.

He was a lovely bloke, and as a matter of fact, born not too far away in Kings Lynn, so living the dream and playing for his local club. He was, like me, a central midfielder, full of energy and running, but skilful with it, so not your typical midfield terrier. He had a bit of class about him and could spot a pass or an opening. He wasn't adverse to having a pop at goal either, getting one from about thirty yards out against Nottingham Forest once. So, a good all-round player, of who Ken Brown said, 'If you cut him open, his blood will flow yellow and green.' He'd come through the schoolboy and youth teams at Norwich so he was a good pick for me to follow, look after and keep an eye on, just as he would, bucking the trend a little bit, and keeping an eye out for me.

Ken Brown and the coaching staff wanted me to play like Peter. So they told me to watch him whenever I could, whether it was in training or a game. Watch his runs, how he made space, found his man, got forward when the chance arose. He was a busy player. Never stopped running and gave his all for ninety minutes. When he got the ball, he'd take a touch, maybe two, then, more often than not he'd have moved it on and be running ahead, looking for the return pass. He'd be the fulcrum of the side. The lads at the back would tidy up an opposing attack, retain possession and look up, and there'd be Peter always wanting and looking for the ball, never shirking, even if he was having a bad game, which wasn't often. He'd be available for the pass, take it, take responsibility and move on, finding someone else. All teams need that sort of player, someone who makes everything go around them.

Norwich had a few good ones like that in the past. We had Gary Megson, and the team that won the League championship under Nigel Worthington in 2004 had Gary Holt. Stick a player like that in the centre of midfield alongside a more creative player, a playmaker, and you've got the makings of a successful partnership. Hence, later on at Norwich, Chippy (Ian Crook) and I combined well in the middle. I'll leave you to work out which of us did what job. Peter would also have been in a side that featured a lot of flair players. Mark Barham was one, a great player and good lad, one of the best crossers of a ball I've ever seen, and he came from Folkestone! He was also good enough to play for England. Dave Bennett and Louie Donowa were another two, both played wide and both could run like you wouldn't believe. The only thing is, when Louie got the ball at his feet, bang! He'd be off and away, never mind the shape of the team, just watch me go. Peter would have to stay put, minding the gap in the midfield and looking out for opposition players nudging themselves forward. That was his game and it was mine as well, no wonder Ken Brown and Dave Stringer went on at me to watch him all the time. I must have known Pete's game almost as well as he did after a while.

The playing mantra for me never changed. Get the ball, pass the ball and move. Get, give, support. Get, give, support. This was drilled into me all the time. It was what I heard and, through watching Peter Mendham play, what I constantly saw as well. It was not only learnt from him. There were other players at the club when I was starting out who'd also mastered that way of playing, people like Mick McGuire and Martin O'Neill. Everyone at the club knew their job, they were all good at it, and they were all, without exception, decent players. Ken Brown put a hell of a good side together in the mid-1980s, good enough to win the League Cup at Wembley. That side had a great mix. The old timers, like my old nemesis Channon and Asa Hartford, along with the solid old pros, the been there and done that, like John Deehan, Dave Watson and Peter. Finally, there were the youngsters. Louie Donowa was twenty on that day at Wembley; Paul Haylock was twenty-one on the day of the final, while Denis Van Wijk, my old snooker mate from the Stracey Hotel, was twenty-two. At Christmas that year, they'd been a comfortable tenth in the table, a position born on the back of some good wins in the league against clubs like Everton and Arsenal. Something clearly went wrong somewhere because after winning the League Cup, Norwich only won three out of their last thirteen games and got relegated. This was something that, due to the poor run of form, hadn't exactly come out as a bolt of the blue, it hadn't been anticipated by the club or the supporters.

Ken Brown and his assistant, future Norwich Manager Dave Stringer, were hugely responsible for helping me improve immeasurably, grow professionally and develop into the player I was. Not, I should add, as the player I eventually became. That came later and brings someone else into the story. But they certainly filed off the rough edges, and ended up with a professional footballer who just needed a bit of polishing to be near the finished article. And I mean no disrespect to them by adding that, had I remained the player that they helped make me become then, long term, I wouldn't have made it. No question. Under their guidance I grew into the game and into the club, and became a pivotal member of the Norwich City Youth team during my first season at the club, a vital stage in my development. That jump, from playing at schoolboy level to getting a regular place in the youth team, is as difficult as the one that takes you from the reserves to the first team. You're growing up physically and emotionally as well. Add to that all sorts of other potential distractions along the way. You're seventeen/eighteen/nineteen for goodness sake. Parties, loud music, beer, girls and having a good time. To forgo all those things you could be enjoying, in order to commit to the hard work and effort required to stand half a chance of making it as a professional footballer, is quite a challenge. I wasn't that sort of a lad and didn't really need all of that stuff to make me happy. But it's one of the things that takes its toll on young players as they grow up, with even those that do well at youth level fading from the game.

I was working hard, though I didn't have to motivate myself to do so as Dave and all the other coaches did it for us. They'd seen the raw material that I had within me, now they wanted to turn me into a footballer. They certainly liked what they saw on the pitch in training and games. That side of my character had no problems. I was confident (there's a surprise), I'd shout at the other players, let them know what I wanted or where I wanted them or the ball. I got stuck and (forgive the cliché) I let my football do the talking for me. I was aggressive, honest, and committed. I would run until I dropped, or would drop if they ran me hard enough to drop in the first place. Normally I was still standing while everyone around me was throwing up. We were all good footballers, but they wanted athletes. We never stopped running or working hard. My sweat and blood will forever be all over that old training ground at Trowse, we all gave body and soul in training. You hardly ever saw a ball some days; it was all about 'get fit then you can have a ball to play with. But running was my thing and I ran all day, happy as anything. I didn't have much pace. That was Louie Donowa's big asset. Boy, could he shift. It was unbelievable, he was electric. So too were Keith Bertschin and John Deehan in the first team. They got a lot of goals for Norwich and much of that was to do with their speed, either the pace or their speed of thought, being in the right place at the right time, anticipating, creating chances through instinct.

Look at how John Deehan made the goal that won Norwich the 1985 League Cup final, the lad playing for Sunderland. David Corner had the ball out by the corner flag at his end, he could have seen it out, cleared it, made a long pass down the flanks, anything. But he hesitated for a second too long, that was enough for Dixie. He'd have been watching, second guessing what might have happened, and, when the time came, he nipped in, won the ball on the touchline and set up the move that got Norwich their goal. Speed of thought and reaction makes a good player, a great one.

The coaching staff were certainly keeping a careful eye on me at that time. After one training session, Ken Brown called me over and said, 'Son, we think you're a little bit too slim, you need building up a bit.' Slim? Of course I was slim, it was all the running. But Ken carried on, adding, 'Football is physical and there are times when it shows with you. You're getting knocked off the ball far too easily; we'd like you to start doing some exercises with the weights.' To be fair, Ken was not the first to say this. My dad had long been suggesting I started pumping a little iron to build myself up. I'd always stayed away from the weights as a youngster, as I tended to think that too much of that sort of work and muscle build-up dulled your sharpness. But how could I now question both Ken Brown and my dad? I still contemplated doing just that until Ken had another word with me, suggesting that I supplement the weights by buying £1 worth of steak every day, and having that as part of my afternoon meal with a can of stout. Doing that wasn't exactly a hardship, and, after all, I was only following the club's suggestion. But it worked and I began to fill out and get stronger. Little by little, I was settling into my new surroundings and both Norwich and Norfolk weren't quite so strange and unfamiliar. To help me become a little more independent in and around the city, as well as make the journeys home a little more bearable, Dad spent £60 on a car for me. What fond memories I have of that motor, a little blue Mini. It couldn't go any faster than 55 mph but it was my little haven. Me, my Mini and the dozens of cassette tapes I had in there, of all my favourite bands – what a great life I was leading. Work meant spending time playing and learning my trade alongside some great professionals, with both their guidance and that of the coaches that worked with them and us. When I had a day off I would set off somewhere to do some fishing and while away the time on the side of a river somewhere. Looking back now, I guess some people might have seen me as a bit of a loner, doing the football thing every day, totally committed to that and the training, and, when I did have some time to myself, spending it either eating steak and drinking the odd stout, or off fishing somewhere! It was great and I loved it.

Fishing was quite big at the club at that time and we had some pretty committed anglers among the players. Mark Barham, Peter Mendham, Keith Bertschin, John Deehan and Dave Watson were all into it, as was the club's official photographer, a really lovely and genuine chap by the name of Roger Harris. Roger is a top man. He took so many of the lads under his belt, and helped them get away from the pressure cooker of football by introducing them to fishing and the tranquillity that surrounds it. We all used to fish at the River Yare in Cringleford, a small village to the south-west of Norwich. Another place we'd go would be Barford Lakes, which was just outside the city. Not that I'd go with them though. I preferred my own company and having time to myself, rather than being off in a big group somewhere. When I did go out it would have been back home in Kent with the family, just as it is today. If I am going out then the company I most like is that of my wife, Margaret, and my twin boys, Joseph and Jacob. Family has always been the most important thing in my life and nothing changes.

I did have a bit of a social life of course. I had money in my pocket for the first time in my life and continued to enjoy exploring the city. There was also hanging out with Denis Van Wijk and our snooker. As time progressed, and as much as I had loved my time at the Stracey Hotel, I did begin to feel as if I was getting into a bit of a rut, and both the place and my living arrangements began to lose a little bit of their lustre. Luckily for me, just as I was beginning to develop these itchy feet, I found myself in the right place at the right time. One Sunday evening, I was playing snooker (what else?) at the Stracey Hotel with some friends of mine, Wally and Shirley Tolliday. They'd recently got married and moved into the city, and, as we chatted away, they let slip that they had a spare room in their new place. Well, Gossy, how would you like to move in with us, we've got the room and the extra money would come in handy, so how about it?

How could I say no? It was a wrench, of course, to leave the Stracey Hotel. Carl and Diane had looked after me so well and done so much to help me settle down into the first place I could call my own, but the problem was just that I was on my own, perhaps more than was good for me. So I moved in and started to experience a little flavour of that precious family life that I'd left behind. It was more of a home life for me with them. I cooked in their kitchen, had a big room all to myself and generally felt like part of the family. But, in many ways, even though I was growing up fast, I still had a lot to learn about life.

There was one early evening when Wally asked me if I fancied popping over to the pub for a quick drink. I had just come in from a gentle jog. After a hard day's training under the watchful eye of Dave Stringer at Trowse, I liked to unwind in the evenings by going out for a run, and was sat in front of the TV. I heard what Wally had asked me but wasn't really sure why he wanted to go, or why he wanted me to go with him. In any case, I didn't drink. 'Come on Jezz, let's have a quick half in the pub around the corner. Are you up for it?' 'Wally, mate, why do I want to go out for a drink? I'm not even thirsty, and besides, I'm going to be in bed by 8.30.'

Wasn't thirsty! I had a lot to learn about life and socialising. But I was happy. Training was hard and there was a lot of pressure on me to excel every day, to constantly prove ourselves. But I didn't want to do, or be, anywhere else. I was happy to do whatever needed to be done, to put up with whatever challenges and difficulties came my way in order to get a full-time professional contract. Maybe, just maybe, if I got that, I'd end up going out with Wally for that drink. But, right then, right at that moment, training was everything. I'll always be grateful to them both for taking me on back then, and am delighted that they went onto have two sons, William and Daniel. I am the proud godfather of William.

I'd pitch up at Trowse every morning in the Mini, noting, as I arrived, the other players and the cars they drove. It was a bit different in those days mind. No sign of a baby Bentley or rows of smart 4x4s with blacked out windows and state-of-the-art audio systems. Ken Brown, for example, had a massive Volvo that would have drunk up the fuel like you wouldn't believe. It was a sensible, albeit thirsty car, for a sensible and level-headed man. Not like our goalkeeper, Chris Woods. He had a Ford Capri with spoilers on the outside, and the front the car was so pimped up that it looked like the Batmobile, so much so everyone started calling him Batman. Well, I did anyway. Most of the players had beat-up looking Ford Fiestas or similar, so my Mini didn't look too out of place, unless I ended up parked near Keith Bertschin, who had a Porsche. It was an old one mind, but it was still a Porsche.

Denis van Wijk had a Saab. A very old Saab. One day, as we were both driving into training, we found ourselves at the petrol station just outside of Trowse. I stuck a fiver's worth in the Mini, which would keep me going for the rest of the month. Denis is still filling up, chatting away to me as he did, oblivious to what he was doing. He was oblivious, that is, until I looked at the pump and discovered about £50 worth of petrol has gone in his car that he was still filling up. This, not surprisingly, gave Denis a bit of a shock. He stopped what he was doing and said (imagine a tinge of Dutch here if you please) 'My God. What is going on? What is happening here?' Denis' Saab had a huge leak in its petrol tank and, as quickly as he was putting the petrol in, it was flowing out again all over the forecourt, so much so that we were both standing there in a massively expanding pool of petrol!

He was a lovely guy Denis, a real gentleman. The girls all loved him. At one time, when I was still at the Stracey Hotel with him, Robert Rosario came to lodge there as well. So there was me, lodging and going out with two of the best-looking blokes in the city, and me not being at all streetwise. Not like Big Rob. He had it all, the looks, the credibility, the patter. On the odd occasions I went out with him, he'd be looking a million dollars, while I would look like a bag of cement. We'd be somewhere in Anglia Square and I'd be this little 'Billy-no-mates' sat all on his own at the end of the bar, pretending he's having a great night out while all the girls are gathered around Rob, a man who looked like Andrew Ridgeley, one half of '80s pop duo Wham and old mucker to George Michael. I, on the other hand, looked more like David Gower. So there was no contest really, the girls all wanted to talk to him, not me. Not that I'd have known what to say to girls anyway. I enjoyed my own company. We had some great times, me and big Bob, and I'll always be grateful for his close friendship and support, a top man who had the total respect of many. He was as confident at training as he was socialising, and soon got his chance in the first team, making his senior debut in a game against Watford at Carrow Road on 7 April 1984. Not a bad way to start either. We won 6-1 and Rob had the luxury of playing alongside John Deehan, who more than showed the new boy how it was done by scoring four goals. Rob was only just eighteen when he made his debut, doing so a little over a month before I made mine, even though he was over a year younger than me. It also showed, and not for the first time, that Ken Brown was willing to give the youth team players their chance at senior level, and, in fact, that was very well illustrated during that 1983/84 season, where seven of us were given a chance in that campaign.[1]

Big Bob was ahead of us in that aspect, he had that self-confidence, swagger and ability in leading the line that meant he was accepted by the first-team players, despite his age and non-league background. The most important of these was Mike Channon; he pretty much ruled the roost at the club then, and if he accepted you, then everyone did. For such an experienced and capable professional to have that faith and acceptance in such a young and relatively untried player says a lot for Bob, both as a person and a footballer. I was delighted for him, but also determined to have that same level of acceptance myself.

I looked up to all of my teammates at the club, the senior professionals who were making a good career in the game for themselves, earning the plaudits and respect that goes with it, and not just from youngsters like me but in the game as a whole. Respect is enormous in football, it doesn't really matter how good a player or manager you are, if your teammates don't respect you then you're fighting a losing battle, and it'll be very hard for you to be accepted as one of the boys. Respect can't be bought, it has to be earnt, and through deeds rather than words. Many of the first-team boys at Norwich at that time had proven themselves as top professionals long before they joined the club. Two of the best examples I can think of were our main strikers at the time, Keith Bertschin and John Deehan.

Everyone listened to them and you could understand why. They'd long proven themselves at the top level, Keith with Ipswich Town and Birmingham City, and John with Aston Villa and West Bromwich Albion. He'd also won a League Cup winners medal with Villa a few years before he joined us, as well as having been picked a number of times for the England Under-21 team, where he scored something like six goals in seven games. So that respect was immediately there for him, just as it was for 'Bertsch', who'd forced his way into a more than decent Ipswich team that featured fellow strikers such as Paul Mariner and Trevor Whymark. He'd also played alongside Trevor Francis at Birmingham.

So they both knew what it was all about and it showed. They were wonderful characters, so full of self-confidence, players that went into every game thinking they'd score. I'll never forget Keith's goalscoring celebration of dancing around the corner flag, he was doing it long before players like Roger Milla and Lee Sharpe made it fashionable in the '90s. He loved scoring goals; he'd puff out his chest and strut about the place as if he owned it. He was also seriously fit, a really committed all -ound trainer. And, being a bit of a fitness fanatic myself, I admired him for that. There wasn't an ounce of fat on him, not one bit. He worked so hard at his game, someone who it was really easy to look up to, an honest bloke who you would love to have alongside you in any team. As for Dixie Deehan, well, he might not have been as keen on training as Keith was, but he didn't need to prove anything to anyone, he was a very clever footballer. He was a typical goal poacher, yes, but also someone who knew a lot about the game and could fill in just about anywhere on the pitch. He had a great first touch and great vision, the sort of player that all teams need. He complemented Keith very well and it was a pleasure, as well as an education, to watch them play together.

Another big player who was at the club when I joined was Martin O'Neill. Now he was a footballer as intelligent on the pitch as he was off it. He had two spells as a player with the club as well as a short one as manager in 1995, so I knew and worked with him in both of those roles. While he was a player at the club he always had time for the youth-team players, and would often show up among us saying 'Come and join me in the gym', and off we'd all go in his wake, how could you not? Besides, when someone like Martin O'Neill told you to do something, you did as you were told, no questions asked!

He'd get us playing head tennis or something before training began, or he'd get hold of a tennis ball and challenge any of us to try and take it from him, adding that if any of us managed to do so he'd give them his car. Quite an incentive. But no one ever did, that ball would be stuck to his foot and he'd keep controlling it, playing keepy-uppy with it, anything at all. He was very keen on doing little exercises with tennis balls was Martin, along with Mark Barham, who'd sometimes join in. Mark was another who was brilliant at helping out with the younger players. The theory with that exercise, of course, is that if you can control something as small as a tennis ball, then in theory, a full-sized football would be easy. It was a very simple but hugely effective exercise, and you could see by the way he put those little sessions together, and how he related to and talked to the players, that'd he'd go on to be a top manager in the future.

Our goalkeeper, Chris Woods (the man with Batman's car) was like Keith Bertschin. He was a fitness fanatic, someone with a great work ethic who'd train all day if you let him, and one of the best goalkeepers I've ever seen. He was the last line of defence in that team, but on the field and the dressing room the team was ruled by our central defenders, Dave Watson and Steve Bruce. Another was Aage Hareide the Norwegian, a lovely man and a real gentleman, who joined the club from Manchester City towards the end of 1982, and who fell in love with the club and the city so much he found it a real wrench to leave. Mick McGuire, who played in midfield, was a strong character and one-time captain of the club, who went onto work for the PFA. Peter Mendham, the lad I was told to watch week in, week out, in order to learn to play like him, must have known that was what the club wanted. He'd often take me to one side and say, 'Gossy, if you need any help with your game, just ask me.' Cheers Pete. He was another lovely fella who I still bump into today, usually in the gym.

So Gossy, you're now wondering, who was your apprentice when you were a first-team player? What poor young lad did you get to do all your fetching and carrying for you, averting their eyes when they came into the dressing room in case you saw them and demanded a song or a quick comedy routine from the 'new boy'? My apprentice, as it turned out, did quite well in the game, and continues to do so in business today. It was Dion Dublin. I still owe him £25 from Christmas a while back that was meant to be his yearly tip, and I never got around to giving it to him. Sorry about that Dion, remind me if we meet up sometime, I'll see you right then if I've got any money on me. Dion was a good lad. He listened, he learnt, he put those skills into practice. And he proved Norwich wrong because the Canaries released him before he'd even played one first-team game for them. Now, admittedly, clubs release players all the time, the turnover of youngsters being told that they aren't good enough has always been enormous. Most do their absolute best to prove the clubs right and drift out of the game altogether. But not Dion.

Four years after he left Norwich he'd gone to Manchester United, playing and scoring in the Premier League at Old Trafford. If you're going to show a club that they made the wrong decision in letting you go, that's not a bad way to do it. Norwich eventually saw the error of their ways of course and brought him back to Carrow Road in 2006, nearly two decades after they'd let him go. He was thirty-seven then, with bags of experience and know-how, and the proverbial wise, old head at the club during what was a pretty bad time for them towards the end of Nigel Worthington's time as manager. He went on to play under Peter Grant and Glenn Roeder at the club before he retired from playing in 2008.

Mind you, he had it easy when he was working with me. The apprentices didn't have to do any of the mucky, repetitive jobs that we always did then, it was all about playing and learning just the one trade – how to be a professional footballer. I'd be there for all of them of course; a little chat here, an arm around the shoulder there, that sort of thing. They were all learning things like the Coerver football coaching programme, one that was inspired by the teachings of the great Dutch coach, Wiel Coerver. It was light years ahead of some of the stuff that we did, and you couldn't be surprised that those that took part in it, people like Dion, went on to become such technically good players throughout their careers. He's a lovely guy is Dion, a brilliant and captivating character who people can't help but like. Dion mate, that £25 is on its way.

So yes, we had to work bloody hard all over the training ground, football stadium, wherever and whenever we were needed. If we cut the mustard then they might let us play a bit of football. We worked hard, listened to our coaches, did as we were told and committed ourselves to our game. And we were a good group of lads, so good, in fact, that we went on to win a rare League and Cup double with Norwich, testimony not only to that group but the footballing nous of Dave Stringer. To this day, Dave remains the most knowledgeable football man I have ever known, and, as I am sure Dave would remind me, a 'proper' Norfolk person through and through. He was a man whose help and guidance during my first two seasons at the club is something I'll never forget. Little did any of us know just how successfully Dave would guide that team of fresh-faced and hopeful youngsters to that FA Youth Cup win in 1983, seeing us suddenly regarded as future professional footballers rather than a bunch of young hopefuls with stars in their eyes. Yes, of course some would fall down by the wayside. But what grounding and education that 1982/83 season gave us, and all thanks to Dave Stringer. And that whole initiation thing? Stripping naked, standing in the middle of the first-team dressing room, having things thrown at me as I sing three songs – even today I'm still waiting for it to happen!

---

[1] In addition to Gossy and Robert Rosario, who signed for the Canaries from non-League Hillingdon Borough rather than coming through the youth team, the other five teenagers given their first-team debuts that season were Paul Clayton, Louie Donowa, Mark Farrington, Daryl Godbold, Jon Rigby and Tony Spearing. Farrington joined Norwich from their 1983 FA Youth Cup final opponents Everton shortly after the final.

5

Youth Team to First Team

And then it got worse. The waiters came over to get everyone's orders. Now this was another problem for me. I had barely eaten at a restaurant in my life. I didn't know what to do or ask for, I didn't have a clue. I got away with the starter, luckily enough, by asking for the soup, which was tomato, a meal I was familiar with. Things could only get better now, or so I thought.

When the first round draw for the 1983 FA Youth Cup presented us with a home tie against Southend in the October of 1982, I suspect a few us of were dreaming of getting all the way to the final the following spring. That's not to say we didn't think we were good enough. Far from it. We were, even at that stage of our league programme in the Southern Counties East League, focusing on doing well in that and, if at all possible, looking to repeat the success of the Canary side that had won it three years earlier. This had been not long after John Bond, upon being appointed Norwich Manager in 1973, had successfully lobbied for the club to be admitted into it.

That's a little story in itself that deserves a retelling. When Bond took over at Norwich, the club's youth set-up was, to put it mildly, nothing short of a shambles. It's not that the club didn't have a youth set-up, they did, and it had been good enough to bring lads like Steve Govier, Paul Kent and Paul Cheesley up through the ranks and into the first team. But they didn't have any proper competitive games or a league to play in regularly. Instead, friendlies were arranged against some of the local teams to Norwich, clubs like Kings Lynn, Gorleston and Great Yarmouth. Now, as you can imagine, the lads in these teams used to relish the opportunity of playing against Norwich City, even if it was just, in their eyes, 'the kids'. It certainly wouldn't stop them kicking a young prodigy 6 feet up in the air just so he could boast about it to his mates in the pub afterwards. John Bond, unsurprisingly, didn't want this happening to his best, young players so he approached the FA to ask if Norwich could be entered in the Southern Counties East League, a properly organised league competition that included the young sides from the top teams in that part of the country, like Arsenal, Tottenham, Chelsea and so on. Unsurprisingly, the FA said no. Norwich couldn't enter the league because Norfolk was too far away and the costs and logistics involved with other teams having to travel there was too much. You would think that would be that. But Bond persisted, claiming if they were admitted then Norwich would play all of their games away from home. How could the FA say no to that? So the Canaries were in, and, for two seasons, they did just that, playing all their games away from home before eventually being accepted as full members playing each team in the league home and away. They went on to win it in 1980 so we had a lot to live up to.

We started the season well. By the time that FA Youth Cup tie against Southend came along, we were unbeaten in the league and looking good to have a real go at winning it for the second time in just four years. This would have been no mean feat when you consider that calibre of opposition. Again, the youth teams at Chelsea, Tottenham and Arsenal who just happened to have, among others, Tony Adams and Niall Quinn coming through their ranks at that time. They were going to be decent opposition whenever we played them, just as all the teams we played would be. And despite their perceived lowly status, that would include Southend. Their lads would be up for playing us and would want to get a good result, a chance to go on a little run themselves.

It wasn't as if the smaller teams never stood a chance in the FA Youth Cup. The competition for places at the big clubs was so great, then and now, that a lot of decent youngsters would opt for a so-called lesser club, thinking they'd have a better chance of making it into the first team there. There had been some decent sides in the competition who'd recently won it that had not been seen as a 'glamour' clubs. Millwall won it in 1979 and Crystal Palace won it two years prior to that. Then there was Bristol City and Huddersfield, both of which reached the final during the previous decade. This was testimony that if you had a decent set-up and encouraged the best of the young lads to sign for you, rather than Liverpool, Arsenal or Chelsea, you could do well. It would have been all the inspiration that those Southend lads needed for that game, but it would have been for us as well. On the night we wanted it just that little bit more, beating them 6-0 at Carrow Road with Jon Rigby scoring a hat-trick; Mark Crowe, Brendan McIntyre and Paul Clayton scoring the others.

Mark Crowe was, perhaps, of all the players in our squad that season. He was named the youth team Player of the Season at the end of that campaign, something that, in a team that did the League and Cup double, was some achievement. He made his first-team debut as a substitute in the game at Brighton that December when he was still seventeen, and was our captain and an England Youth International. Everyone talked about him. Mark Crowe, the next big thing to come out of Carrow Road, even the fans knew who he was. Yet that appearance against Brighton turned out to be his first and last for the first team. He had 16 minutes of glory before, for whatever reason, he slipped out of the game, joining Torquay before moving onto Cambridge United and then into non-league football. He was, without doubt, a very gifted footballer who had all the attributes needed to make it in the game, yet didn't. It's not for me to judge Mark of course, or make suggestions as to why his career peaked with us that season, but what it does illustrate is that glory and honours at that level, whether it be winning cups or playing for your country, is by no means a guarantee that you are going to make it in the game. This is a fact that is as relevant and pertinent to any team that have done well at that level.

If we were ever going to slip up (and we didn't think we would) then it would have been in our game against Arsenal in the next round. But we drew 2-2 at their place, got them back for a replay at Carrow Road a week later and stuck four goals past them, going one better in the following round when we beat Aston Villa. This was a team I might, had things perhaps turned out a little differently, have been playing for myself. I wonder if any of their staff that night remembered me? But no worries, we were better than them all over the pitch and won 5-2.

By now, the Norwich fans were getting a little bit excited about the prospect of their youth team going all the way in the competition, and nearly 4,000 turned out at Carrow Road to see us beat Watford 3-1 in the fourth round. That win gave us the plumb tie in the quarter-finals against Manchester United at Old Trafford, a game no one except us thought we'd win. But we did, 1-0, with Louie Donowa scoring. That home gate more than doubled for the second-leg game of the semi-final, against Luton Town on 7 April, which we drew 0-0, one of the rare occasions we had failed to score at home that season. The good work had already been done mind you, a 3-1 win in the first leg at their place putting us into the final, Jon Rigby and Paul Clayton getting the goals, two guys who couldn't stop scoring that season. Big things were expected of them as well, I thought they were brilliant players and felt sure they'd go on to become big names in the game. Sadly, that didn't turn out to be the case, just as it hadn't with Mark Crowe. I don't think I was alone in thinking that both would make the grade either, we all thought they would. Paul ended up making fifteen appearances for the first team, but at that level his scoring prowess seemed to abandon him, and as a striker you are judged on your goals, not hard work or other attributes to your game. He scored eight goals in our Youth Cup triumph that season, also scoring for the reserves, but he didn't quite make the final step up.

So there we were, in the final – mission accomplished. Well, almost, we had to win it first. We'd already won the league, walked it without losing a game. Yet Everton, our opponents in the final, started as favourites. But that suited us. And, let's face it, win or lose, getting to the final was a massive achievement for us, the first time a Norwich City side had ever got that far. Along with it, the crowds and expectation grew. For the first leg of that final at Carrow Road there were around 12,000 people there. In the league games, we were certainly used to playing in front of a couple of hundred people. That game ended in a narrow 3-2 victory for us, and is especially memorable for me as I scored our winning goal. It came from a set piece, with the ball coming nicely to me on the edge of the penalty area. I just got my head over the ball and drilled the thing. It absolutely flew into the net – what a feeling.

But the job was only half done. For the second leg at Goodison Park there were near 15,000 spectators, the great majority of them expecting Everton to turn it around. Massive ground, massive pressure to get a result. I loved it, loved that pressure and all that went with it. I couldn't wait to get out there, especially having scored that winner in the first leg. Yes, of course there were doubts before kick-off. Can I cope? Am I good enough, strong enough, fit enough? This is a big game, will I be able to rise to the occasion? It would be, by far, the biggest game I'd ever played in, in my life. For some of the players involved, it would be the biggest game they would ever play in their entire careers. So yes, I was a little frightened beforehand.

There was, as I have already said, a lot expected of us and you felt that. But we were a good side with some good players. Jon Rigby and Paul Clayton were a tremendous pair in attack, they got forty-eight between them in the League and cup competitions that season. Then there was Tony Spearing, a fantastic attacking left-back, who went on to have a good career in the game, with seventy-odd games for Norwich and about the same for Leicester City. Tony was a fantastic person to have in the changing rooms, confident, comical and a leader. I loved being in his company and seeing him in the team as he took no prisoners, a very strong, brave and reliable player. He now heads up the European scouting network at West Brom and is doing well for himself, just as it always looked he would, even right back then.

Dave Stringer had us playing in a strict 4-4-2 formation, and you played that way back then whether you liked it or not! We knew, after that first leg, that meeting Everton on their own ground was going to be as tough a match as any we had yet had, probably in our entire careers to date. Everton were a good side, make no mistake about it. Their centre-forward, Mark Farrington, was a big threat; he'd scored their two goals in the first leg and had put himself about a bit, giving our defence a hard time. We would need to keep a close eye on him in the second leg, a game that we'd have to play very well in to win.

And we played well in that second leg but it wasn't quite enough. Everton won 3-2, our first defeat of the season, meaning the final score was 5-5 on aggregate. But no golden goal or penalties back then. We all had to go back and do it again, Everton winning the toss and electing, not surprisingly, to play the deciding game at their ground, nearly a month after that second game was played. It gave us a lot to think about, and it meant that our season was anything but over. We'd done well and we knew it, but nothing changed.

We got back to Norwich late that night and the next day it was back to Trowse and back to work. Cleaning boots, answering the telephone, keeping an eye out for the gaffer (Ken Brown) and his assistant, Mel Machin, who'd seize on any opportunity to have a little dig at you. There was no time to sit back and bask in the glory of what we've achieved already, and no point trying to do so, Dave Stringer would never have allowed it. So we remained focused, working hard at our game and our jobs until the day of the decider, then it was off to Goodison again for the deciding game, which we won 1-0, Paul Clayton getting the goal, much to the suprise of the 22,000-strong home crowd, who fully expected their side to win. Winning the Youth Cup that year was one of the greatest achievements of my life, I feel so proud to have been part of such a magnificent team.

There's one thing about those games at Everton I'll never forget. Before one of them it was almost my birthday. Just before that game, my mum came up to me and gave me a little gift; it was a ring that I have worn ever since then and one I'll wear forever. My family were so proud of me, they saw these games and the success I'd had with the youth team as a culmination of all the sacrifices they'd made for me, all the driving around and late nights over the years, as well as the love and support they'd constantly given me when things weren't going as well. It's funny, on that day, when she gave me that ring, not long before kick-off at Goodison, she went and lost hers. It seems almost symbolic doesn't it, like passing on the torch or something. And here we all were, at one of the most famous football stadiums in the country, with me so close to making it. I was so close and yet, at the same time, so far. Because there was so much to do still, so much hard work, effort and application. For those two games, I did allow myself to sit back for a moment and take everything in that I'd achieved so far, with the climax of all of that about to start. It was something I could proudly share with my parents.

But of course, I hadn't made it. We had two cups and two sets of winners' medals in our hands, souvenirs of a great season. Some of the lads had already made their first-team debuts, but even they knew that didn't mean they'd made it. There was still so much hard work to do to push on. Indeed, those next few months would probably be as hard and challenging as any that I had yet faced in the game to make the stellar leap from the youth team to the first team. But achieving that alone was not good enough, not for me. Remember Mark Crowe, the classic case of an outstanding, young player who went from a successful youth sides to play a few games for the first team, before almost totally disappearing from the game altogether. He'd made his senior debut for Norwich in 1982 with the footballing world at his feet. Less than seven years later he was playing for Thetford Town, the success of that season with all of us and his England Youth side call up all but forgotten.

For one thing, I still had to look after Mike Channon. He'd wind me up all the time, socks up one tree, shorts in another, watching me clamber up the tree to get them and giving me a hard time in the process, as if it had been me that put them there in the first place. And, when I did get them, he'd want them washed, dried, pressed and made ready for him to use. Ah, the glamour. And, double winners or not, we still had to knock on that first-team dressing room door and wait to be asked in, our achievements meant nothing to the denizens of that exclusive little enclave. Every one of them, everyone at the club, they were watching us, waiting, looking to see what happened next. Would we push on or would we fall away, some of us thinking we were the finished article and getting a bit of the 'big time Charlie' about us? Pressure, pressure, pressure – nothing had changed.

But, aside from all that, one thing bothered me the most, and, at the same time, made me determined to make it into the first team and become a regular starter. It came from one of those first-team lads whom I was so nervous about, Keith

Bertschin to be exact, and a piece I read about him in *Shoot!,* or a similar magazine at that time. It was one of those pieces that the fans love and the players grudgingly respond to. It was a list of questions about themselves, including some personal ones like their favourite TV show and so on. The last question in the piece was a very straight forward football one, asking him which player, out of all those in our successful youth team, that he thought stood the best chance of going on to do well in the game? Keith's answer stood out a mile for me ... 'Jeremy Goss.'

I read it and read it again, and I started to shake. If Keith Bertschin, a successful professional, respected player and proven goalscorer at the highest of levels, one of the 'players' in more ways than one, thought that of me, then how the hell could I even think about letting him down? I couldn't, I couldn't let him down, not after he said that. I resolved, then and there, to work even harder at my game, frightened of being a disappointment to Keith, a legend at Norwich, after the very public faith he'd placed in me.

By the time the 1983/84 season began, I was eighteen and ready and wanting to make my first-team debut at some point during that season. It was at the back of my mind that quite a few of my team mates had already done so. Mark Crowe, Louie Donowa and Mark Metcalf had all come off the bench at some point the previous season to play, although, in every case, that was as many appearances as they made that season. At the start of that campaign I wasn't anywhere near the first team. Peter Mendham played in my position and was as nailed as a starter in Ken Brown's first XI as it was possible to get. Ken had previously called me into his office at the end of the previous season; a moment I met with some trepidation, thinking 'This is it, I'm gone, he's going to let me go'.

But of course, it wasn't that bad. I went in and he was quick and to the point, 'Gossy, just sign this professional contract will you? It's for a year and this is what you'll be earning.' No room for negotiation and certainly no agents. I don't think anyone had heard of them back then, or at least we hadn't. I didn't need to read or check it though. I was delighted. I sat down, signed it with the club secretary by my side and walked away with it with an enormous smile on my face. I got to my car, that £60 blue Mini my dad had bought for me, still smiling, and drove all the way home to Folkestone to big hugs all round. 'Guess what? I'm a professional football player with Norwich City.'

We had a bit of a celebration, as you can imagine. And, if I'm honest, it all brought a tear to my eye. It was my reward, the culmination of that dream that I'd been holding close to my heart for the last few years. It also made me think, again, of the people who'd helped me get there. Especially Mum and Dad. I was happy for me and for them. But, as it all sank in and I planned my training routine for the summer, it began to dawn on me that things were going to be a little different that following season. For a start, I'd be changing in the first-team dressing room and wouldn't have to knock before I went in anymore. I'd still sit there as quiet as a mouse, mind, as a first-year pro. I couldn't, and wasn't, going to throw my weight about. And guess what? I now had my own apprentice. I got Dion as I've already said, but I can't remember who my first one was. I would have been soft on him mind. Little things, like coming off the training pitch and throwing my boots down onto the big pile of them at the edge of that pitch, there for the apprentices to go through, clean and return to you. Only a few months earlier, I'd been working my way through that never-ending pile, now I was contributing to it. Another thing I remember, small but so significant, was filling in application forms which asked what your occupation was, I could put 'professional footballer'. That gave me such a buzz, or at least it did until I got an insurance quote back and the price of the premiums had gone through the roof because of the perceived risks involved with my occupation. It now cost me a fortune to drive around in that Mini.

But look, the novelty soon wore off. I was one of a group of around twenty-two players, all of whom wanted to be in the first team and thought they should be in the first team. That meant, especially as back then there was only one sub picked for every game, there'd be a lot of disappointed footballers every week. I spent much of my time in the reserves, including at training where we had to act as the 'opposition' to the first team in practice matches and set pieces. In other words, Mel Machin would set us up as whatever team we were due to be playing that week, which meant taking set pieces like they did or setting up defensive walls as they did. Mel would get me to take the corners for example. And I had to do it properly, do it exactly as the named player from the opposition would do, else Mel would give me a bollocking, in fact, he'd batter me.

He was a hard man, but as a coach I thoroughly respected him, he knew what he was talking about. Mel often told me that I was a coach's dream. Was that because of the way I played? No, it was because I did as I was told. If he wanted fifty press-ups, I'd get on and do them. A hundred? No problem Mel. Run around that training pitch a dozen times. Sure thing. Mel was playing the game, keeping an eye on me, seeing how this new addition to the senior ranks would react, how he'd behave or be able to follow instructions. I did everything I could to make a good impression. It must have paid off. On one of the early away trips at the start of the 1983/84 season, I was named as a member of the first-team travelling party. There was my name, right at the bottom of the fifteen or sixteen who'd been selected to go.

I was made up because I knew it meant I had a small chance of being picked as one of the twelve the next day against, I think, Aston Villa. There was a slightly bigger chance that I'd also be the gopher on that trip, making all the teas and coffees for the first-team players, running up and down the aisle of that coach and making sure all their needs were being seen to. They respected what I had achieved, but it was still a case of 'Well done Gossy on getting your pro deal, but you're still the youngest here, so you'll have to do as you're told'. And I did. Mind you, that journey was nothing compared to the fear that went through me when I found out who I'd be rooming with. It was only Mike Channon, yes, of all people, it had to be him. Rooming with him, even just for one night, was going to be one of the scariest things I'd ever done in my life. All sorts of thoughts were racing through my mind. Will I have to talk to him? Will he expect me to run around after him making him tea and coffee? What if I snore and he doesn't get a good night's sleep before the big game and it's all my fault? Seriously, I was bricking it. We got to Birmingham and all went up to our rooms, then, for one reason or another, we ended up being late going down for dinner that evening, Mick was going on at me: 'Come on, come on, we've got to be down there'. Maybe I'd been in the loo or something, first night nerves, whatever. In the end, when I did get downstairs, I found that I was the very last of all the club party there that night to arrive, I was late and I was last.

Imagine then, how I felt when I finally made it downstairs to the dining room. All of the other lads were sat down, and, what's more, they had pulled two tables together and arranged it so that there was absolutely no room for me to sit with them anywhere. The table was full. There was one space next to Ken Brown and Mel Machin on the staff table, they were sat away from the players, along with Tim Sheppard our physio. I therefore had a dilemma. Do I casually pull up another chair and manage to make myself a little bit of extra room on the two main tables with all the other lads? I wasn't quite sure how I could, but there were some spares about the place so it was sort of possible, although it would mean a lot of messing and moving about. Or, do I go and sit down away from all the lads on the staff table, sat there, bold as brass, the first away trip and with Ken Brown and Mel Machin? It's a problem and one I struggled to work out as my mind was doing nothing but saying 'Oh shit, what do I do?' over and over again!

Then the decision was made for me. Tim Sheppard looked up at me and called across the room, 'Gossy, there's a spare seat here. Come and sit down son.' So I did. Except that I was now sat directly opposite the first-team table, trying desperately not to look at them or make eye contact as they are all looked at me, pointing, stifling giggles and enjoying every second of my embarrassment.

And then it got worse. The waiters came over to get everyone's orders. Now this was another problem for me. I had barely eaten at a restaurant in my life. I didn't know what to do or ask for, I didn't have a clue. I got away with the starter, luckily enough, by asking for the soup, which was tomato, a meal I was familiar with. Things could only get better now, or so I thought. By now, the other lads were starting to lob a few suggestions over at me, the banter is starting with questions like 'What's the team tomorrow then Gossy?', and 'Gossy, ask the gaffer if I'm starting tomorrow?' It was getting beyond embarrassing and I opted to get stuck in to my soup in the hope their attention will go elsewhere. Still, feeling my cheeks smarting with the shame of it all, I broke up my bread roll and dunked it into the bowl of soup that had been placed in front of me. As I did, Mel Machin slammed his knife and fork down onto the table with an enormous crash that made everyone jump and look up, before he glared in my direction saying, 'You disgusting filthy pig'.

It had all gone quiet now. Everyone was looking in my direction. I couldn't go any redder if I tried. My face was, I knew, the colour of a Liverpool shirt. I looked up at Mel, the bread still in my hand, dripping soup back into the bowl, and managed to squeak a reply in his direction, barely audible but he hears it. 'Erm, sorry, what Mel?' He said it again. 'You disgusting filthy pig. Who are you, to sit here, next to me, whilst I'm trying to enjoy my dinner, dip your bread in your soup like that? You disgust me.' Mel put a long, hard emphasis on the word 'disgust'. I just wanted to slip under the table and, politely and quietly, die.

As the meal continued, I'd occasionally glance across at the lads all eating together on the other table and every time, behind Mel's back, they would smile at me as they all dipped their bread into their soup. I soon lost my appetite and hardly ate a thing. When the meal was over, I disappeared back up to the room and hid away until the next morning. Mel had been testing me, seeing if I would come out of my shell and how I would react. I later learnt that it was a little ritual he went through with all the young lads, a bit of a 'shock' tactic in a very public situation, seeing, for him, what we were made of. I've never forgotten it. Indeed, many years later when I bumped into Mel again, I reminded him of that trip and the incident itself.

I'd gone along to Bournemouth where he was a director of the football club. He and another board member were interviewing me for the job of youth team manager there and I mentioned it to him during the interview. He remembered. He added that he had seen me grow and achieve so much with Norwich City since then and that I was a completely different guy to the one he had challenged that evening. He gave me a lot of compliments that day in fact, and I have to say, I learnt a lot from him throughout my career.

It was a constant battle in those early days. And, whatever Mel was trying to do, it took me time to feel part of things. I remained the quiet lad in the background, not getting involved in the banter and laughing at everyone else's jokes. I got as far as the sub's bench, but that's as far as it seemed to go. In fact, I hold the record at Norwich City for being picked as substitute for the most consecutive matches. Eighteen times. The sight of me jogging up and down the old asphalt running track by the stand at Carrow Road became such a regular one that the fans used to take the piss, especially if I was running near the chap that was selling the hot dogs, coffees, and Mars Bars from a little tray he had with him. Someone in the crowd would shout ,'Oi, Gossy, get us a Twix will you?' Then someone would add, 'I'll have a coffee and a hot dog Gossy, I'm in Row G, get it up here for me mate.' I hated it, absolutely hated it. One week I'd be on the coach and part of the first-team squad going off for a big game somewhere, the next I'd be stood at the side of the pitch at Carrow Road, all these fans having a pop at me. It was all good banter and they probably thought it was funny. I didn't. I was disillusioned and wondering what I had to do to push on. Even when I got near to getting a regular place in the team, the club would then go out and buy another midfielder. Mike Phelan came in, then Ian Crook, then Andy Townsend. Every time I thought I was getting close, and about to get a run, they'd go out and get someone else in, spend money when they had me raring to go, ready to prove my value and place. Then the younger players started getting runs of games before me. Some got it and were released or moved on. But I was still there waiting, always waiting for my time to come.

The lustre of signing that first ever professional contract was beginning to wear a bit thin. I did at last (as far as I was concerned) finally make my debut for the first team. It came in an away trip to Coventry City for our penultimate fixture of the 1983/84 season, and over a year since our triumph in the FA Youth Cup. Strangely enough, out of the eight players from that side that had beaten Everton over those three games, I was the last to make an appearance for the Norwich City first team. But not only that, even Mark Farrington, the Everton striker who'd played so well for them, eventually ending up with us after they decided not to give him a professional contract, made it into our first team before me. So, as you could tell, by the time my debut finally came along, I was getting more than a little frustrated.

It was the usual routine, travelling up as part of the official party, finding out the night before the game, from Ken Brown, that I was going to be on the bench. Good and bad news really. Good, obviously, because it means that you have a chance of playing. But bad because there was only one substitute allowed back then, and managers didn't usually bring them on unless for an injury, which none of us wanted to happen to any of our players, myself included. As it turned out, I did get on. Tony Spearing and John Deehan collided with each other as they both went for a header, with the end result being that Dixie received a bad cut above the eye and had to go off. My big chance had finally arrived.

I don't really recall much of the game. I know that I ran about a lot, showing all the enthusiasm and energy that you'd expect, but I don't think I touched the ball more than two or three times. So I provided nuisance value really. We lost the game 2-1, which meant no win bonus that week but, for me, it was another box ticked, another achievement that I had set out to do accomplish. So I was a happy man. It also just happened to be the day after my nineteenth birthday, so I am pretty sure I would have been up celebrating with a few beers until early the next morning. Or, more likely, back home and straight to bed with an early morning run planned! Nothing changed there.

It was just a shame it was so near to the end of the season really. Norwich met Liverpool three days later for their final game of the season, drawing 1-1 at Carrow Road, Mark Farrington getting the nod for that place on the bench this time. No matter. I'd made the first team; it was now up to me to convince Ken Brown that I needed to be in his thoughts as soon as the 1984/85 season kicked off. That meant a summer of very hard work lay ahead. But I was ready and willing.

I wonder if Ken Brown had picked up on my frustration? All the effort, the hard work, the total and utter commitment to training. Whenever someone asks me about my career, I often tell them that I saw myself as a 'nearly man', in terms of the game and Norwich City as a whole. So near and yet so far, something that perfectly sums up that season. Last to make his debut out of that eight and, when I did, it was for a meaningless game at the end of the season. I'd only got on because John Deehan cut his eye. Was Ken Brown doing me a favour, was it a nod to me for all the work and effort I'd shown, or did they think I'd deserved being selected on merit and for my football abilities alone, which is how it always should be. But then, if it was for that reason, then why did I wait so long for my debut? Mark Metcalf made his first-team bow eighteen months before me, coming off the bench to replace my old mate Mark Barham in a game against West Ham. A game that was hardly a 'nothing' match, as Norwich had gone into it one game off the bottom of the table having just lost at home to Notts County.

You need players who can battle all day long in games like that, and I felt I fitted the bill. Mark was a decent footballer but he was more of a creative player than me, one who liked to take his time on the ball and find the pass. You needed a bit more than that at Upton Park when your backs are against the wall. You wanted someone who was more able to put his foot through the ball and win tackles, make things happen. And I felt that player was me.

So yes, I was that nearly man. Seven of my teammates got their debuts before me, with both Mark Crowe and Louie Donowa joining Mark and playing for the first team before the Youth Cup final. Why them and not me? As you can imagine, it was frustrating the hell out of me and playing havoc with my mind. Ken Brown hadn't given even a thank you, a reward, an acknowledgement for all my efforts, an end-of-season sweetener even, before they let me go. No doubt about it, I was worried for my future.

True, I was doing the miles with the first team. Up, down and across the country on the coach with the senior players, always part of things, always involved, and still (not that I minded) running up and down the aisle of that coach fetching the hot drinks for the rest of the squad. But I was also doing what seemed like miles and miles up and down the side of pitches all over the country, trying to stay loose, to look keen, to be ready when needed. And, aside from that gesture of an appearance at Coventry, I was getting nowhere. So, as I said earlier, the thrill of being a professional, of all that involvement was beginning to wear a little bit thin. I was fed up with the same small group of fans taking the piss out of me every game, and all those jokes that went with it. I was fed up with being part of the squad every week and then, when the team was announced, being on the bench-again. I also started, like most players, to get some niggling little injuries, nothing serious, just minor stuff that put me back a week or two. But it meant that the 1984/85 season was a very frustrating one for me, especially as it started well, with me coming off the bench (replacing John Devine) for my second senior appearance in a game at Tottenham on 1 September. We lost 3-1 and, in truth, we never had a hope of getting anything. Tottenham put on a great attacking display that afternoon with their winger, John Chiedozie, causing us all sorts of problems with his pace and trickery.

I made three more appearances from the bench that season. The first, four days later, against West Brom, was my senior bow at Carrow Road, and an enjoyable night as we won 2-1. It was an especially good night for Mark Farrington, who I'd played against in those FA Youth Cup final games against Everton, he scored our first before creating the second for Peter Mendham. Mark had struggled a bit since he joined us and had been warned, prior to the game, that his place at the club was by no means guaranteed, so it was good for him to answer back in such a fashion. His goal was a bit special as well, a 20-yard volley that Baggies' 'keeper, Tony Godden, who was no mug, had no chance with. I came on for Dale Gordon near the end, Ken Brown electing to play me alongside Peter Mendham, in the centre of midfield, to keep things solid and hold on to our lead, no easy task against a side that had some real attacking quality in its ranks in Cyrille Regis and Tony Morley.

I missed out on our next game against Southampton, but then got the nod to start on the bench again for the game against Stoke City on 19 September. This time, I came on for Peter as we fought out a 0-0 draw, one of the highlights of the day being on the same pitch as Alan Hudson, once of Chelsea, then thirty-two, but still showing the class that made him one of the greatest English midfielders in over a decade. His promptings and little one-touches lit up Carrow Road in what was, for the most part, a dull game. John Deehan could have won it for us, his shot was goal bound, until Mark Chamberlain somehow cleared it away. What a difference to our season it would have made if that went in.

Six games into the season and I'd featured in half of them. I'd yet to make a start but I was beginning to feel it wouldn't be that far off. John Devine, who we'd signed from Arsenal the previous summer, was reducing my chances of starting. He was a very versatile player who could either play in the centre of midfield with Peter Mendham, or slot in as a full-back, which is what he did at Sunderland in October, seamlessly replacing my good mate Denis van Wijk in the back four. Any hopes I then had of being called up to play alongside Peter Mendham were swiftly dashed, as Ken Brown then went out and signed Asa Hartford to pep up our midfield. Asa duly got the nod to start that game alongside Peter and that was that.

Frustrated again. See what I meant by the 'nearly man'? Every time it looked as if my big chance had come (and in my mind, it was due) something or someone would come along and give me a kick in the teeth. I could hardly argue with the club getting hold of Asa Hartford when the opportunity presented itself; he'd played in the top flight for nearly two decades, with long spells at Manchester City, Everton and Scotland, going to two World Cups in 1978 and 1982. He was a couple of weeks short of his thirty-fourth birthday when he signed, but with someone like Peter Mendham playing alongside him doing all the running, he hardly had to exert himself. Thus, like Alan Hudson had been doing at Stoke, Asa became a great influence in and around the club, especially to still-impressionable young pups like me. Despite the fact he'd come along and nicked our chances of getting a few games, we would listen to all and any advice he could give us.

I wasn't totally out of the picture though, as no doubt with experience of big games and expectations in mind, Ken Brown named me on the bench for the game against Manchester United on 1 December – a nice early Christmas present for the player now labelled as 'young Gossy'. They weren't the world giants they are today, certainly as far as winning trophies and big crowds are concerned. However, the attendance of 36,635 was still the biggest we played in front of that season, even if they get over double that now. No matter. It was still an enormous game for us, playing against a team that was full of quality. Players like Paul McGrath, Bryan Robson, Gordon Strachan, Mark Hughes and Norman Whiteside for example. We were up against it from the start, and it came as no surprise when Robson headed home a Hughes' cross after little more than 10 minutes to put them ahead. Shortly after that, John Deehan got a knock and had to come off, meaning I was on, with 70–75 minutes to make an impression and really stand out in our midfield. With Dixie (Deehan) coming off, we just had Mike Channon in attack, with me making up one part of a central midfield trio alongside Asa Hartford and Peter Mendham, and Louie Donowa and Dale Gordon providing the pace on the wings. We worked hard but they were formidable in defence, McGrath and Gordon McQueen easily dealing with whatever threat we were able to create. It was more about damage limitation than anything else, especially with Channon, then thirty-six, the lone striker! It came as no surprise when Mark Hughes ran onto an exquisite pass from Jesper Olsen to stroke their second past Chris Woods after half an hour. After that, it was game over. We'd lost but I'd come on and done reasonably well, getting some decent touches and making a few good passes, linking up play and running my nuts off. I also remember making a stack of mistakes but I didn't care about those. I was learning to adapt to the pace of first-team football and what a place to do it, at Old Trafford and against some of the best players in the League. I certainly thought I'd done enough to warrant the chance of a start against West Ham at Carrow Road the following week, but it wasn't to be. Dixie was still unfit so Ken Brown recalled Mark Farrington to play alongside Channon in attack, with Mendham and Hartford resuming their duties in the centre of midfield.

The news before the game that Mark Barham was, after nearly a year out with injury, now almost ready for a recall to the first team was good to hear, on a day that we won 1-0, thanks to another outrageously good goal from Farrington. This was tempered for me by the fact that he would be another rival for a first-team place. I'd started the season with a fair chance of a run of games, but now, with Mark almost fit again and Asa Hartford having signed had two more players ahead of me in the queue, I was the nearly man once again.

At least I made my full League debut early in the New Year, in a home game against Southampton at Carrow Road, a week after Ken Brown had started me in an uninspiring 0-0 draw at Birmingham in the FA Cup. I remember that the pitch was iced over for that game and it was hard to keep your balance as a result. In fact, the match should probably have been called off. One thing I do remember was passing back to Chris Woods from about 30 yards and Mel giving me a massive bollocking! Funny how things like that stick in your mind.

The Southampton game felt special as they had once rejected me. They had a team that included, shall we say, a few 'characters'. Characters like Mark Dennis and Joe Jordan, both of whom were good players, but were able to get stuck in and let you know they were there. Dennis, in particular, took no prisoners if he felt the occasion warranted it, being sent off twelve times during the course of his career. Ken Brown must have had that little bit of extra midfield steel in mind when he picked me to start alongside Peter Mendham. Our job would have been to boss that area and limit the number of chances the Saints got, or limit the number of times that Danny Wallace would have had of creating chances for Jordan. The game nearly didn't go ahead at all, a concern that started my 'nearly man' worries up all over again, but after strenuous efforts were made to clear the pitch of snow prior to kick-off, it went ahead. The conditions, which were icy and slippery, meant it wasn't a classic, one in which we eventually scraped a single goal, John Deehan, scoring it. Dennis had a quiet game by his standards but, as feared, Joe Jordan had an impact; his challenge on Dave Watson led to our captain needing lengthy treatment before being stretchered off.

That game was played on 12 January 1985. Following the welcome three points it brought us, I slipped completely out of the first-team picture as far as the league was concerned. I was playing in a reserve-team game when I injured my right knee, ending up, almost before I knew it, in hospital and needing to have an operation to fix things. This was a complete nightmare. Not only was I going to miss a lot of games through injury, but I was going to miss the club trip down to Wembley where the lads beat Sunderland in the League Cup final – a huge personal disappointment.

My next first-team game was on 6 December 1986, not far short of two years later, when I started at Goodison Park against Everton, a game we lost 4-0. I was only in that game because Ken Brown had nine first-team players missing due to injury or suspension, so our heavy defeat was hardly a surprise against an Everton team that would end the 1986/87 season as champions. Naturally, I was glad to be playing again, but I had only got selected as nine of my clubmates were unavailable. Is that what it was going to take at Norwich for me to get a game, near enough a full team to be missing before I got my chance? We were so low on numbers that the manager had called up his son, Kenny Brown, junior to the side, and in addition to that, we'd signed a lad by the name of Mark Seagraves from Liverpool on loan a couple of weeks earlier. He was twenty and hadn't made a first-team appearance for Liverpool, yet here he was, straight into the first team and expected to make, in all likelihood, as immediate a positive impression as the last lad that Norwich had brought down from Liverpool, namely Dave Watson. Luckily for me at that time, I had another option lined up for the second half of that season-but it didn't do my confidence any good to head all the way into December of that year and get just the one game, and that because, seemingly, the club had to pick anyone who was available and fit.

It was so, so frustrating for me. And I'd had enough. So much so that at one point later on I went up to see Ken Brown and poured my heart out to him, explaining my disappointment at the lack of first-team opportunities, asking him for advice on what might be the best thing I could do. He told me to hang in there, saying, 'You've got a good future at this club Gossy, your time will come son.' It never did, and at one point I was all set to rejoin Mel Machin, who'd left the club at the end of that 1986/87 season in order to join Manchester City as manager.

Today, Manchester City are one of the world's top sides. Money seems to be no object to them in terms of players or infrastructure, and they very clearly have people in charge who will stop at nothing to ensure that they win the Champions League, then do so again. Things were not quite as good when Mel joined them. They'd ended that season in one of the relegation places, which meant Mel's brief, upon appointment, would have been to the point – get us promoted back to the top flight again. There was no doubt their board were aware of just how tough an operator Mel was, and how much he expected from his players. It really was a case of 'my way or the highway' with Mel, and any slackers in their squad would soon find themselves bombed out of the club. I was certainly flattered that Mel wanted me as one of his first signings. He certainly sold the club to me, got me up to Maine Road for a look around and told me of his plans for them. I was impressed. The ground held around 35,000 people when it was full, and Mel was determined to build a side that went up playing the sort of football that would mean the crowds packing into the place every time they played. It was an easy decision to make really, and as far as I was concerned, even though I was dropping a division to play my football, it didn't matter because I would be a regular first-team player getting loads of games.

Mel said he wanted me to operate in the centre of midfield, playing alongside some of the more creative players at the club, the likes of Paul Lake and David White, doing what I did best, winning the ball and doing all the running to ensure players had the time and space to take chances and score goals. Brilliant! Just as I was about to sign, their chairman, Peter Swales, and his contemporary at Norwich, Arthur South, fell out over something. So that was that, the deal was off. Naturally, I was more than displeased that I had to pay the price for their little tiff, but there was little I could do about it. Looking back, I'd approached everything in the wrong way. I should have spoken to Ken about Man City but, instead, I went behind his back. That was stupid. To his eternal credit though, Mel never forgot me, and a few years later, when he took charge of Barnsley, he was onto me again about joining him there. I went to meet with him at Oakwell and was again impressed. My mind made up, I went to see Dave Stringer who had, by then, taken over from Ken Brown. I submitted an official transfer request, expecting the whole thing to go through without a hitch. However, Dave rejected it out of hand, saying I was going nowhere and, on top of that, offered me a new three year deal at Norwich.

I'd been desperate to get away from the club so I could play and enjoy my football regularly, yet with that gesture, Dave made me believe that the club still wanted me. It didn't take me long to agree to what was on offer, and within a few days, I had committed myself to Norwich City again, now more determined than ever to make it at the club I was swiftly regarding as my own.

6

From Sweden with Love

My attitude was way out there for anyone to see. A case of go on then, sack me. I don't care. I'll get another club, no problem. Because I'm sick to death of being the nearly man, of the tag 'young Gossy', of hearing Dave Stringer say, 'Gossy, your time will come son.' Well it hadn't and it wouldn't. As far as I was concerned, I was finished at Norwich City.

Mel Machin's attempts to sign me for Manchester City and Barnsley were not the first time that another team wanted to lure me away from Carrow Road with a view to my playing my football elsewhere. While Mel had been unsuccessful on both occasions, the first approach was made did more to boost my confidence and self belief than anything that had previously happened in my career, including that FA Youth Cup win back in 1983.

It came towards the end of the 1985/86 season. The previous one had ended on a bit of a low point for both me and the club. We'd won the League Cup at Wembley, beating Sunderland in the final. My chances of featuring or being anywhere near that, however, were zero, thanks to one of those niggling little injuries I'd picked up. Mind you, there is a nice tale around that. After we had won that game, Ken Brown came round to see me in his Rolls-Royce, complete with the League Cup for me to see and hold. We then went for a little drive around with it, me in the back of this Rolls with the trophy. I just sat there, enjoying the moment and looking at Ken and thinking, 'This is the best man I've ever met in my life.' And I really thought that. He'd given me that first contract as a professional footballer, my first-team debut at Coventry, and earlier in that 1984/85 season, my first start in the game against Southampton, one of the clubs that had, of course, rejected me when I was a schoolboy. So I had good reason to like the man, all the more so because he'd bothered to bring that trophy round to me, injured and fed up, making me feel very special and appreciated.

And yet I didn't feel as if he had any real faith in me. I missed all of the following campaign, one that saw the club win promotion back to the First Division, after winning that League Cup and getting relegated in the same season. Injuries didn't help of course, but, even so, new players kept on coming in, almost three at once in the summer of 1985. We're talking Mike Phelan, Garry Brooke and David Williams, all good players and all midfielders. How do you think that made me feel? It didn't appear as if Ken had any long term faith in me, and as a result, my morale, which was already low, dropped and then dropped some more, so much so that I even began to wonder if I had a future in the game. But I didn't think that way for long, I wouldn't allow it. So, by December 1985, with me fit and ready to play, I went to see Ken again and, like before, laid my cards on the table. I told him straight, I wasn't happy, I wanted to play and that I had to get away, someplace else, where I could at least get a game every week, no matter where it was.

Ken understood straight away. 'How about a loan move?' This was great. That meant I'd get a move and some games, but that the club still wanted me, that they didn't want to sell or release me, but get me a good loan deal somewhere so I could play and come back to Carrow Road a better player. A player that was finally ready for the first team. After all, since I'd signed that first professional contract at the end of the 1982/83 season, in the three seasons that had followed that, I had made the grand total of one start, plus five more appearances off the bench. It was a good suggestion, the proverbial no brainer. 'Yes gaffer, anywhere to get a game. Thank you.' His next line threw me a little mind. 'How about Sweden?' I hesitated for perhaps a quarter of a second. 'Yep, great. Tell me more.'

The club that were interested in talking me on loan were IFK Luleå. They wanted me straight away, for a six-month spell lasting until the following July. They were based in a small town on the north coast of the country, one that only had a population of around 45,000, a town in local term is the same size as Kings Lynn. They played in the Swedish First Division, the equivalent to our Second Division which is now the Championship. They wanted me and I was desperate to join up with them. Ken got the ball rolling and soon there were three representatives from the club watching me in training. We got together after the training session, they were impressed, asking me if I wanted to play for them and I gave an unequivocal 'yes'. And that was that, it was pretty much sorted out overnight, with me flying out there to join them within a week. And what can I say? It was magnificent, a real boost to me and my character in every conceivable way. My game developed, my personality grew, I became a better player and a more confident individual as a result. And I soon found myself loving absolutely everything about Sweden. The country, the people, the food, the places and their attitude to life itself. But also the football, the way we trained and, of course, the way the game was played. There was none of the frenetic stuff that you experienced every week in England, it was all one and two touch, very technical, a game where the ball was always played to your feet and everyone, no matter what their position, was comfortable with the ball.

Luleå played with a sweeper, a 'spare' man who sat behind the back four. His role was to dictate the tempo and direction of the game. Thus, when the 'keeper got possession, his two full-backs would push up as high as they could, usually to near the halfway line, while the two centre-halves would take a position on the edge of the 18-yard box. Now this immediately gives the two opposing strikers a problem – who do you keep an eye on? As an opposition, it's a lot easier to master a flat and predictable back four, but this more mobile one is more of a challenge. Did they push up alongside the full-backs or stay central with the two defenders in the middle? More often than not, they'd push wide towards the full-backs, meaning there was time and space for the 'keeper to roll the ball out to the sweeper. He'd then advance in the 'D' on the edge of the penalty area and start the move, ball at feet and options ahead of him.

People rave, and rightly so, about Barcelona and the way they play the game today, the famous 'tiki-taka'. But listen, they were playing that type of football in Sweden nearly three decades ago. It wasn't anywhere near the level of Barca of course, but the strategy was the same; whoever was on the ball should have at least three passing options around him. It was all one- and two-touch, keeping and supporting possession, but at a slower pace than you'd see in England. The game was slower and very precise, possession was everything. I loved it. In England, I'd been so used to the way the full backs would get the ball and bang it 30 yards up the pitch with everyone pushing up quick to win the drop downs. It wasn't like that in Sweden, and it was a delight to experience and play that type of football, something that was a great learning curve for me.

One thing became very clear to me after I had been in Sweden for a while. The way of life and the style of football suited me down to the ground. I still had the 'run all day' and aggression factor as part of my play, which the Swedish players loved. And, while I brought a different level of fitness to the team, I was also developing a better touch on the ball as I was getting a lot more possession from the type of play they favoured. I had no doubt that I could have made a decent living for myself out there, maybe I would have progressed at Luleå and, with a bit of luck, eventually got a move to one of the biggest clubs in the country, clubs like as IFK Göteborg, Malmö FF and AIK. I could have won medals and would have been playing in European football every season – who knows? The prospect crossed my mind more than once, it was a very tempting one indeed. After all, here I was, every week, playing a style of football that suited me, with people who I really liked and got on well with. I picked up a bit of the language too. In essence, I loved out it there, and what was the alternative? Scratching around in the reserves at Norwich or sat on the bench for week after week, running up and down the side of the pitch in order to stem the boredom while some old fan in the crowd asks me to lob a Mars Bar their way.

What would you do? The thing was, I still had a massive drive to prove myself in English football at Norwich, to show the critics and detractors how wrong they were. Maybe if I'd gone to Sweden after having done even moderately well at Norwich then things might have been different. But I had yet to really achieve anything there and it was playing on my mind. I also had my family back in England, and being a family-orientated lad, I missed them. It was, for a time, a quandary. Luckily for me, Norwich took steps to solve it for me. I got back in time for the start for pre-season training in the summer of 1986 and without warning, was offered a new two-year deal by the club. Now, they'd obviously had some good reports so when that offer was made, I had little hesitation in accepting. It was a guaranteed two years, a lot of security and a lot of time to finally push on and achieve what I wanted to achieve at the club.

I still went back to Luleå the following December for a second loan stint with them and, again, thoroughly enjoyed myself and the football. It helped, of course, that I looked like one of the locals; that blond barnet came in handy after all. On a serious note, I found myself fitting in with all things Swedish very easily. My first loan stint with them went well, and during the second, they took me on for pretty much all of the Swedish league season. This was one of the reasons why I only made one appearance for the Norwich first team during the 1986/87 season, in that match at Everton where they were looking for anyone who was fit and available. I headed back to Sweden and Luleå soon after that match, and soon felt right at home among the very companionable and laid-back Swedes.

While I was out there, I also became very fond of a brand of Swedish sausage called Bullens Pilsnerkorv – see, I told you I tried to fit right in! It is (I'm putting my *Masterchef* hat on here) a sausage product that was named after the Swedish actor, Erik Berglund, who was also a food writer. You don't cook or grill the sausage though, the best and only way to enjoy it is to warm it in a hot broth, ideally the one that it comes with it in the jar. My likeness for these became a bit of a standing joke among my teammates, so much so, that after I had returned to England, a local sports reporter who I got to know out there, by the name of Peter Lundgren, used to send consignments of them back to me in Norwich. Even nearly thirty years later, as we were researching this book, one chap who Ed was in contact with asked him if Jeremy 'still liked the Bullens Pilsnerkorv?'

In my two spells at the club I played a total of twenty-three games, scoring two goals. I also played in a significant friendly game, one which, as it turned out, was one of my last official 'duties' as a IFK Luleå player. Relations between the club and Norwich City had become so cordial that, on 3 August 1987, they met in a friendly match, one of six that Norwich played in Scandinavia prior to the beginning of the 1987/88 season with me playing against my own teammates! It was a good game and I gave it everything, as I always do, even though I was disappointed with the result at the final whistle, as Norwich beat us 3-1.

I remember not daring to tackle Ian Crook during that game, either I didn't want to risk hurting him or I didn't want to mistime it and have Chippy make me look stupid. So I shadowed him for the whole game, playing and learning at the same time. And I noticed the difference between the game I'd been playing in Sweden and how Norwich played. They were fitter than us and faster than us. Yes, we were strong technically and good on the ball. But they were just so fit, physical and full of pace and energy. They ran us into the ground and we were all shattered after that game. That was where the Swedes were miles ahead of the English. They knew all about lactic acid build-up and how to deal with it.

The best way? Jump into an ice bath. Except we didn't even have to do that. We just ran and jumped into the nearest fjord. We'd stand around in that for a while, the water would be icy but beautifully clear, and then, once we were done, it would be straight into the sauna. Peace, tranquillity and relaxation. In the sauna with all of your mates, eating some of that Bullens Pilsnerkorv which gave you a massive energy boost. Good times. I look back on it all with nothing but fond memories. For the places, the people and the football. I'd like to go back there one day with my family, show Margaret, Jacob and Joseph a little of the country, maybe introduce them to the sauna. I don't think they'd enjoy jumping into the icy fjords quite so much as I did.

So, the second spell at Luleå was over, it was fond farewells and back to England. The 1987/88 season was about to kick off and I wanted to play. I wasn't expecting to walk straight into the team but I was going to make sure that Ken Brown found it difficult to leave me out. The club, as usual, had brought some new players in. Mark Bowen had arrived from Tottenham for the start of the season, as had Simon Ratcliffe, a former England Schoolboys captain who'd joined from Manchester United. Norwich were clearly hoping to build on the very good previous season they'd had, one which had seen them finish fifth in the First Division with players like Steve Bruce, Kevin Drinkell and Mike Phelan, all players who made a big and favourable impression on the game. My once youth-team colleague, Tony Spearing, had also started thirty-nine out of Norwich's forty-two league games that season.

I was delighted for Tony. But with that delight came back that old feeling of frustration. He was in, he was a player now. So why wasn't I? It didn't help that the club had a poor start to the season, losing seven out of their first ten league games. That led to Ken Brown getting the sack after a 2-0 defeat at Charlton, one that had the Norwich fans waving white hankies in protest at the end of the game. Two days later, Brown was gone and Dave Stringer, my old manager from the youth team was installed as his replacement.

Now Dave knew me, knew what I had to offer. We were struggling and I thought that maybe I'd have a chance with him in charge. He knew I'd never let him or the team down in terms of work rate and commitment. Plus, I was a different type of midfield player compared to the others at Dave's disposal, and could easily see myself playing alongside the likes of Chippy, Mike Phelan and Ruel Fox. They were all good players, yet they were players who created, made things happen. They needed, I thought, someone alongside them who could win the ball and give it to them, make sure they had the opportunities to make things happen. And, it seemed, Dave Stringer, initially at least, agreed with my way of thinking. His first match in charge was at home to Arsenal on 21 November 1987 and there I was, a starter, with No. 10 on the back of my shirt in a midfield quartet with Chippy alongside me in the middle, and Mike Phelan and Dale Gordon in the wide positions.

We lost 4-2 but I expected to keep my place in the team. One thing you didn't do with Dave Stringer, however, was be complacent, because I was out again for the next game with Trevor Putney taking my place. I returned the favour to Putters on Boxing Day, against Derby and finally had a good run in the first team, playing in all bar one of our remaining league games that season, as well as a couple more in two FA Cup ties against Swindon.

I also scored my first goals for the club in that run. The first was against Chelsea at Carrow Road two days after the Derby game. We battered them 3-0, I got the second with about 20 minutes left. But it got better. My second that season was at White Hart Lane against Tottenham. Ossie Ardiles was playing for them, and it was an honour for me to be on the same pitch as him. It was a shame that Chippy was injured and missed the opportunity to orchestrate our play in front of him and the Tottenham management. No worries though. There were about 10 minutes of the first half left when I got onto a cross, connected with it perfectly and sent the header flying past Bobby Mimms. I got a knock as I made contact, probably courtesy of Terry Fenwick, but we were on our way and we went on to win 3-1, a great result at a ground where it's never been easy to come away with something. Am I pleased with how things were going and how my career was picking up under Dave Stringer? You bet. I was buzzing.

I ended that 1987/88 season having made twenty-two league appearances for the club, of which only two came from the bench. The team had picked up after its bad start as well, in fact, we got as high as ninth at one point but ended up in fourteenth place, well clear of the relegation places. There had been some controversies and disappointments. The repercussions of Ken Brown's sacking went on for a while and, for a time, Robert Chase the club chairman was an unpopular figure (a signs of things to come). We also witnessed the beginning, and end, of John O'Neill's career as a player for Norwich City. He came in as a more than capable replacement for the Manchester-United-bound Steve Bruce, making his debut for us at Plough Lane, the then home of Wimbledon.

Wimbledon and Plough Lane. Wow. It was always an experience. As the away side, you'd always be in the smallest of dressing rooms, with little or no room to hang your stuff, one loo that might or might not work and perhaps one functional shower head with no hot water, but cold, if you were lucky. The home team would be in their own relatively luxurious dressing room right next to you, and all you would hear as you got ready for the game was their ghetto blaster at maximum volume, constantly on, playing some track that had a constant, loud bass and beat – bloody awful stuff. Then the Wimbledon lads would be banging on the walls, letting you know they're there with threats and promises all: 'We're coming to get you', that sort of thing. Class A intimidation, there was no one better.

Anyway, John was with us and completely up for his first game as a top-class replacement for Steve, slotting in alongside Shaun Elliott, a lad who been signed from Sunderland at the start of the previous season. It had been Watson and Bruce for so long but now, a way down the line, we had Elliott and O'Neill. Would it have worked? It was hard to tell. The tragedy for John O'Neill is that he never got the opportunity to show what a good player he was in a Norwich shirt. He'd played over 300 games for Leicester City, as well as having had the experience of two consecutive World Cups with Northern Ireland, and at twenty-nine he had a few years of top flight life left in him yet. I've already said how I didn't like new signings coming in if it meant they were going to push me out of the side, but you couldn't argue with someone like John coming in. I was on the bench for the game and, true to form, Wimbledon were at us from the start. Big, long balls humped up field for John Fashanu and Alan Cork to chase, the rest of them getting in our players faces as much as they could. It wasn't personal, just the Wimbledon way. Vinnie Jones remains their best known player, but there were others who could put themselves about. Eric Young was one, a strapping, very old-school centre-half who went by the nickname of 'Ninja'. Then there was Dennis Wise, skilful enough to go on to play for Chelsea and England but right at home in the melee on the pitch, a good player and one who you could see would go onto better things if he could ever tear himself away from Plough Lane.

Then there was John Fashanu. He always seemed to play well against us. I don't know if it was because Norwich had bombed him out after he'd made only seven appearances for the club. His older brother, Justin, got all the early fame and attention during his time with Norwich and beyond, but, if anything, leaving Norwich and being under the radar seemed to suit John and he did well for himself, getting back into the top flight with Wimbledon after spells with Lincoln City and Millwall. His goal gave Wimbledon a 1-0 win, meaning we were stuck in twentieth place; not the best place to be, even at that stage of the season. Yet, slowly, we began to put together some good little runs, including seven games without defeat from late January to the middle of March. Unfortunately for John O'Neill, the injury he sustained in the Wimbledon game meant that he never played another competitive game again, a tragedy for both him and the club as he was a quality player.

Dave had also added Robert Fleck to the squad, and after so sadly losing John to that injury, he brought in Andy Linighan from Oldham Athletic. We finished the season in fourteenth place. If we hadn't had a terrible run of games at the end, one that saw us win only one in nine, I reckon we could have finished in the top ten. But, whichever way you looked at it, we ended the season as a side that looked as if it had a lot to give, one with a core of good players at its heart, like Mark Bowen, Ian Culverhouse, Bryan Gunn, Mike Phelan and Robert Fleck. After all, having been an ever-present feature in our last twelve games (despite coinciding with that poor run) I had reason to believe that I would be in Dave Stringer's plans at the start of the following season. My time, I concluded, had finally come.

How wrong can a man be? I came back for pre-season training in the summer of 1988 like a man obsessed. Fitter than I had ever been and faster, more committed and twice as dedicated. Dave Stringer had put a lot of faith in me towards the end of the previous season and I was determined to prove to him and my teammates that I would start the new one as I meant to go on – in the first team, willing, able and capable, a man that his manager and his mates could trust and someone who wouldn't let them down. Not getting games didn't come into it. I'd made the breakthrough, played the games and even got a couple of goals. I was ready.

But it was as if the last half of the previous season had all been in vain, that it was a fluke, an aberration. As the season started and went on, nothing changed. I couldn't believe it. But hey, listen. That wasn't because I was getting complacent or above myself. Not at all. I knew I had to fight for my place in the team every week. No one during my time at Norwich ever took their place in the team for granted, no matter who they were or how important they were to the club. Bryan Gunn, Mark Bowen, Ian Crook, Chris Sutton. All of them. We'd wait for the team to be announced, dressing-room etiquette stating that, until you knew you were playing, you stayed in your suit and tie. And yes, that included the likes of Gunny, as certain a starter as anyone while he was at the club. Along with everyone else, he waited to see what the team was before he started to get changed before a match. If someone got a little absent-minded, a little ahead of themselves, the lads would soon let them know all about it. 'Oh, playing today are we?' 'Good to see you're starting, what's the rest of the team then?' 'Look lads, the gaffer isn't picking the side today, so-and-so is, am I in mate, can I play?' They'd get battered. So, with that in mind, added to the fact that I was still only twenty-three and a veteran of less than thirty career league games, how the hell could I assume I should be starting?

Except I thought I should be. But what did the gaffer do? He only went out and bought another midfielder, that's all. This time it was Andy Townsend. And he was a decent player, playing against us at Carrow Road the previous season and hitting the bar from a free kick (although Gunny would have said he had it covered).

Joking apart, it was a body blow for me. Dave Stringer didn't even start Townsend in our opening game; the midfield quartet was Dale Gordon, Ian Crook, Trevor Putney and Mike Phelan. Putters, one of the funniest blokes I have ever met, was the steel alongside Chippy. I liked Putters a lot, he was top man. But he was wearing my shirt. When Putters got sent off at Derby I should have got my chance. But I didn't, Andy Townsend was straight in and kept his place, more or less, for the rest of the season. I can see where this was all going and I had had enough. Dave Stringer had always been, and still is, like a second Dad to me, I have so much respect for him it's unbelievable.

But I was banging my head on a brick wall here. I'd put in the transfer request by now that saw Mel Machin take an interest in me going to Manchester City with him. But the little tiff between Peter Swales and Arthur South put paid to that. No one else had shown much of an interest in me, and besides, as much as he won't play me, I don't think Dave Stringer is all that keen on letting me go either. I was up in his office, more times than I care to remember, asking him why I wasn't in the team? 'Why is Mike Phelan starting ahead of me?' 'I think I can do a better job than Andy Townsend.' Questions, questions, questions.

Yet, every time Dave Stringer just looked me in the eye and uttered the same phrase. 'Gossy, your time will come son.' At this point I was thinking I should do something drastic. I wasn't ready for a season in the reserves, or on the bench (if I was lucky). To make things worse, a couple of lads who were younger than me were now getting a look in. Ruel Fox was one and Robert Rosario another. Big Rob was another good lad and a good player, you ask Fleckie how much he enjoyed and appreciated playing alongside him. But Rob came into the team straight from school, making his debut when he was just seventeen, back in 1984, a few weeks after I'd made mine. He wouldn't have been far off 100 appearances for the club that season if he kept his place.

What hope did I have? Should I have packed it all in? Was this stupid talk? Well, no, it wasn't. I wanted to become a professional triathlete, run around the world, run the length of the Great Wall of China, run across America. I was fit enough, God knows I slogged my guts out at training every day. And for what? Nothing. I just wanted to get out of Norwich and run, run and then run some more. Why carry on wasting my time here, I thought? I was getting older (I'd have been twenty-four at the end of the season) and I was still seen as 'young Gossy', even though there are lads younger than me getting regular games. Think back to that reserve-team game right at the beginning of this book, the wet, cold evening at Oxford United. Yep, that's where I was. Bleeding sweat for this club and getting nowhere.

Yet, even after that frigid afternoon at the Manor Ground, I still loved the game too much to quit. I couldn't reject it, not yet. But what I could do? A little act of defiance, a little bit of rebellion, let my standards drop a little, let myself go a bit? Well, I did. Late nights became the norm, that and a few more beers than usual. Me and the rest of the lads on the graveyard shift – that's what we called playing in the reserves – would get together and sound off a bit, moan and groan into the bottom of our glasses. We were all good enough for the first team so why, we collectively argued, weren't we playing? Yet, every time I asked Dave Stringer that question with regard to myself, the answer was always the same: 'Gossy, your time will come son.'

As I came out of my shell, that rebellious part of me just grew and grew in the years that followed. I was still in the first team under Dave, but I had slowly become one of the lads, always looking for a chance to get a laugh or show everyone what a good lad I was. If it came with the added bonus of letting me work out, so much the better. On one pre-season trip (it might have been to Holland), we were all sat in a restaurant having our evening meal when, for a laugh, I decided to do some weights. We were based in some woodland, and on one side of the driveway that led to the hotel was a huge pile of logs. And not the sort of logs you put on the fire to keep you warm; these were big buggers. In my playful state of mind, I reasoned that all of those logs would look better on the other side of the driveway, and that it was my job to shift them there, one by one. Besides, I'd had some beers and just wanted to let some aggression out. So, off I went, all the lads watching me out of the windows as I jogged to this massive log pile. 'What's Gossy up to now?' They were all agog, wondering what I was planning.

Suddenly, and without warning, Rob Newman was out there with me. He'd just signed from Bristol City and had already ingratiated himself into the group well, and we got on famously. So there he was, stood at my side, acting all excited like a puppy that knows it's going to be taken for a walk. 'What's on your mind mate?' It was all he could do not to jump up and down with excitement. He was, as always, laughing his head off. Rob was a different class of person, always upbeat, positive and confident. He also wanted to have a great time in everything he did and with everyone he was with. He was a brilliant player to have alongside you in the team. He and I got up to some really hilarious things, mainly me doing something stupid and him laughing at it and me.

'I can't believe what you're doing Gossy, you're bloody nuts mate.' Maybe I was. But I shifted all those bloody logs. It half killed me. But I did it. In a strange sort of way, the fact that I was acting up a bit and coming out of my shell got me some respect from the lads. I'd had enough and was rattling the cage. They noticed. My attitude was way out there for anyone to see. A case of go on then, sack me. I don't care. I'll get another club, no problem. Because I was sick to death of being the nearly man of the tag 'young Gossy', of hearing Dave Stringer say 'Gossy, your time will come son'.

Well it hadn't and it wouldn't. As far as I was concerned, I was finished at Norwich City. The other lads and I, on that graveyard shift, once went on a pre-season tour to Hong Kong. We drank the bar dry every night. Lee Power, Tim Sherwood, Mark Walton and me. On the shots all night. I didn't care. I had given heart and soul to the club, so much hard work, dedication and effort. And for what? No reward, no recognition, nothing.

Talk about feeling bitter and twisted, that's where I was. I missed the craic of playing, the camaraderie of being part of something. All I was part of was the graveyard shift, sat on the bench, at best, 5 minutes here, 10 minutes there, if I was lucky. I hated having to go round the dressing room after a match, shaking hands with Andy Townsend, Ian Crook and all the lads after they'd won. I'd get to the midfielders with a hand held out with all the platitudes. 'Well done lads, different class today.' 'Chippy, fantastic mate.' It felt like I couldn't even look them in the eye, and, as for Townsend, I'd be thinking 'but how come you're in the team instead of me?' A pattern was forming, I was ticking off names and faces in my head, players who I'd done this with after games, right back to Martin O'Neill and Asa Hartford back in the early days, probably when I really meant it and wanted to be like them. Now it was people like Townsend who came to the club in the summer of 1988 and pretty much slotted into the first team straight away. It was easier to drop me than it was him. He was a bought player and would shout and scream more than me if he didn't play.

I was working hard in training, running my nuts off every day. That never changed. I really was a case of 'work hard, play hard', whereas before I'd been 'work hard, don't play at all'. But I was still the nearly man. The 1988/89 season came and went in a blur of reserve-team games and nights gallivanting around the city centre. What made matters worse is that it turned out to be the best in the club's history. We finished fourth in the First Division and reached the FA Cup semi-finals, a fantastic achievement and testimony to Dave Stringer's unquestionable ability as a manager. No arguments there.

But I wasn't part of it. Not at all. The club used eighteen players that season. Hey, how times have changed, a club can used fourteen in one single match now, and all, bar five of them, made at least ten first-team starts. Look down the appearances table for that season though and where am I? Not on it. Look, even Paul Cook played in four league games, and that really did my head in. Paul Cook! Now don't get me wrong, I'm not going to slag Cookie off. He was a good lad. He came to us from Wigan after doing well for them, but was he needed? He was a left-winger but got a chance in midfield before me. No wonder I was disillusioned. The nearly man? Invisible man more like. When it became clear to Cook that he wasn't going to play for Norwich, he got his move, a good one as well, to Wolves, where he played around 200 games for them. At the time of writing this, he's the manager of Chesterfield. I bet he doesn't remember the angry lad with the blonde barnet at Norwich now.

Time dragged on. I was almost beyond caring by the time the 1989/90 season rolled around. My attitude was, if I'm going to be bombed out by this club, then I'm going in style. I got very close to Mark Walton and Henrik Mortensen, probably my two best mates at the club at that time. Henrik left, having never really had the opportunity to show what a good player he was, which was a shame, as was the fact that injury eventually ended his time at the club. The three of us were very close, as I was with Rob Newman, my mate among all those logs, who joined us in the summer of 1991. Having close friends, someone you can talk to and share your frustrations with, makes a big difference. During that bad time for me, that three-year spell from around 1988–91, lads like Mark and Rob made a lot of difference, especially Wally (Mark Walton) who is one of my closest friends to this day. I was lower than the proverbial snake's belly for such a long time but they were always there, even if it was to just slither along the graveyard shift with me. Cheers lads.

What's especially galling is that I had some great games for the reserves. I'd be on fire, hitting 30-yard passes to feet, part of little one-twos in the middle, making things happen. With only one man and his dog there to watch, if they were even watching at all. The club 'honoured' me for these performances by making me captain of the reserves. That sums up where you are doesn't it? 'Well done Gossy, we've noticed how well you're doing for the reserves, you're now captain'. Hey thanks, do I get a little trophy for the mantelpiece or something? What a load of bollocks. I despised the fact I was captain, it made me even angrier, even keener to get away, to be kicked out. Every Tuesday night I'd be out with Wally and Henrik after training. 'Right lads, where are we off to tonight?' Normally we'd start at Hectors House in the city before moving onto Chicago's. Every Tuesday and Saturday night without fail. Out on the town. It was like I'd reverted to being sixteen/seventeen years old again, having the youth that I'd never had when I was that age. We went out to blot the memory of playing reserve games. Even when you played the bigger teams, you'd never play at their grounds as they all wanted to keep the pitch pristine for the first-teamers. So, if we went down to Arsenal, we'd be shunted off to some college playing field near Enfield or something; we'd play the game there on a terrible little pitch with hardly any facilities.

But hey, I was captain. Wally and I went out together but we also worked together, anything to get that aggression and frustration out of both our systems. We'd stay behind after training and I'd just ping balls at him, hour after hour, me practicing my shooting, him his goalkeeping. We were looking out for each other, taking care of them as well as ourselves.

I must emphasise one thing though. Despite all the bad times, the anger, the frustration and dejection – and the nights spent at the bar – it never affected my training or the times I did play in a game, even if it was for the reserves. Not once. The time may have been a blur and much of my recollection of that time is exactly that (and you can probably understand why). But what does remain clear and sharp in my mind is my continued and absolute dedication to the practice of my profession. That never changed, and it's probably what saved my career. The fact that I was now a lot more outgoing, confident and relaxed certainly made an impression on the other lads. It got me noticed, got me a little bit of respect.

I was opinionated, forceful and, if need be, aggressive, as occasion demanded it. Your teammates see that in you and they recognise them as qualities that they want alongside them in the footballing trenches. In the heat of a big game against quality opposition and players who can hurt you, the communal thought is 'who do I want alongside me today, who's strong enough to stick up for me, who has the aggression and the strength?' They saw me, saw that new focus and aggression and suddenly regarded me as an asset to the team, a good man to have alongside them on the pitch, someone who wouldn't hide or back down. Ironic isn't it? The attitude I had partially lapsed into as a result of not caring anymore had won me the respect of my peers and, ultimately, the manager and his coaching staff. It meant that I was going to be playing for the first team again.

I'd come into a team that was now changing, and quickly. All the players who had been around when I signed my first professional contract were either on their way or had long gone. You look at the list of players who made at least one appearance for the club during the 1983/84 season and then fast forward to the end of that decade. There's only me left. Gunny has come in, all of the lads from Tottenham have come in, Ruel Fox has come in, David Phillips. Some came and went, like Garry Brooke, for example, another who came from Tottenham and who got games ahead of me. Jan Molby, what a player by the way, he came in on loan and played ahead of me. But, bit by bit, Dave Stringer was rebuilding the squad. And I was the only one who survived. It meant, naturally enough, that I thought I had a chance of playing, especially as I thought I was the perfect midfield partner for Ian Crook. But Dave didn't seem to think so at first. He even played lads out of position alongside Chippy, in some games, rather than put me in.

Andy Townsend did a run of games. We used to call him Shaky after Shakin' Stevens, the rock and roll singer. Andy came into training one day dressed head to toe in denim – jacket, jeans, the works. So he became Shaky after that. We battered him, and I'm still waiting for him to do some of his TV work with that old denim jacket on.

Dave could tell that I wanted to go. He knew. And he would have known that Mel Machin had been on the phone to me about my joining him at Barnsley. When Mel rang, he said all the right things, about me and his new club. He said how he respected me, how I'd always be playing, how he wanted the club to go places with me as a part of it. I went up there with my dad, who drove, incidentally, all the way from Folkestone to Norwich to meet me before we went up to Barnsley together. We met Mel, had a look around the town and the ground. It suited me, no question. As we were driving back, I'd said to Dad, 'It's time to go, I'm signing for Mel.' My mind was made up. I'd get back to Norwich, go and see Dave and put in the transfer request.

The club wouldn't turn it down, I was acting up and I wasn't in the team. I was finished there and couldn't see any problems. 'Do what you need to do', said Dad, 'but yes, maybe it is time you moved on, had a fresh start.' So, we got back and I immediately went to see Dave, told him I wanted out. He had little choice really. I was about to go out of contract anyway, and would be on the PFA list of free agents that was circulated among all the other clubs. I was free to go. Dave listened then asked me to join him outside. At this point, I wondered what was going on. He put his arm around my shoulders as we walked out onto the pitch at Carrow Road, standing in the centre circle. Then we walked back to the touchline and walked around the pitch, Dave talking to me as we walked. 'Look around you Gossy. Look at this stadium, look at the pitch. Look at the players we've got at this football club. You belong here. You love this club as much as I do. You're Norwich City through and through. You know that. But you want to move? Let me say this. The grass is not always greener on the other side. You'd be moving to a new area, a new team, new fans and teammates. The only person there you know is Mel. But everyone knows you here. And they have a great deal of respect for you. I want you to stay, stay because...' The next four words sent a shockwave through my body. 'Your time has come son.'

And, with that, Dave offered me a new three-year deal to stay with the club. And what did I say, bearing in mind I wanted out, I'd had enough and that I wanted, desperately, to link up with Mel again at Barnsley? 'Thanks Gaffer. I'd be delighted to sign it.'

Naturally enough, after all I'd said to Dad as we'd driven back down from Barnsley, I now had to tell him I'd changed my mind, and, was not only staying put, but had committed myself to another three years at the club. But Dad, as always, was completely behind me, supportive and positive about whatever I chose to do. 'Go with your heart. Do what feels right and what makes you happy. I will back you all the way, as will your mum and the rest of the family.' How could I fail with support like that?

Dave Stringer had not been the only one to notice that my attitude was changing. As far as I was concerned, I was rebelling, taking certain things to the limit and seeing how far I could go, maybe even testing the club out. Would they sack me, for example, if just kept up with the nights out and the 'I don't give a ****' attitude? If they had done it, it wouldn't have bothered me. I'd have taken the opportunity to run around the world, something I'd always wanted to do, before coming back and finding another club.

I was sure of it in fact. Yet, despite all the partying and carousing, one thing never changed, and that was my attitude to training and playing. I always gave my utmost every time, no matter what. Yet, because I was frustrated and angry at the situation I was in, I was training and playing in a far more relaxed manner than I had been previously. It was the old club physio, Tim Sheppard, who pointed this out to me one day. 'Gossy, when you used to play the ball or make a pass, your body shape was tense and severe. It was like you were trying too hard to make the perfect pass. Now, you are a lot more relaxed, its coming more naturally to you and you're doing things you weren't capable of a little while ago.'

He was right. I was more relaxed. If I made the pass or won the ball, great. If I didn't, hey, it was no big deal. And if one of my teammates gave me a bollocking for mucking something up then I'd just give one straight back to them. Don't mess with me, focus on your own game. That raised a few eyebrows. 'Hello', they were thinking, 'What's got into Gossy?' They were beginning to notice that I was sticking up for myself and not letting myself get messed around with. By anyone.

7

Semi-Final Heartbreak

And that was that. The end of our dream, our season, everything. Is losing a semi-final worse than losing a final? I don't know, I haven't played in one. Neither had any of us. But Dave Stringer had. And I reckon, for him, that it was one of his worse days in football.

The funny thing is, even though I'd finally got to hear the words I'd been waiting to hear from Dave for so long and, had started to build a real foundation of trust and camaraderie with my teammates, it turned out that, as far as the 1991/92 season was concerned, I couldn't wait for it to finish, to play our final game, say thanks to the fans and clear off for a few weeks holiday to get away from football.

We were all hurting and wanted to clear off somewhere, to forget how the season had ended and have a little time away from the game, before we started off all over again for what would be, as we all soon found out, the very first season of the new FA Premier League. That would be great, make no mistake about it. We'd start pre-season and be totally focused on it. Professional, ready and committed. But that was some months into the future. But at the time of how the 1991/92 season, which had drawn to a painful conclusion, it was just hurt and frustration, individually for me, and for all of us as a team. All the more so because we'd started it with so much optimism, a conviction that we were going to do more than make up the numbers in Division One. Don't forget, Dave Stringer had guided the best side in the club's history to a finishing position of fourth in 1989, as well as leading the club to an FA Cup semi-final. The big disappointment had been how the club had failed to build on that success. To be respected in football you need to be consistent, to follow things through, do it again and again and again. Much like Manchester United have done over the last two decades. Even if you couldn't stand the sight of Fergie and his all-conquering team, you can't deny them the respect their achievements merited. For them, winning was standard. And no matter how many times they won the Premier League or the FA Cup, they enjoyed the success as if it was their first. Well, we wanted *our* first.

Where had all this hurt come from? The FA Cup. We'd reached the last four for the second time in four years, and this time, I was involved. I'd sat on the sidelines that last time, involved, but out of the team, elated to be changed and warming up on the pitch with the lads, but then a strange rejected feeling taking a seat on the bench when the whistle went. But I was still torn up for my mates when they lost that game to Everton, and, despite his not picking me, for Dave Stringer. How brilliant would it have been to see him lead the side out at Wembley, that humble man from Great Yarmouth who was hardly an illustrious footballing name, leading the club to two FA Cup semi-finals and a top-four finish in the season of 1988/89, surely one of the most successful in the club's history? He'd played there twice for the club in League Cup Finals, and lost them both. So he knew what it was like to lose at Wembley as a player. Now, as a manager, he knew what it was like to lose a semi-final, missing out right at the last moment. That made it a hat-trick that Dave Stringer neither wanted, nor deserved. We wanted to put that right, for Dave and for ourselves, for people like the three Ians – Butterworth, Crook and Culverhouse – who'd played in that game against Everton in 1989, and, above all, for the fans. Norwich were certainly given a great opportunity to progress with a game against Sunderland, who were in Division Two at the time. What can you say? Who wasn't dreaming about Wembley Way, new suits and 'Abide with Me'? We were super confident we would win. You couldn't help yourself.

All that excitement and expectancy and we just didn't turn up. We had the tickets and, very publicly, tore them in half and threw them away. Table for eleven Sir, for the FA Cup final? No mate, don't think we'll bother. These Sunderland lads through, they didn't succumb to the big game tension and 'freeze' on the day like we did. My take on that game, looking back, was that we all just tried too hard. It was a career-defining moment under severe pressure. We over focused on producing our best game, and by doing so, tensed up and 'choked' in the moment of glory. We didn't 'bottle' it. 'Bottling it', to me, means lack of bravery, and I believe we were brave but simply cracked under intense pressure. So Sunderland won from a sucker punch of a goal by John Byrne. Was he offside? I don't know. Their midfielder hit a hopeful cross, it drifted beyond my mate, Mark Walton, and there was Byrne with a simple header to make it 1-0. And that was that. The end of our dream, our season, everything. Is losing a semi-final worse than losing a final? I don't know, I haven't played in one. Neither had any of us. But Dave Stringer had. And I reckon, for him, that it was one of his worse days in football, despite having lost two League Cup finals. I know it was one of mine.

The dressing room afterwards was a terrible place to be. The dreadful silence was only disrupted by the euphoric chanting and cheering of the Sunderland fans, who were gloriously making their way out of the main stand above where we now gathered. We just sat there, motionless, Dave Stringer and Dave Williams too, all numb and shocked, unwillingly digesting that desperate feeling of losing a semi-final. The hurt in Dave Stringer's face was obvious, I personally felt I had let him down, and badly. Eventually, after what must have been a good 15–20 minutes, he got up and said, very quietly, 'Come on, we're not hanging about, let's get showered and let's get out of here.' Tim Sheppard, our physio, then slowly started to pack up the gear, consoling everyone with an easy arm round the shoulder or a pat the head. What a gent. What a physio/psychologist. He was big part of the changing room, and along with the two Dave's, he would have to disguise this retched feeling and work hard to install into us some vital confidence and self-belief. Remember, we still had half a dozen league games to play and had slipped down the table; our recent focus and attention was the semi-final and we'd taken our eyes off the league games. So we had a bit to do, and they weren't going to be 'nothing' games like they sometimes are for teams in that situation. The mood didn't improve on the way back either. Normally, after a defeat, you get on the coach, have a few drinks, get the carbs back in with some food and even share a beer if you wanted.

Basically, recover, chill out and get into some light-hearted discussion. You get over it, and by the time Monday comes, you're ready to kick on again. But this was different. At the time, the hurt was too much; the consequence of losing such a big-time match was just too serious. Silence followed us all the way home. I sat alone in my thoughts, thinking of I had done wrong in the game. Beating myself up quite nicely to be fair. Then, the fans popped into my head; 25,000 fans gathered in one section of the stand was a magical sight to see. That same Yellow & Green Army would very soon get the opportunity to air their anger and disgust at the team, no holding back, just loud and clear abuse at top of their agenda for the next home match I'm sure. It was so, so low. How could something so bad come from a day that had started so well?

It's funny really. It wasn't at the time, but we stopped halfway back for a little break to get some fish and chips. We were right next to a churchyard, which felt appropriate. Everyone slipped away to have some time for themselves, Wally (Mark Walton) was sat up against a gravestone, tearful and inconsolable. It hurt me bad to see him in that way and I remember Gerry Peyton, who was at the club on loan at the time, was trying to comfort him. He's a good lad Gerry, a really nice bloke. But it didn't really help Mark, he was devastated. Everyone was. Someone said that it wasn't just our best chance of getting to an FA Cup final, it was probably the only chance we'd ever have and we'd blown it. I didn't agree with that. A lot of us still had many years left at the top of the game with Norwich or, if it happened, at other clubs. There was always interest in our players, that's how it had always been at Norwich, the old joke about having a revolving door was true enough, except ours only went one way and that was out. So yes, there was always interest there. Robert Fleck had been on a number of club's wanted lists for some time and rightly so, he was a great player. There'd also been interest in Gunny (Bryan Gunn) and Ian Butterworth. I think Mark Bowen had been linked with a move back to Tottenham. Was anyone interested in me? I'd never heard anything and you usually get the gossip from the papers around the training ground. 'Is it true Newcastle are in for you?' That sort of thing. 'No mate, load of bloody rubbish' would be the answer. But that player would invariably be clearing his locker and saying his goodbyes the next day. The powers that be at Norwich liked the colour of the buying clubs' money back then.

This was why there was no reason to believe some of those players wouldn't have another FA Cup final one day. Next year with Norwich maybe, or with another club. But you know what? None of them did. If you look at the line-up for that day, we all thought the team Dave Stringer picked would have been good enough to get to Wembley. Did they ever play there again? Where are they now? I'll tell you. In goal, Mark Walton. One of my best mates in football, a giant of a man and a gentleman. He was only in the team because Gunny was injured. But he was a great 'keeper, no doubt about that. He went on to play for quite a few clubs after us, including Fulham and Brighton. He didn't get even a sniff of Wembley in that time. He must have known that getting to even another semi-final would be a big ask. As I said, he was gutted afterwards, desperate. His Dad hadn't been able to make it for the semi-final, but he'd said to Mark beforehand, 'I'll be there for the final. I'll be the proudest man in the stadium.' How Wally must have felt about that I'll never know, and he's a big mate of mine. People accuse footballers of being selfish, with no heart or soul for fans or club. That's crap! They should have seen how cut up Wally was after that semi-final.

Ian Culverhouse? Great player and a good coach. I was at the club with him for a very short time when he was there with Paul Lambert, while I was helping out Chippy (Ian Crook) with the reserves. Ian could have played at a higher level but he loved it at Norwich. So did Mark Bowen. I'm sure he had his chances to move on as well, so yeah, he might also have got some medals if he had. Neither got anywhere near Wembley, neither did Colin Woodthorpe. Another good lad. Norwich bought him in, a complete unknown, from Chester City. He was never a first-team regular, but he could slot in most places at the back, that sort of versatility is essential for any team. He still played over 150 games for Norwich, scoring against Liverpool and playing against Inter Milan. So not a bad old career really. But no cup final for him or Ian Butterworth. Butterworth was another who could have played for a bigger club if they'd have followed up their interest. John Polston moved onto Reading eventually. Funny guy, loads of stories. He wouldn't have looked out of place at any top club.

Foxy might have made it. He got some decent moves. Newcastle, Tottenham. But it wasn't their time when he went there. Or Flecky. He was desperate to play in that game, so much so that he spent time in an oxygen chamber to try and speed up his recovery from injury. All to no avail. Even a half-fit Flecky was a danger to any opposition, but sadly it was a game too soon for him. Rob Newman, a fantastic mate of mine and a room partner for a good few years. He was another great player, so underrated, strong and so versatile. A brilliant striker on the ball, he'd scored a fantastic goal in the quarter-final replay against Southampton, one any striker would have been proud to own. But he never got to Wembley (unless you count Manchester City, where he's now scouting). Rob would have preferred to have played mind. Even Chris Sutton, who was still a kid then, went on to great things, notably at Blackburn with his Premier League winners' medal. He also won the Scottish Cup with Celtic, so fair play to him. He was with Chelsea when they got to the final in 2000, but he wasn't even on the bench. Still, he got a medal. I don't know what do you do with a medal when you haven't even played in the match? I bet Sutty's still got it though. Somewhere. He's probably lost it. I've a funny story about Sutty I'll tell you it later.

There you go. A good team and some very good players. And, just as we'd all thought, none of us ever got anywhere near an FA Cup final. Even for Sutty, getting there and not being involved at all, that would have been hard and he wouldn't have enjoyed it. No wonder we were all devastated. We knew. That was it. Wembley gone, and a magical opportunity blown away.

Dave Stringer knew it. He looked done in. He'd been at the club for nearly five years and it had taken it out on him. He quit a day before the last day of the season, he'd had enough, said it was time for a new man with new ideas to take over. He later said to a reporter that he was 'filleted'. Again, you look back to that game against Sunderland, that lost opportunity for so many of us. Dave might have thought that would have been the perfect way to go out, an established team in the top flight, a great squad of players and an FA Cup final. Well, sometimes football does seem to be scripted. The Matthews final, England winning the World Cup in 1966, Liverpool coming back from 3-0 down in a Champions League final. You know it's still going to happen even when it looks as if there is no way it will. It didn't work out that way for us. Sunderland got to the final and played Liverpool. They lost but they had the day out, the whole experience. You can't ever take that away from them. We didn't even have it to be taken away from us.

The problem was, we still had the League programme to finish after that game. Oh whoopee-doo-dah. Six games, six games to raise ourselves out of the pit we were all in and make sure Norwich stayed in Division One. We'd been distracted by the cup. At the end of November, beginning of December, all was looking good. We were comfortably in the top ten with some good wins and performances accompanying that. We stuffed Chelsea 3-0 at Stamford Bridge for example. Flecky scored two, Chelsea didn't forget that. However, in the lead up to the semi-final, and immediately afterwards, our form fell to pieces. We beat Everton 4-3 at Carrow Road on 21 March in a crazy, crazy game. We all looked great in that match, but looked nothing like it in the remaining ones. We lost to Villa, Man Utd, Arsenal, West Ham and even to Notts County, and at home! No disrespect intended, but we should have beaten them. We had battered them at times. Flecky hit one of his trademark volleys, a goal all the way, but one that was saved – unbelievable. But they started having a go back and we got a bit frustrated, as did the crowd. Then they brought this kid on, looked like he should still have been at school (so did I sometimes), he swung his leg at the ball late on and it got deflected in. Suddenly, it was 'come on lads, we're in a massive trouble here now, look at the table'. We were eighteenth after that game, just five points clear of the relegation places with three games to play. The pressure tap was definitely turned to 'on'. Sheffield Wednesday were next up and they were flying, they comfortably beat us 2-0 and barely broke sweat in the process.

Now it *was* looking dodgy. We still had that gap, but our last two games were against Wimbledon, which were the last team you'd want to be playing, and Leeds United, probably the second-last team you'd want to be playing as they were looking set to be crowned Champions, and all because of some inspirational Frenchman they'd signed, who would, in another season, go on to 'scythe' me down in a game at Carrow Road, dumping me near the advertising hoardings in the process. *Merci*, Eric.

Relief then, at home to Wimbledon. Flecky put us ahead after 20 minutes or so, the first goal we scored in the opening 45 minutes of a match since that win at Everton seven games ago. That's how badly we'd been playing. We only needed a point to absolutely guarantee safety. Had we lost, well, going to the new champions on the last day, needing a win – no thanks. But all was well. That was until Gary Elkins scored early in the second half. They were all over us, buzzing, looking for a win. They had a new manager in Joe Kinnear and they were fighting for him, winning every tackle, bombing the ball forward. John Fashanu was playing, the Norwich old boy, but he didn't seem to be the raging bull he usually was. Maybe John didn't want to hurt his old club, the one where he and Justin grew up? He still put himself about and all the old chat was there, but we managed to hold on. Thank Christ for that, we were safe, we could just go up to Leeds and relax knowing we would be playing them and all the other big clubs again next season. Not Notts County mind, they had gone. Never recovered from it either. For the sake of two more wins, they could have stuck around and that might have changed things around there a hell of a lot. Because, although we weren't really that aware of it at the time, things were changing, and our staying put in Division One was a lot more important than anyone might have realised at the time.

That was the penultimate Saturday. The following Friday, we got the news. Dave Stringer had quit, he didn't even want to see the season out. Like he went on to say, he'd had enough. We were safe, job done, time to go. I had, and I still have, a huge amount of time and respect for Dave. He had been my youth-team, reserve- and first-team manager, and had nurtured me from boy to man. On the pitch, he put time and energy into making me a better player, and off the pitch helped me develop that all-important self-confidence. Above all, he had given me a chance in the game. Something I'll always be grateful for. Dave also ingrained into me the way I should play, the way we should all play. I'd be on the bench, or, more likely than not, sat in the stands, and he'd come up to me before the game and have a few words. It would always be the same thing.

'Gossy ... you're not playing today but look. Make the most of being here. Watch the lad playing in your position this afternoon. Look at how he plays, what he does. Watch him. Learn from him. That's what we want from you, that's how we want you to play.'

But that what's he told everyone. That was the Norwich way. Right down through the teams. Look at the first team for example. Let's say Denis Van Wijk gets a knock in training and is ruled out of the weekend game. Who's the reserve left-back? Tony Spearing. He's been having that little chat from Dave Stringer as well. So he's been sat, just like me, watching Denis play. Knows his game as well as he does. That means he can slot in and know exactly how he should play, exactly how the team plays. The reserves mirrored the first team, the youth side mirrored the reserves, the school kids mirrored the youth team. Later on, we had Mark Bowen as left-back. Taff was one of the best left-backs you'll ever see – brilliant and funny. What a role model for Rob Ullathorne, who was cover for him. Taff played a lot of games for Norwich over the years so Rob didn't get much of a look in. But his education at Norwich didn't do him or his career any harm. He might not have made it here, but he went onto play for Osasuna in Spain and was the first ever 'Bosman' in England, as well as playing for Leicester in the Premier League. So he was a good player, he just had Taff ahead of him. He learnt to play the Norwich way under Dave and look where he ended up, playing in Spain. Doesn't that show you how good his coaching was, that and the club's philosophy on how football should be played? I think it does.

Mind you, although I think Dave is of a 'different class', I did get tired of the lack of first-team opportunities and our little chats. It's all very well being encouraged to watch and learn, to do this, that and the other. I must have heard it hundreds of times. But I wanted to play, and if the player in ahead of you isn't, in your opinion, as good as you, then you're going to ask the manager some questions. Now this is where my character came to be tested to the max because I was never the type to shake my cage hard enough or loud enough. My dad would always tell me to get in there and tell the manager I wasn't happy, so either play me or sell me. He believed that I was too nice and I would have achieved more in the game if I had a bit more aggression and nastiness, Vinnie Jones and Roy Keane style. And, as always, he was spot on. I idealised my dad's strength of character, I really wish I could have been a bit more like him in that respect. He has such great presence and, with his military background, he has that respectful, but authoritative, tone of voice, and the ability to look 'in charge' and 'special' without saying a word. But you are who you are and I was always, for a long while, the quiet lad. Mel Machin labelled me a 'coach's dream' because I never moaned or bit back, I just effectively did what I was told to do but now, at this point of my career, I had to change and start saying something that would help my cause. To be confrontational wasn't easy for me, but the word was suddenly staring me in the face.

Other lads in the same 'stuck in the Ressies' position as me were Tim Sherwood, Lee Power, Ruel Fox and Chris Sutton, who all had no problem in opening up and speaking or even shouting their minds. But I did. So there I'd be, every Monday, knocking at Dave's door instead, demanding a 'chat' and asking why I wasn't picked on Saturday. I'd want to know why these people were in the team, why they were playing instead of me. 'Gaffer, why do you keep picking Micky (Phelan) ahead of me, he's struggling and we aren't doing well, get me in, I'll make a difference.' It didn't matter who it was, I'd be there on Monday morning, same old, same old. 'Gaffer, I gotta say this, Andy Townsend had a stinker on Saturday, I'm a better player than he is, get him out and get me in the side.'

This was me talking a load of bollocks really. I knew these lads were good players and doing well, but I was getting my 'I'm not happy' point over. Dave had heard it all before and not just from me. And, to be fair to Dave, he'd listen. After all, he knew me and realised how hard it was for me to get these words out. He'd sit there and let me say my thing, and, after all, I was slagging off the other players, he could have slung me out of the door. But he'd listen because it was constructive criticism. Eventually, I'd get it all off my chest in a calm-mannered way. Then he'd look me straight in the eye, and simply say 'Your time will come. I understand your frustrations but I promise you your time will come.' He would then go to praise me. 'Gossy you're one of the fittest players I've ever seen and your attitude to training and playing is different class, but I can only pick eleven players out of thirty-five and at this moment I'm happy with my midfield. But you're next in so keep doing what you're doing and your time will come.'

He'd then see me out and get ready for the next glum-faced reserve-team player in line. I knew that my audience was over then, but I was pleased to have spoken my mind in my own manner and in my own way, and got off to training with the rest of the lads – including all those who I thought I shouldn't be in the team. 'All right Andy mate, you played a blinder on Saturday, put Gazza in the shade pal.'

I got a lot of games that season to be fair, probably around forty in the League and Cup – so my chats with him must have worked. I still didn't think my time had come, mind you, I still didn't think I was part of things or had arrived. But at least I was getting games. I'd appeared in an FA Cup semi-final and now I was set to complete a decent enough season by playing at Leeds in that last game. Naturally enough, I wanted to win. That was always enough incentive for me. But being up against someone like Eric Cantona or Gary Speed (Gary's death shook me – shook us all!) was an extra incentive. I wanted to be the best, so I wanted to play against the best, be tested by them and come out on top. It was the end of the season and I wanted to make an impression on whoever would be taking over. I wanted to give a good impression of myself and prove worthy of a place in the team. Phil Neal, whatever. Look at me. Make sure I'm in your team. I wanted the next season to start straight away and was full of energy going into that one.

But the game didn't turn out that way. We just went through the motions, us and Leeds. It was like a pre-season game. No big tackles. No aggro on the pitch. They were celebrating winning the title (had they won it or had Man Utd lost it?). It doesn't matter. As a player, you hate being at games like that, when all the focus is on the other team and the match is just incidental, gets in the way almost. So we were the sideshow really. I'm not even sure their fans noticed we were there, we were uninvited guests at the party. Rod Wallace scored in the first half and that was enough for them, they showboated a bit after that to be honest. David Williams was in charge for the day, one of the very best coaches in the game. A few of us thought he might be in the running to take over from Dave. When he spoke, he made so much sense, made the game sound easy, no wonder he was at Man United with Fergie for so long. Class is rewarded. But he either rejected the chance or was never asked. Very few, including the players, knew what was going at that boardroom level, the players were always last to be informed to be honest.

It was a real mess. Not long after that game, David Williams did leave the club, joining Bournemouth. You do wonder at that sort of move. Had he got a chance of the main job here? I don't know. Most of us would have been happy for him to have a go, to get the nod. It would have been continuity and that never seemed to have done Liverpool any harm. It hadn't for us either. After John Bond left, Ken Brown got the job, and Dave afterwards, all promotions from within. David Williams seemed the obvious choice. But, with him gone, that was it, our managerial and coaching team were no more and the lads thought that someone new was going to come in. That always unsettles you as a player. Straight away you're minding your back, never mind the rest of them. Is he going to like me, rate me, give me a game? Or will I be out? Will he be bringing players he knows and trusts in? John Bond came to us from Bournemouth and brought half of his side with him, I bet that put a few of the squad out at the time. Because you're thinking, oh, not good enough am I? And straight away you're imagining the new manager doesn't like you, he's got it in for you, so you've got the hump with him. Yet nothing's happened and no one has said anything! That's how a footballer works – himself first, second and third. We were all on edge. Some of the more high-profile lads, well, they might have thought, hey, if he doesn't like me, I'll get a move, no problem. And yes, the likes of Gunny, Butts, Mark Bowen and Ian Crook would have done. But me and some of the others? Well, you might not have had another top-flight club come in for you, it might be one in the Second Division. Yeah, it might have been a good club, I'd previously had the chance to go to Barnsley, remember, and they had a nice set-up, an ambitious manager in Mel Machin, who I knew. So I'd have certainly gone there just to get some games.

At the back of my mind I'm thinking, you're dropping a division, is that really what you want to do at this stage of your career, shouldn't you be pushing on? And what about the money, is it going to be as good? And I'll have to move house, all of a sudden it's not such a good idea. I wanted to stay. Anyway, I loved the club and felt I still had something to prove to the fans. Dave had given me a run of games and I thought I'd done well. But, of course, this new manager was going to come in and bomb me out. Except, of course, he wasn't, because no one had been appointed, nothing was happening. All we had to do was think about going on holiday and meeting the new gaffer when we got back.

Right: 1. Me (*right*) and my brother Tim, along with ex-Liverpool legend and current BBC pundit Mark Lawrenson.

Below: 2. With former BBC *Grandstand* presenter Frank Bough, who is interviewing me about my call up for the England Schoolboys squad. Note I have the FA blazer on! (May 1982).

3. Kent Schools line-up. I'm bottom row, third from left.

4. England Schoolboys line up for the camera this time – a proud moment. I'm sat on the bottom row, third from right.

Above: 5. Stretching at Trowse as a young player at Norwich, along with Peter Mendham and Louie Donowa.

Right: 6. Running hard as usual at Trowse, Dave Stringer watching in the background.

Left: 7. A very posed promotional shot for the IFK Luleå club handbook.

Below: 8. In action for IFK Luleå in August 1986, and the recipient of much attention from four GIF Sundsvall players.

9. My second appearance as a Norwich player was against Tottenham Hotspur at White Hart Lane on 1 September 1984, a great experience as I came off the bench to replace John Devine. Seen here fighting for the ball with Spurs' Paul Miller (No. 5) and Gary Mabbutt, with Keith Bertschin offering support.

10. One step forward, two steps back. It's Tottenham again, only this time I'm playing for Norwich Reserves against their second-string side at a deserted Carrow Road in April 1986. Tony Spearing is my Norwich teammate in the background.

11. Playing at Old Trafford against Manchester United, as good as it gets! Up against Paul McGrath (No. 6) and Remi Moses, with Asa Hartford and Greg Downs backing me up.

12. Ian Crook was the midfield maestro I had the pleasure of playing alongside on so many occasions, but even he could have a bad day in training!

Above left: 13. Training in the snow.

Above right: 14. Dave Stringer was a huge influence on my career, a man who I will always have time and respect for.

Below left: 15. Celebrating an FA Cup win with my good friend and teammate Mark Walton.

Left: 16. Mike Walker passing on some pearls of wisdom from the touchline. I am listening, even though it might look like I'm not!

Below: 17. Me and the lads line up prior to the start of the 1992/93 season. The gaffer is looking sharp in his suit!

18. With Gary Megson, two obvious candidates to model the very latest in Norwich City leisurewear.

19. In the process of scoring the goal against Leeds United at Elland Road that won the BBC Goal of the Month Award for August 1993, with Leeds players Jon Newsome, later to become a teammate and captain and Tony Dorigo looking on. Mark Robins is the Norwich player who had also been challenging for Ruel Fox's perfect cross. Our performance in that game, a 4-0 win, was as good as any I've ever been involved in as a player.

Above: 20. The entire Norwich City travelling party line up for the camera the night before our UEFA Cup match against Bayern Munich in the Olympic Stadium. A great trip with some wonderful memories.

Left: 21. That iconic photo of my goal against Bayern Munich given a little special treatment.

Right: 22. Celebrating *that* goal with Ruel Fox and Chris Sutton.

Below: 23. Post-match at Carrow Road after our 1-1 draw against Bayern Munich. I've got Lothar Matthaus's shirt on; he took mine in exchange but I was later told he threw it away!

Above: 24. With Margaret and our parents on our wedding day. A quiet day involving family, just as we wanted. My mum and dad are standing either side of me, along with Margaret's parents, Rodney and Janet.

Left: 25. With Margaret, all dressed up and ready to celebrate Christmas!

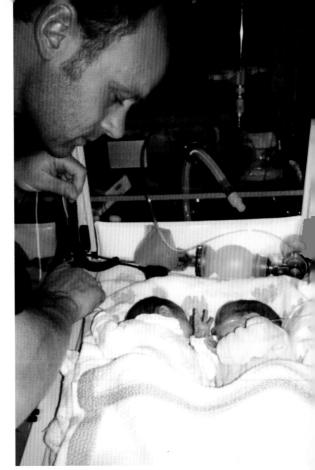

Right: 26. Watching over Jacob and Joseph in the SCBU.

Below: 27. With my lads in Spain – looks like it was a tough day in the sun!

28. Another memorable goal from my collection, the last ever to be scored in front of the old Kop at Anfield. Surely Razor Ruddock isn't ducking?

29. Celebrating that goal at Anfield. Rushie doesn't look too happy about it.

30. At the end of a special game in front of some very special fans at Anfield (I'm far left). The Kop salute both sides at the end of that game which ended Liverpool 0 Norwich 1 (Goss!).

31. Margaret and I are very proud of our table-tennis-playing twin boys. Joseph (*left*) and Jacob (*right*) are shown here with some of their trophies, along with Albert Cadmore in the centre. Albert married me and Margaret, and also christened the boys. He is president of the Great Yarmouth Table Tennis League and a good friend to all of us.

Left: 32. The first (of many thousand) turns of the pedals, as I set out from Norwich Cathedral on the Back to Bayern ride for the NNAB – an unforgettable experience.

Below: 33. My favourite times are always those spent with my family – me, Joseph, Maggie and Jacob. Perfect!

Things soon started happening. The big news was that Flecky wanted away. He'd promised to stay on for one more season, on the understanding that the club helped him get a good move. Well, now that time had come. The club, of course, didn't want to know by then. The manager had gone, they didn't want one of the club's best players to go as well. But he dug his heels in, even when the club were mucking about with the fee, always asking for a little bit more. He went in the end; Chelsea signed him. A deserved move because he is a top-man and a great goalscorer. The relationship he had with the fans was extraordinary, they loved him so much and vice versa. We would miss him big time.

Then, all the gossip was about how Phil Neal was going to be named new Norwich manager. He hadn't long been sacked by Bolton, and he'd done an OK job there, but he'd never managed a First Division club, so was he the right man? I wasn't sure. I didn't know enough about him to judge him, but he was a top player, won just about everything with Liverpool, but Norwich manager? Football is a small world and players know players, who know managers, and your character and personality is spread throughout football before any mention of your ability.

A typical chat between the lads summarising a certain player would be, 'To be fair he's Billy-big-time, a right asshole. Decent player though.' So, it soon got round the changing rooms that Phil was a good lad and a decent coach, which sounded good. If he had a reputation of being a 'prick' you'd start worrying. But then, it didn't matter, because, all of a sudden, it was announced Mike Walker had got the job. Stories went around, there are always stories, that Neal had all but got the job, but, right at the last moment, made it clear he wasn't prepared to uproot and live in Norfolk. So that was that. The board wanted someone committed and I don't blame them. You don't let all your players live hundreds of miles away, well, Norwich didn't anyway. So that was that, Mike got the job. And you know what? I was really pleased. For him, for the club, and naturally, for me. Because my time really was about to come.

8

A Whole New Ball Game

I wasn't having that. So I ran over and smacked right into him, hit the sweet spot. He never saw me coming. He was down on the floor squealing, but that was too bad. I took him out because he crocked Chippy. So now he was down on the floor and I was standing over Moncur, feeling and looking, no doubt, a bit like Russell Crowe in Gladiator – and yes, I was ready to kill him, I really was.

Mike Walker was the right appointment for the club. He'd been reserve-team manager, so he knew the players, the way the club played the game. He knew his way around. Was he a safe option, a cheap appointment? The fans would all have been either wondering who he was or thinking it was a disaster. But he was absolutely the right man for the job. The players knew and respected him, I certainly did. Right back to John Bond, we'd been a side that wanted to play football the right way. From Bond to Ken Brown, and onto Dave. Now you'd expect Mike to keep that tradition going, that of playing 'good' football. People ask me, how do you define 'good' football? Well, for us, it was simple. You start with the 'keeper, ask him, no, *tell* him, engrain in him to throw the ball out, to find a man and start a move from the back, not to just hoof it out. Do things that way, pass the ball, always look to pass the ball and keep the ball below knee height. The big crime was giving it back to the opposition. If they haven't got the ball, then they can't hurt you, right? Watch Norwich play when John Bond was manager, or Ken Brown. Watch them now. It's the way the club has always done things. Mike respected that. Some of us, like Foxy, Chris Sutton and me, didn't know how to play any other way, it was all we had known, the only way we could play the game! Then you've got the lads that came in from Tottenham like Ian Culverhouse, Mark Bowen, John Polston and Ian Crook. They'd all been brought up to play that way as well, it was coached into them, just as it was us, at an early age.

So, Mike Walker getting the job was absolutely the right thing, the best appointment the club could have made. Was it an accident, or was someone at the club thinking along those lines? I don't know. But you can look back now and think what would have happened if Phil Neal had got the job after all? I think for my mates, the club and me, things would have been very different.

Mike was great for me. In every sense of the word. He knew me and I knew him, he knew I wouldn't let him down. Listen, I'd have run off a cliff for him. He came in and straight away said to me, 'You're going to be in my team. I trust you, I like you as a player, you'll be playing. I'm going to build the entire side around you and Ian Crook in midfield. He'll make things happen, you'll help make them happen.' How brilliant is it to have that chance, that belief from your manager? I was hardly one of the leading lights in the team, or one of the main men, so to speak. But he still made it clear how important I was to him and the team. He believed in me, he knew my character, he trusted me.

And I could be trusted. I was fit. Fit? Come on, you should know by now. There was no one fitter. I ran for fun. I had passion, determination, and real fire in my belly. A perfect foil for a craftsman like Chippy Crook. Mike had all that in me, he had the template. Now he could start to turn me into a better footballer, work on the technical side of my game. No one had done that before, but he did. He worked on my passing, my tackling, my distribution. He helped me achieve all that I wanted for myself, to have the belief and the footballing capabilities. You then find out ten other blokes who, one way or the other, are working to those same goals. The foundation is that belief, that determination to work hard and to be there for each other on the pitch. That, on its own, is a powerful thing. Look at Wimbledon in the eighties. Mike wanted to add some footballers to that, and he had them at the club.

You worked as a team and you thought as a team. A collective. He banged it into us, again and again and again, you don't just need to have the coaching to know where you need to be on the pitch, you need to know where you're going and where everyone else is as well. So, that was the tactical side of things, that was the coaching, for which we had John Deehan. But John had spent a long part of his career at Norwich as well, so he knew what to expect when he came back. Get the ball, give it to someone else in a yellow shirt. How easy is that? Control it, move it on. Simple. Don't over-elaborate; don't try to be too clever. We may be wearing yellow shirts, but we're not Brazil. If you get caught on the ball, if you lose possession that's your fault, you waited for too long; you didn't know what to do. I'd be on the training pitch, we'd be playing a seven-a-side game or something, and I'd suddenly hear Mike Walker's voice booming out from the sidelines.

'Gossy! Wherever you are, if you get the ball and Sutty's free, give it him. If Foxy is on and looking for it – give it to him. Always go forward. If no one is on, keep possession and wait for someone to be available. They will be. Don't you dare go backwards or lose it.' I used to hear those voices in my head all the time, those phrases, 'Don't give it away' and 'Get it, give it.'

But it paid off. I remember one day pre-season, in 1992/93. We were playing another practice match (Mike liked to play little games like that all the time). It was a baking hot day. Everyone had been working hard, everyone had a big sweat on. You were looking for the water bottles. If you'd worked really hard, and, especially if it's hot, you would want to throw up. We used to have what we called 'Terror Tuesday's' in training. You ran your nuts off. Seriously. And then you ran some more. And, just as you didn't think you'd even be able to walk again – you ran again.

Football? What was one of those. We never saw one on those days. We'd have a 3,000-metre run, then a sprint, then a longer run, then another sprint. Long, short, long, short. Shuttle runs. Bleep tests. You then had Wednesday's off – which you needed. But suddenly, in the middle of one of those exhausting sessions, it dawned on me. Remember how I had previously thought that I still hasn't arrived despite all the games, the cup semi-final, the last league game at the home of the new champions? Well, now I realised I had. I felt a million dollars, fitter than I had ever been or expected to be. I could manage the runs. I could run a marathon in under four hours, run the hundred metres in about 12 seconds. I was all over the pitch, winning the ball, making the runs and tackles, and working really hard. And it was all second nature to me, it was ... well, it was easy. And from then on in, I knew we could have a good season, because, if everyone else was feeling the same way, we were going to be a team to be reckoned with.

I slept well that night. I knew I wasn't letting anyone down. I felt I belonged, that I belonged in the FA Premier League, or whatever it was when it started. I was ready. We all were. I was a first-team player, wearing the right coloured top, playing alongside the right people. We had the right players at the club. And they all, except Flecky, stuck around. They'd been there for several years, they were all approaching the peaks of their careers. We had a good player in every position on the pitch. There wasn't a weak link. Look at Ian Culverhouse at right-back. In that position, you're judged on how many crosses you let the opposing winger get in. He didn't let many in. He knew how to tackle, knew how to pass. He was a brilliant player who should have played for England. Same on the other side with Mark Bowen. He did it for us, week after week after week. He never got less than a 7/10 from me.

He did it for Wales as well, I played and trained alongside him for the national side, he was just the same. And when he spoke up? Well, you listened. Same with Ian Crook. We complemented each other perfectly in that midfield. Chippy had spent a few years watching Ardiles and Villa in the Tottenham midfield, a team that needed players like that to keep him out of their side. He'd tell me stories of the training sessions they had there, time spent just trying to get the ball off Ricky Villa! You look at him and think he was just a makeweight in the Ardiles deal. But he could play. Ardiles and him, as small and slight a professional footballer as you like and they couldn't get the ball off them. Could they do him for pace? No. Could Ossie ping out 40 yard passes, to feet, with those old Mitre balls? Yes he could. Ian Crook watched him and learnt. And now we had Ian Crook at Norwich who could land a ball on half a sixpence from that distance. I didn't need to worry about doing things like that, I just wanted to get the ball and make sure he got it next, if at all possible. He was a craftsman, an artist with a football. I was more of the grafter at his side, the artisan. My game was focused on strength and stamina, getting up and down the pitch supporting everyone.

It was a great pre-season for me. Like I have said, I felt, I knew, that I had finally arrived. Mike had worked under Dave and seen what I could do. Now he was going to give me my chance, make me one of his pivotal players. Because of that, because the manager was very clearly demonstrating his faith in me, others then started to see me in a different way. There was no more banging on the managers door, no more 'Your time will come'. Hopefully the younger players were now saying that about me, wanting my place in the first team. The established players, they'd see me in training and in the pre-season games, they'd be thinking, 'Look at him, look what he's doing, look what he's bringing to the team.' On and off the pitch, I did that, wanted to prove it. I would go to war with these lads, go to war for them and on my own if I had to. I stuck up for myself, maybe I hadn't done that enough in the past. So yes, all the scuffles and scrapes you get at all clubs, I'd be involved. A few drinks, arm-wrestles, fights. I'd be in there, showing I wasn't someone to mess with. I'd fight my teammates if I had to, and I'd certainly fight the opposition.

I remember a game against Swindon. For no reason that I can think of, other than, maybe, he knew he was a nothing player in comparison, John Moncur went over and absolutely battered Ian Crook, sent him flying. Chippy was down on the floor, he was obviously hurt, and there's John Moncur, standing over him, shouting and screaming abuse at him. I wasn't having that. So I ran over and smacked right into him, hit the sweet spot. He never saw me coming. He was down on the floor squealing, but that was too bad. I took him out because he crocked Chippy. So now he was down on the floor and I was standing over Moncur, feeling and looking, no doubt, a bit like Russell Crowe in Gladiator – and yes, I was ready to kill him, I really was. The red mist was dancing in front of my eyes and all I want to do is hurt him for taking out my mate, a player with more class and talent than Moncur will ever have.

Mind you, it's not as if my little squabble with him is an isolated incident because it was all kicking off by now, probably down to me. I'd been interviewed on one of those midweek sports shows in the days leading up to the game about a few bits and pieces, when, in closing, the interviewer asked me about our pending league game with Swindon Town who were, as they had been all season, struggling near the bottom of the league, while we had a European run to our name sitting pretty in about ninth place. We were flying. What I should have said was 'it'll be a tough game, they're playing at home and will make it difficult for us; they've got some good players and will want to show their fans that they mean business and want to get away from the relegation zone.' Respect in other words. But what I actually said was, 'We're playing well and they're not that good a team, so look, we shouldn't have any problem going there and turning them over.' I said it because I was on top of my footballing world. Wired, fired, ready for war. I wasn't frightened of anyone and would probably have said the same about any team. But I needed to learn some charm and subtlety. Modern players have lessons in how to deal with the media. We hadn't. So I just sounded off and thought nothing more about it.

Naturally enough, my words and the sentiment behind them swiftly found their way down to Swindon. They were all in the local press, with, naturally, a little dash of the, shall we say, embellishment that journalists sometimes like to give to stories. In other words, it became of case of Goss looks down at Swindon and doesn't just write them off, he slags them off. Which meant that I'd pretty much done John Gorman's pre-match team talk for him. He'd have wound his lads up good and proper by telling them what a big-time-Charlie I was, and who the hell did I think I was? They'd have been climbing the walls in their dressing room before kick-off. Their fans, mind you, had kicked off long before that.

I was jostled and spat at by the Swindon fans as we walked from the coach to the dressing rooms. They were riled, and completely so, and didn't mind letting me know in the most obvious and threatening manner they could. Once we got to the relative safety of the dressing room, the gaffer had a quiet word. 'You are going to get battered today Gossy, but you bloody deserve it because what you said about them before the game was out of order. Completely out of order ... but hey, bollocks to them, get out there.'

Moncur was at it from the start. Niggling away, making little comments, crafty asides to the ref and playing to the crowd, who were loving it, especially when he took Chippy out. He'd had a second or so of glory before I was on him. Now, the crowd, who had been cheering for him after he'd nobbled my mate were howling in protest, 'off, off, off, off'. It was all boiling up nicely, especially as they were now in amid us and spoiling for a fight. A couple of the more sensible Norwich boys started to get inbetween warring parties: 'come on lads, don't be silly, break it up', that sort of thing, while the ref was darting from one group to another blowing his whistle and saying to no one in particular 'I'll send someone off, I will, I'll send someone off.' It didn't really look as if anyone was taking much notice of him.

Then, out of the chaos, a figure appeared. Massive, big strides, shoulders you could land a light aircraft on. Ladies and gentlemen ... Mr B. Kilcline. 'Killer Kilcline' to his friends (and enemies). He's a big lad to say the least. Big enough for there to be an unwritten law in football which stated you don't mess with Killer Kilcline. The first person he saw was Rob Newman, hopping from foot to foot and imploring everyone to 'calm down, calm down', a bit like 'Harry Enfield's Scousers West Country cousins'. Naturally enough, Killer thought this must have meant that Rob had started it all. Simple enough logic. So he grabbed Rob, put him in a headlock and started rubbing the top of Rob's head with his fist, walking away from the carnage a bit like a lion dragging some helpless antelope off for its dinner.

'Come with me old son, I'll teach you to muck about with my mate.' Rob was panicking now. Who wouldn't? 'It wasn't me, it wasn't me. You've got the wrong man.' All for one and one for all? 'It was Gossy!' Killer turned around, think the Terminator dropping the box of roses as he starts to fire the shotgun. A growl. Think

Jurassic Park. I'm one of the little kids in the kitchen. 'Where's Gossy?' By now, of course, the Swindon fans were really wound up. I was a dead man as far as they were concerned. Their sense of outrage and anger, however, is tempered, albeit only slightly, by the fact they're winning the game 3-2. And it stays that way until there is around 5 minutes left, when Chippy, somehow in one piece after his scrap with Moncur, made an uncharacteristic charge for goal, before letting fly in that artistic way of his, a shot that hit the crossbar. Temporary relief for the Swindon players and fans, until public enemy number one (me), beat everyone to the loose ball and tapped it into the goal to make the score 3-3, which is how it finished. Good move Gossy. It was pandemonium when the final whistle went. The lads formed a guard around me as we went off the pitch, the Swindon fans desperate to get at me. We got in the changing rooms in one piece and, to the soundtrack of the growing anger outside, got changed. There wasn't going to be any social in the players' lounge after this game.

Just as we were ready to go, Tim Sheppard popped his head around the changing room door. The noise got louder and there were cries of 'Get the bastard!' Tim shut sit again. 'Right', he says, 'you go out of the back way and sneak in through the emergency exit of the coach, we'll distract them by going out this way. They won't notice you're making your way by another route.'

But I wasn't having that. 'No way. I'm going out the front with the rest of you lads. Come on, let's go.' And we do, to more cries of 'There he is, get him, do him!' And yes, I took some hits and some spittle en route, but the lads are around me and its nothing serious. I bombed onto the coach first and sat at the back, safe once the rest of the lads were on board. And then we were away, the Swindon fans going nuts but we were fine, sat back in our seats, laughing about the events of the day and cracking open a few beers. As we headed back, one of my teammates made the pithy observation that perfectly summed up how I'd changed since I had rebelled against Dave Stringer, and the fact I wasn't being given a chance in the side not so long ago. A lot had changed and his little comment was spot on.

'Gossy. You're a fruitcake.' But I was. And they respected me. I'd gone from being the quiet one, quiet in words and deed, to one of the lads. A bit loud, a bit out there, a bit in your face. And the lads in the team liked and respected me for it. They knew I'd run through brick walls for them in training, or in a match, they knew I'd look out for them, just as I had with Chippy. I was one of the boys.

This was something that had started at the beginning of the previous season, around eighteen months before that Swindon game. I'd worked hard in pre-season and been lifted by Mike saying he was going to shape his team around me. Another season. Except this time, I felt I really belonged, with the lads beginning to accept me as one of them. I'd never gone into a new season feeling better. And it wasn't any old season either, it was this new Premier League, the FA Premier League as it was back then. We didn't really know how it would change the game, or that it would as much as it did. There'd been a lot of hype for it on Sky, what with all their adverts for it, a 'whole new ball game' or some such rubbish. Nothing much changes for the players though, you just want to play. New League, new name, same game. And, as it always seemed to be on the first day of the season, it was boiling hot. We were at Arsenal, as tough an opening game as you could ask for. We had finished one season with a game at the champions, starting the next one at the ground of one of the clubs who were favourites to be the next champions. But that was what I wanted, what we wanted. Big games and big-name players appearing against us. Arsenal had a few! David Seaman, Tony Adams, Paul Merson, Ian Wright and Anders Limpar, who'd been all over the Sky ads. I wonder if they looked down our squad list, even bothered at all? It didn't matter. We were ready for them. We'd got the disappointments of the previous season out of our systems, whatever had been left had been sweated, even puked out of us by Mike Walker. So it was a case of bring on the Arsenal, and we were going there to win, not just to make up the numbers. Not in that game and not during that season. We wanted to win and I wanted to prove myself as the top, top player I knew I could be.

Flecky had gone but Mike did a good bit of pre-season shopping, bringing in Mark Robins from Manchester United. Now Robbo is the biggest moaner in football. He really was. And he started just as soon as he arrived at Norwich. You could tell which car was his in the players' car park because it was the biggest, shiniest, fastest, most expensive looking one. He'd got a good move, a nice car, playing regular football with a great bunch of lads. Was he made up for himself? Oh no. Moan, moan, moan. 'Why are we training today, we never used to at United on Mondays.' 'I don't like the food here.' 'The dressing rooms are too small, they were much bigger at United.' 'The houses here are too expensive, they're a lot cheaper in Cheshire' (yeah, course they are Robbo). He was a handy player, a natural goalscorer. But he did like a moan.

After he had first got into management, I was doing some coaching at Norwich, helping Chippy out with the reserves soon after Paul Lambert had arrived. Robbo, back up north, was Barnsley manager at the time. Anyway, we were at Colney, training had finished and a few of us were having a cup of tea. The phone rings, Chippy answers. It's Robbo. Chippy's chuffed, it's been ages since he, since any of us, had spoken to him. So it's all 'allo Robbo mate, great to hear from you? How's it going up at Barnsley? Gossy's here mate, he'll have a word with you. We must all meet up, have a few drinks.' But Robbo's wasn't listening and Chippy's happy face soon faded away. There was silence for a few seconds and Chippy then said, all quiet, 'Yeah OK, Robbo, we'll let you know. Bye then.'

Me and the other lads were all agog, all asking Chippy how he was and what he'd wanted. Chippy was stunned, saying 'it was like he was reading out his shopping list!' He then mimics Robbo, and fair play, he's got Robbo spot on, monotone, staccato. 'Hullo Chippy, it's Robbo. I was wondering if you had any players I could take at loan. I'm at Barnsley, I need players. No one has any to spare. I dunno what I'm meant to do. It wasn't like this at ...' Same old Robbo!

The other player Mike brought in that summer was Gary Megson. He came in on a free transfer from Manchester City. He was a similar sort of player to me, red rag to a bull there! As it happened, we often played in the same team and I noted then what a good player he was. That, and a fantastic pro, one for the kids to learn from. We very nearly didn't get him. Robert Chase, the Norwich chairman at the time, wasn't going to sanction the signing. He thought Meggy was too old and too expensive. Hardly. He was on a free and wouldn't have been earning as much as Robbo. Mind you, if he had, Robbo would have had a right old whinge about that as well.

It became quite a battle of wills between the manager and his chairman, Mike was determined to get Meggy on board because he knew what he could do for the team and club as a whole. We got him in the end, and straight away, Meggy's professional attitude was standing out. He was thirty-three when he came to us and went on to play more football in the Premier League, as well as in Europe. Because he'd looked after himself, he was fit and he wanted to play. It was a great signing by Mike, even though the chairman, and probably the fans, didn't realise it. He made a massive difference and was a big influence on us that season. Mike wanted the club to feed off his influence and professionalism. So Meggy was in the starting line up for Arsenal, playing with me in the centre, with Ruel Fox and Dave Phillips on the wings. Steel in the middle, pace on the outside. Mike wanted us to get in behind them to expose the weaknesses of their full backs to pace.

Weaknesses? Lee Dixon and Nigel Winterburn were two of the best full-backs in the country. They, plus Tony Adams and Steve Bould, were as good a back four as you'd see, or play against, anywhere. But Mike made us feel they were fallible, that we could get at them and give them a game. That sort of self-belief is crucial in football, it makes good players think they are great ones – they might not be, but they play like it. And for as long as you can keep that self-belief and confidence on the go, they'll play like that for you all season. Don't get me wrong. We had some very good players at the club, but maybe because we were at Norwich, we didn't think, or believe, we'd ever become great ones. Wouldn't we be playing for Arsenal or Manchester United if we were? Mike shook us up a bit, made us believe that the stage we were now on was as much for us as anyone else playing that day. By five to three, we were so fired up we were bouncing off the walls. In the past, Norwich teams would have been sat there thinking 'this is Highbury', and been fixated on that, the tradition, the heritage, the history. We were thinking, 'so what if it's Highbury. Let's get out there and win.' Eleven blokes stood, not sat, there, shouting and screaming the place down, like mad dogs about to be let off the lead. A new season, a new era in football. We were ready. Let us play. As for our resident midfield maestro, our resident footballing genius, the Norfolk Platini called Chippy? He's on the bench. Your time will come son!

I'm not going to rattle through each and every game of that season. The records are all there for everyone to see, and you don't need me to give a running account of them. But that Arsenal game, I will dwell on for a moment. Because it set us up for everything that was to follow, everything that happened in the crazy two years or so that came after that game. Yes, we were 2-0 down at half-time. Some of the lads might even have thought it would be a case of damage limitation in the second half. But that wasn't Mike Walker's way; it wouldn't have been Dave Stringer's either. Anyway, we were sat there in those massive Highbury changing rooms, two down, sweat pouring off us, getting liquids on board and waiting for the bollocking that never came. Mike is calm, considered ... hell, he's confident even.

Not bad lads. You're maybe giving them a little bit more space than we should. But, on the whole, I think we can be happy with that. No reason why we can't get a result here. Just get in among them a little more, get some early balls played into their box. And Robbo ... [here Mike nodded in the direction of Mark Robins who'd started on the bench] ... keep warm; you'll be coming on after 10 minutes or so.

Such confidence. You can't help but feel 8 feet tall when you play for a manager who gives you that sort of belief. Here we were, two down at Highbury on the opening day of the season, needing at least two goals against one of the most disciplined defences in English football history. Yet he thinks we can go out there and turn it around.

What does that sort of confidence do for you? I'll tell you. It's infectious and you believe it. And we did. We went out there full of ourselves, absolutely convinced we could get a result. The look on the Arsenal boys' faces was priceless. They'd probably expected us to come out with our heads down, shoulders slumped, just wanting to get it over with. Yet we were out of the traps from the kick-off. There was no fear, just belief. And that included Robbo, who came on and scored two, his second and our fourth. It was a quality chip over David Seaman, from at least 25 yards out, that not only sealed the win and put the wheels of a great season in motion, it also had the Arsenal fans applauding while the Norwich fans danced a jig of delight in the late afternoon sunshine.

It felt great. We'd put down a marker for the rest of the season and got some momentum going, which just kept going throughout that season and into the next one. Would we have had the same sort of campaign had we lost that game? It is difficult to say. We were still a good team with some excellent players and a great manager. So I think we would have done well regardless. After all, we not only lost, but were thoroughly outplayed in our opening game of the following season by Manchester United, losing 2-0 at Carrow Road. But we still went onto have some great results as well as that run in the UEFA Cup. So no, that memorable 1992/93 season didn't happen because of that win over Arsenal on the opening day, we'd have done well anyway. But listen, it made a hell of a difference.

We were in party mode going back as you can imagine. A few beers, a few laughs. Even Robbo might have cracked open a smile. I was bouncing up and down the aisle of that coach, the life and soul of the party ... well, maybe? A long, long way from the lad who used to quietly sit at the front and hope no one saw him or said anything to him, the blonde lad from the Ressies who was good for making you a tea or coffee.

At one point, I waltzed up to Gary Megson, wrapped my arms around him and said 'Hey, come on Meggy, we beat the Arsenal, great result mate, great result and a magic debut for you. Come on, let's make the most of this, have a few beers.'

Meggy, such a professional, looked at me and said, 'Yes, but we should be looking to do this every week.' And he was right. It was the start of a brand new season and we'd played just one game. Yes, we'd won it and we'd done well. But there are often a few odd results at the start of the season. Arsenal would work it out of their systems and come again, we had to make sure we kept it up over the remaining forty-one games of that campaign – starting at Carrow Road against Chelsea in just four days time. It was a special day for me. But it was going to get a lot more special, and in a way I couldn't possibly have imagined.

The party coach was getting closer to Norwich and, as it did, thoughts turned to where we all might go to continue the celebrations. Somewhere in the city naturally, but where? All the lads had differing opinions on where we might go, all, that is, except for me. Because I didn't want to. It wasn't, I should add, because I was reverting back to the shy lad who didn't go out, who wondered why on earth you'd go out for a drink if you weren't thirsty. Far from it. No, I was, quite simply, done in. Knackered. It had been a hard game, played in boiling hot sunshine, and I had, as was always the case, ran my nuts off for 90 minutes. Going out on the town was the last thing on my mind.

Now, don't get me wrong. I felt great. The coach was rocking and the beers were flying. Even Barry, our trusted coach driver from Ambassadors Coach Travel, had a massive grin on his face all the way home. It had been a brilliant day, one of those you get into the game for, put in a shift and get rewards like this. I had a massive smile on my face, being there, experiencing that and sharing the sense of accomplishment afterwards with the lads. There's nothing like it. Every now and again we'd go past another coach, one that was full of our fans, partying just as we were, scarves flying out of the windows. We'd all wave and cheer at them and they'd do the same back. We even stopped for some fish and chips somewhere. Great times that I was lapping it up. But I was nearly dead on my feet. The heat, the grafting, the beers. Time to get back and get some sleep.

'Come on, come on, let's go out!' The cries were getting louder and louder as we got into Norwich. 'You coming Gossy?' Rob Newman was insisting rather than asking. 'We're off to Chicago's.' Chicago's, for the uninitiated, is a Norwich nightclub and bar. It was, and is, popular with fit, young men in the mood for a little liquid relaxation. Enticing as it all sounded, I tried to explain to Rob that I wouldn't be joining them on this occasion. 'You what? Gossy, sort yourself out son. You're coming out and that's the end of it. Most of the boys are going out and are off to Chicago's and you are joining us.' Guess what? I was off to Chicago's.

So I went along. I wasn't going to dance the night away or paint the town red, nothing like that. I took my place at the bar, a quiet little corner of it at that, and stood, sipping a Guinness and chatting to Rob, Mark Walton and Sutty. The little things. The camaraderie among the lads was as good as I'd ever known it at the club. Passing the time of day in good company. And, as the evening wore on and the Guinness started to work its way through me, I popped off to the loo, noticing, as I walked down the stairs, a really attractive girl out of the corner of my eye.

My God, I thought, she is absolutely gorgeous. Then, I thought nothing more of it. I came back, rejoined the lads at the bar and joined in with the chat again, I couldn't, however, get this absolutely stunning woman out of my mind. Was she still there? I took a look, trying not to make it obvious. Yes, she was, with some other girls. I kept an eye on her as I carried on the banter with the lads, and then, suddenly, she looked as if she was making her way across the floor towards us. And indeed she was. This vision was walking straight over to where we were standing. For a second, I thought she was after a drink, or maybe she was going to want to chat with one of the other lads. Sutty was becoming a well known face by now, perhaps she was coming over to say hello to him?

But no, she simply found some space between us at the bar to order some drinks. Then, before I knew it, we started chatting and I asked her if she wanted a drink? I was amazed because firstly, she was interested in talking to me, and secondly, because she said, 'Yes, I'll have what you're drinking, a pint of Guinness.' Wow! Not a sneaky glass of wine, or a subtle gin and tonic, but a huge pint of Guinness. It took me by surprise as well as impressing me in a funny sort of way. I got the drinks in for us both and then proceeded to do the gentlemanly thing of slowly elbowing Sutty and Rob out of the way in order to leave a bit of private space for me and Maggie, before then proceeding to man-mark her for the next thirty minutes or so, allowing her no space to move on. Rob, who always had great vision, read the situation well and gave me excellent cover and support by thrusting a pen and paper in my hand so that I could get her phone number. This was a good move as I didn't want her to side step away from me without my having some sort of end result. And, eventually, Maggie gave me her number, adding that she worked at her parents' hotel in Gorleston. Several days later, I drove to Gorleston, a place I'd never been to before, met Maggie again for a coffee and the rest is history.

That good start at Arsenal did, as I had suspected and hoped, given us the confidence boost and momentum going into the rest of that season. We had Chelsea at Carrow Road on the Tuesday night, and they went ahead. Not a problem, we still won with goals from David Phillips and Robbo, again, his third in two games. What a bargain he was turning out to be. Former Norwich favourite, Robert Fleck, watched from the stands, he'd signed for Chelsea from us in the summer, but, under the terms of the deal, we'd made sure he couldn't have played against us in this game. A wise decision, as I am sure Flecky would have liked nothing more than to put one over on us at Carrow Road.

He's a top man is Flecky. Genuinely so. As loud and in your face as you like on the pitch against the opposition and the fans. He didn't care and wound them up something rotten. And, with all due respect, when you've lived in Glasgow and played in the Old Firm derby as he has up there, Norwich City against Ipswich Town is probably something you can take in your stride. He used to keep an eye out for the younger lads mind, had all the time in the world for them, a word and an arm around your shoulder when needed. When I was having a crisis of self-doubt once, maybe not giving myself as much credit as I should have done for what I was doing, he sorted that out, he got hold of me, looked me straight in the eye and gave it to me with both barrels. 'Listen. You are where you are and in this team because you are a bloody good player, one who is only ever going to get better. So don't let me ever hear you say things like that or doubt yourself again, understand?' 'Yes Flecky, thanks for that. Don't know what I was thinking of.'

Off the pitch, he was as quiet as a lamb. No, seriously. In a game, an away trip, in and around the club and at training he was like Gazza, a massive character, always up to something. But away from the game, away from his work, he was, and is today, as modest, quiet and considerate a bloke as you could ever meet. He spends a lot of his time working with school kids now. He doesn't have to. But he wants to, wants to give something back to the community and be part of something. The kids adore him, even if it's more likely to be their dads who ask him about the football and want his autograph! So, like I said, a top man. But we were all glad he wasn't playing in that game because he would have been a complete and utter bloody pain in the backside for all of us throughout.

Naturally enough, most of the people in the media reckoned our good start wouldn't last. There were the rather predictable remarks about the 'Canaries being on top of the Premiership perch', and we were, after all, the very first leaders of that 'new' division, but we were widely expected to go away and stop bothering everyone by the Autumn.

No chance. After we had played our tenth league game of the season, at Coventry at the end of September, which was a 1-1 draw, we were still top of the table, two points ahead of Blackburn Rovers in second place. It was them up next at Ewood Park, a game we all thought we could get something from. We'd won seven of those opening ten games, scoring nineteen goals in the process, while Robbo was right up there with the division's top scorers with six goals to his name. It came, therefore, as a bit of a shock when Rovers absolutely battered us, winning 7-1, with Alan Shearer, in particular, being unplayable. Even my old mate and Norwich old boy, Tim Sherwood, got in on the act, scoring from a header. It was a nightmare day all round, one which knocked us off the top of the table as all of the pundits and so-called experts in the game rubbed their hands together, collectively saying I told you so.

We were a good team and we bounced back. By early December, we were not only the form side again, the established and well-deserved leaders of the Premier League, we were eight points clear of Blackburn. Eight points clear. That's some achievement by any standard. But, given the quality of the squad that Mike Walker had to call upon, and the confidence and self-belief (those words again) that we had in ourselves and each other, we weren't surprised. The only thing missing for me was that I hadn't yet scored a goal, but that didn't matter as we were playing well, winning games, getting some praise and yes, you know what, we really thought we could have gone on and won the Premier League title that season. I'd even go as far as saying that, as fantastic as the eventual third-place finish was, I was not the only person disappointed once the season had ended. I look back at some of the results and performances and you can see where we'd slipped up. We lost both our games against Ipswich, games we might have expected to win as they weren't having a good season. That was six points gone for a start. Then, there were the games at Blackburn and Manchester United. Yes, Blackburn turned us over but it was a freak result, we should have got a point there at least.

Manchester United away? That was an unlucky one. Eric Cantona was making his full debut for them, but they needed time to get used to him and vice versa. So they weren't that much better than us, or dominant. They scraped it 1-0, a lucky goal from a Lee Sharp cross cannoned off Daryl Sutch, right to the feet of Mark Hughes. Sparky didn't waste such open invitations. Then, Peter Schmeichel saw a goal-bound effort from Robbo come off his feet and away. He didn't know much about it but it was the rub of the green for them, another point lost. Same with Wimbledon, they well and truly turned us over, in mid-March, 3-0. We never had a hope that day. Vinnie Jones and Fash took control of the game from the start and that was that, we were down to third, from first, and, all of a sudden, we looked like we might be slipping off the pace a bit.

But the game that really did it for us was Manchester United at home. They tore us apart. It was, by far, one of the best performances of any team I've ever played against in my career. They'd come to Carrow Road, a week and a bit after we'd beaten Aston Villa, who had been our other close rivals for the title, the result 1-0 with John Polston scoring. That had put us back on top of the table, which meant that United would be at Carrow Road with the onus on them to win, that was where the pressure would be. If we'd won, we would have gone five points ahead of them. In their minds, it might have even put them out of the race altogether. They had, after all, almost given the title to Leeds United on a plate the previous season. It wasn't just theirs to win, but to take home and put on the mantelpiece as well. End of season jitters put paid to their chances then, and you'd have thought that maybe a win for us that night might have done the same thing.

However, you just had to look the team Alex Ferguson picked to know they meant business. And then some. It was a massively attacking line-up, packed with pace. Lee Sharpe, Andrei Kanchelskis and Ryan Giggs were all starting, as was Cantona and Brian McClair. That's five attack-minded players straight off. Talk about making a statement – they'd done it big time. They ripped into us from kick-off, with Sharpe, Kanchelskis and Giggs sat near the halfway line, running the legs off us whenever they got the chance. They were 3-0 up after 20 minutes and those three goals had come in a 7-minute spell from Giggs, Kanchelskis and Cantona. Game over.

Robbo got one back after an hour, but it was cold comfort. They'd completely outplayed us, outfought us and outran us. That defeat knocked the stuffing out of us a bit, and for the first time that season we were a bit down, a bit jaded. We had the chance to make up for it a few days later at Tottenham, but the spark was gone. They won 5-1, and that was pretty much that. The league table after that game had us down in third, a point behind United and two behind Villa. The trouble was they both had two games in hand and they made the most of them.

As is often the case in football, we then had one of our best performances of the season, beating Leeds United 4-2 at Carrow Road. Chris Sutton really announced his class and potential to the world on that day scoring a hat-trick. He was on fire and they couldn't cope with him. He was going on to bigger and better things eventually, of that there was no doubt. I was in my usual place, sat alongside Chippy in the centre of midfield, and just enjoyed the show. When he got his third he was absolutely running on empty, the runs he'd made, the effort and hard work, he placed the ball in the net from an angle, tumbled over and then got up and walked back to get ready for kick-off. He couldn't celebrate, he was that knackered. I like to see that in a player, someone who will give his all, then find a little bit more, and then, as Sutty did in that match, still deliver. Quality.

In the end, it was a Norwich old boy who scored the goal that got us into Europe for the following season. Andy Linighan secured an FA Cup win for Arsenal against Sheffield Wednesday that saw them qualify for the following season's UEFA Cup Winners' Cup tournament, meaning that, by virtue of us finishing third in the Premier League, we'd qualified for the UEFA Cup, the first time that Norwich City would play in competitive European football.

This was the first time we'd play in the tournament but not the first time the team had qualified. Ken Brown had won the League Cup for Norwich in 1985, which meant the team he and Mel Machin put together would have played in the UEFA Cup the following season. Sadly, due to the tragic events that happened at the Heysel Stadium later that spring, it wasn't to be, nor was it to be so when the Canaries qualified for Europe on two more separate occasions – a fifth-place finish in 1987 and then fourth under Dave Stringer in 1989.

The club, therefore, qualified to play in competitive European football in three out of five years, before doing it again four years later. And, for a club of Norwich's size, that was some achievement. Finishing third in the Premier League is now good enough to get you entry into the Champions League, so we sort of missed out there as well. But hey, look. We were all made up and would look forward to whatever new challenges it brought up. Yes, we were disappointed that we didn't make that extra push and end up winning the Premier League in 1993 and maybe if Robert Chase had allowed Mike Walker to strengthen the squad as he'd wanted we could have done so, but it never happened and we all know the disappointments that eventually came, partially as a result of us now seizing the opportunity when it was there.

Not that any negative thoughts were crossing our minds as we all headed off for our respective holidays in the summer of 1993. It was inconceivable, to us, that the club wouldn't make the very best of the foundations that Mike had put in place that season, carrying on the good work that had been started by Dave Stringer before him. Talk was about Europe, adding to the squad over the summer and pushing on in the following season, looking to improve and better what we had already achieved. Me? I'd have probably allowed myself a day or so off before I hit the fitness trail, getting fit in time for pre-season. I couldn't wait to be honest. I'd had a great season, starting twenty-five games in the Premier League for the club, plus appearing in all of the cup games we'd played that season (five in total), one of which, a League Cup tie at Carlisle, had seen me get my first goal of the campaign in a 2-2 draw. I guess most people have forgotten that game now, let alone the fact that I scored in it.

Unbeknown to me, however, I was soon to score a few goals that would get people talking.

9

That Goal, That Game

That tipped Jock over the edge. He flew for Sutty, grabbing him and dragging him down to the spotless floor of that once immaculate dressing room.

It's that moment forever frozen as part of my life, that everyone, to both my everlasting surprise and delight, still want to talk to me about. Even today, over two decades later, I can be out and about somewhere when, out of nowhere, there's a tap on my shoulder and the flash of a smile from a friendly stranger as they tell me how much they remember that goal and that game, the one played in the Olympic Stadium in Munich on 20 October 1993.

'Hello Gossy. I remember that great goal you got against Bayern Munich out there, what a goal that was. Fantastic mate, fantastic. What did it feel like, scoring that goal?' Every time someone mentions *that* game and *that* goal to me, I am touched that they have taken the trouble to do so and have such great memories of something that I was involved in. And, as much as I can, I'll always chat with them about it for a few minutes, how can I not? What's more, I hope people never get bored asking me or talking about it. It was a special time for me and, perhaps more importantly, for the club as well. We'd just had the season of our lives, that third place finish, plus the promise of playing in Europe for the first time in the club's history. But none of us wanted that campaign to be some sort of winding down process after the success of the previous season. We wanted to build on what we'd done, we'd missed out on the Premier League title in the end, but look, we were serious about coming back and having a proper go at it the next time around. That meant we had to be prepared to work right from the off, hard work, more hard work and then some hard work to finish it off with.

Mike and John Deehan took the lads to a pre-season training camp in Denver, Colorado. We played a couple of games out there in a competition alongside three other teams, but the whole purpose of the trip was to get fit. They were, without doubt, the hardest training sessions of my life, Mike literally ran us all into the ground. It was stinking hot and so were we. But it paid off. I was as fit and strong as I'd ever been. And full of confidence. There is one moment I'll never forget while we were out there; we were training, running probably, and I felt great. I was loving it, getting fit with good friends around me. It was a moment of clarity, of knowing I was exactly where I wanted to be, doing exactly what I wanted to do and with the people I most wanted to be with. I couldn't wait for the start of the new season, I was desperate to get started.

As it happened, we didn't have the best of starts. The fixture computer had us playing Manchester United at Carrow Road on the first day of the season, a game and date that Sky soon changed to the Sunday afternoon kick-off for their main televised game. Manchester United and Norwich were the major players the previous season, so everyone expected us to be so again. On the day, they were better than us again, winning 2-0. We never really troubled them to be honest so it was disappointing. Mike soon geared us up again and he had to, the next game was at Blackburn, where we'd lost 7-1 the previous season. We owed it to ourselves and the fans to show up and tell them what we were made of. It was a case of 'Look, you did us last season, we'll admit to that. But we're a good team and we're going to show you tonight just how good we are.'

And we did. They took an early lead, and I suspect everyone was thinking 'here we go again'. But we weren't having it, winning 3-2 in the end, the second and third goals coming within a couple of minutes, with Rob Newman and Chris Sutton the scorers. We were up and running then with another big game to come at Leeds United. The goal I got in that game was the very best I've ever scored and won me the BBC's Goal of the Month award. I've still got it in my house and am proud to have won it, but, believe me, that day and that game was all about the lads and how, on another boiling hot afternoon, we put together one of the best ever performances I've ever been part of as a professional footballer. We rolled them over, we really did. We won 4-0 but it could have been ten and that's no exaggeration. The squad we took to Leeds was the best the football club has ever had, look at that quality in the eleven that started that game, I'll name the team for you: Gunn, Culverhouse, Bowen, Butterworth, Polston, Goss, Crook, Newman, Robins, Fox and Sutton, with Efan Ekoku getting on from the bench. I wasn't the most gifted footballer in the world but I was surrounded by players who were, notably, Ian Crook. I knew what my role was and what I brought to the team. It reminds me of a time when I attended an event at Carrow Road that featured the late and very great Alan Ball, who won the World Cup with England in 1966.

He spoke of how he knew what his job was and what his teammates expected of him. He said he was the team's 'dog'. That's what he had been told by people like Bobby Charlton and Bobby Moore.

Bally, you're our dog and the football is the stick. When we're out there playing the game, you go and fetch the stick, win the stick. When you've done that bring it back to us so we can do something with it. You don't need to worry about anything else. Go win that ball and bring it back to us.

Well, my game was similar, support the ball all over the pitch and give it to another yellow short. I was the worker, the Norwich City dog.

Robbo was desperate for a goal in that game. He did everything but score. He would have been moaning away to everyone. He was in for my goal to be fair. We played it long for a change, out of defence and down their right. Foxy was on it like a flash, taking it to the edge of their penalty area with loads of time to knock it past Chris Fairclough and across the face of the penalty area. Robbo was on his way to meet the pass when it came, even John Motson in the commentary said that he (Robbo) was running in on the near post. But so was I, bombing up the pitch just behind him. I wanted it. Foxy looked before he played the ball. he was looking for Robbo, who I shouted at to 'leave it'. Foxy now saw us both so aimed it right at us, pinging it into where I met it on the volley somewhere near the penalty spot, full stretch, using the pace of the ball to send it goalwards. I've never struck a better ball in my life. There was no power in it, the power was in the cross, my timing and the connection spot on. As I ran off to celebrate, Robbo chased after me, ready for the high fives that would follow. I saw that a lot of the Leeds fans were on their feet applauding me, something I've never forgotten.

There's a great photograph of the moment I made the connection with the ball. Robbo's getting out of the way as I fly in, with Jon Newsome (who later on went to play for Norwich) and Tony Dorigo looking unsure if they were meant to mark one or the other of us. A lovely moment but, like I said, part of what was a fantastic team performance. We'd now won two tough away games on the trot, scoring seven goals in the process, pushing ourselves up to sixth in the table. Four days later, we played Ipswich at Carrow Road and won 1-0, another great and never-to-be-forgotten game for me as I scored the winner, stabbing the ball in from 18 yards out and celebrating with the Barclay faithful. A brilliant night. If you score against the old enemy, your name is remembered forever by the City fans. Four games, three wins and two goals for the lad, Goss. Things were on the up again. Not bad for the team dog!

The big attraction for both players and fans that season, however, would be the UEFA Cup campaign, which started in mid-September with a first round, first leg against the Dutch side Vitesse Arnhem. Interestingly, once our European qualification had been confirmed the previous September, Mike Walker had spoken for all of us when he said how our success that season had to be a springboard to bigger and better things, declaring in the *Eastern Daily Press* that 'We have achieved something which people will say isn't bad in your first season, but we've got to improve on that. That's the goal. We have got to try and win the league next year.'

This was fighting talk, just the sort of thing, as an ambitious professional footballer, that you want to hear. Knowing that the chairman would almost certainly be reading the back page of the newspaper, Mike added, 'I'm looking to bring in two or three new players and no doubt one or two could be on their way too unless we can agree contracts.' Mike was right on one part of what he had said.

The club, for whatever reason, had been unable to agree a new contract with our Welsh international midfielder David Phillips, who had subsequently left the club for Nottingham Forest later in the summer. Comments were later made about the club selling him in order to raise enough money to pay for the under-soil heating being installed at Carrow Road. Which was all a bit silly. Losing Dave was a big blow for us as a team and squad overall, he'd played in all of our league games the previous season as well as contributing nine goals. More importantly, however, was that the club didn't seem that keen to keep him. Dave's decision to join and play for a club that had just been relegated ahead of playing for one that had qualified for Europe seemed an odd one. There must have been some sort of 'fall out' between player and manager. Then there were the 'two to three new players' that Mike had wanted to bring in. Yes, he did bring in two new faces, Spencer Prior and goalkeeper Scott Howie. Good lads and good players, their introduction putting pressure on all the other players competing for a first team spot, a healthy state for any club to be in.

If the club was to push on, and was really serious about doing so, then we should have sought to bring in some real quality, players who could look to slot straight into the first team and make a difference. But it didn't happen. We'd signed Efan Ekoku from Bournemouth that March, but, as good a player as he was, he was twenty-five and had yet to play a game in the Premier League. He went on to show us that he was a brilliant striker, the fastest player I've ever seen and a brilliant character, deadpan funny. I was surprised we hadn't been in for more of the players who had excelled during that 1992/93 season, players who might have fancied stepping it up a bit, career-wise, even if the move might have been seen as a step down for them, in terms of the size of club we were.

We had a great manager, a young and ambitious squad, we were on the up and we were playing in Europe. We'd lost David Phillips to Nottingham Forest, but shouldn't it have been the other way around, shouldn't we have been looking to sign some top players? There are two reasons why I think such players didn't come to Carrow Road. Firstly, the club was struggling to find enough money. And secondly, Mike was only ever going to bring in players who would be better than those in the existing squad. If that player was identified as available, did he want to join Norwich and could we pay him what he would be asking for. This was a lot to consider when bringing new players to a club where Mike had to do things on a shoestring budget.

Yet, rather than us being ambitious and attractive enough a proposition to lure away the top players from clubs that had been relegated, we were selling our own best players to one of those clubs that had gone down. With all due respect to Scott and Spencer, the club did allow Mike to go out and sign some new players, but when he did, they joined us from Clyde and Southend United. The year before, Mike had ended up having a battle of wills with the chairman because the latter didn't want him to sign Gary Megson, even though Meggy came on a free and had a great couple of years with us. Mike must have found it so frustrating. He was on the brink of achieving something really special with us, he believed he could, as did I and all the other players. I'm sure that, even by the time that we played Vitesse, it was already nagging at the back of his mind that he wanted to add to the squad if we were to seriously progress, despite the good job the lads had done up to then.

A further sign of how little the make-up of the side had changed came when Mike named his team to play Vitesse in that first-round game. It had been a year since our memorable win at Arsenal, yet here we were with a team that featured ten of the players who had also lined up at Highbury over a year earlier, the one exception being Efan coming in for David Phillips. As the squad had done it once, they thought they could do it again. But football is a game that demands even the greatest of sides to be constantly updating and improving. Look how that fantastic Liverpool team of the late '70s and early '80s kept reinventing itself, winning just about every trophy there was to win, yet, despite that, players leaving with new ones coming in. We, on the other hand, seemed to be standing still. As a player, you can't let these matters affect you, you just get on with your game. We'd been together for a few years and built up a team spirit and consistency that was a benefit to everyone, but that lack of money or interest in adding to the squad would come back to haunt us.

The first half of the game against Vitesse was a revelation to just about all of us; remember, most of the lads in the squad had never played top-class European opposition before, and certainly not in a competitive match. The team had obviously come with the well-established plan of getting a 0-0 draw to take back to their own patch, and by half-time, that's what the score was. To be fair, we hadn't troubled them that much. They were also doing that decidedly un-English thing of playing with a sweeper system, which we were struggling to work out quite how to play against. There would have been a few raised voices in the dressing room at half-time, but Mike was calmness personified, spelling out to us what we had to do with clear, simple instructions.

'Don't watch them, get into them.' Simple eh? But it was like a revelation. We had been standing around admiring them a little bit, like you do, I guess, when something is a little new and different to you. We'd showed them too much respect, had almost stood off them and admired the way they kept the ball in that slow European way. We needed to change tack and take the game to them. And they couldn't deal with it. Efan put us 1-0 up with a brilliant shot from an angle, I made it 2-0 from a Chippy cut-back in the box, before John Polston made it safe with about 20 minutes to go. Mike had been right, 'getting into them' had been just what the game needed.

What a feeling, my first European game and goal, a great result that sent out the message that we were a decent team. Vitesse would have needed to have played the game of their lives to get anything from the second leg, and in reality, they probably already knew their chance had gone. I remember the magnificent Norwich supporters that night, crammed into a tiny away section, shoulder to shoulder, all singing their hearts out for us.

Needless to say, Vitesse got right into us from kick-off, the referee not helping by giving them a few dubious advantages and handing out a few ridiculous yellow cards. And, the longer the game went on without them scoring, the more physical they became. Late on, for example, Foxy was down on the ground and got deliberately stood on by one of their players. I, being me, quickly lost it and grabbed the lad by his neck, causing a bit of a skirmish. We managed to hold on to 0-0 draw, a brilliant and professional job, especially for a club that was new to this level of football.

When we were drawn against Bayern Munich in the next round, the immediate attitude from the lads was 'Yes! Bring it on.' Massive excitement followed, we were going to play one of the best teams in Europe and the favourites to win the UEFA Cup. Wow! This was dreamland stuff for us. The gaffer and the coaching staff soon calmed us all down, however, and started to map out a game plan with one thought in mind – how to beat them. It was going to be a great trip, playing in one of the then most spectacular stadiums in Europe and against one of the Continent's best teams, in fact, one of its best ever. Admittedly, they weren't at their absolute best. They'd have been playing in the European Cup if they were. They were having a good season and were right on track to win their first Bundesliga title since 1990, which they went on to do. And their squad wasn't too bad either, a quick look at some of the players whom we'd be up against was quite an eye opener – Jorginho, Christian Ziege, Jan Wouters, Mehmet Scholl and, of course, the captain and leading noise in German football at the time, Lothar Matthaus. But the bigger they are...

Mike had warned us not to let the game distract us from our Premier League progress and we didn't, winning 2-1 at Chelsea a couple of days before we were due to fly out to Germany. That meant we were still unbeaten away in the league that season. In fact, of the six away games we'd played, we'd won four and drawn two, scoring nineteen goals in the process. The win at Stamford Bridge lifted us up to second place in the Premier League, a great boost to our preparations and confidence. We'd shown, we'd proved that the great season we'd just enjoyed hadn't been a fluke or a one-off and that we were, again, genuine title contenders. Now we had to prove our win against Vitesse hadn't been a fluke either.

There are two things about that game that I'll never forget, and no, neither are my goal. Well, all right, make it three things including the goal. The first was the night before the match when we got the chance, as you do, to do some training in the ground where the match is going to be played, get the feel of the turf and the look and lay out of the place, that sort of thing. It wasn't meant to be a serious or heavy session at all, just a light one, a few stretches, some jogging, a little ball work. Nothing too strenuous, for the simple fact you don't want to run the risk of losing someone to injury so close to the game, especially one of this magnitude.

So you'd think we'd have been taking it easy. Dream on. We were training in one of the greatest stadiums in the world, everything about it is immaculate, top class, the best of anything and everything available. So we were going to enjoy it, and you know what, the management could not get us off that pitch. We just wanted to stay out there, we'd have trained until midnight if we could. John Deehan was doing his nut shouting at us, literally coming out onto the pitch and trying to drag us off. 'Come on, get off, go to bed, get some rest.' All that sort of thing. Which we did, eventually. And very reluctantly.

Then there's the night of the game itself. We've arrived and are settling ourselves down, we've had a walk around the pitch, grabbed a programme to look through and are getting ourselves focused for what's to come, chatting on the running track or just having a little self-time, taking it all in or maybe looking for friends and family in the crowd. The calm before the storm thing.

As we were all doing that, Chris Sutton dashed back into the away team changing room to go to the loo, quite a regular pre-match ritual for some players, Sutty would have been no different. Anyway, while we were all outside preparing, Jock Robinson, the club's kit man, had been hard at work in the dressing room laying everything out. And it would, as always with Jock, have been immaculate. In fact, it was fantastic, it was one of the biggest nights in the club's history and Jock had done a job to fit the occasion. The place was beyond pristine. All of our kits were laid out in perfect little piles where we changed, a towel on top of our slips, socks, shorts, T-shirts and the match shirts. Then there were all the little things, the finer details like strapping for the players that wanted them, bits of tape for various reasons (I had two pieces that I used to cover up my rings). Jock's attention to detail was almost military in its precision, that dressing room looked absolutely immaculate. Anyway, Sutty had just come out of the loo and wanted a towel to dry his hands on so just grabbed the nearest one he could see. He pulled that off the pile and the whole lot fell to the floor, typical Sutty. He walked on, using the towel and tossing it down somewhere.

Just as he did this, I walked back into the dressing room, I was one of the first back in and just in time to see Jock take notice of what Sutty had done with his nice clean room. He went absolutely ballistic, ripping into Sutty, giving him verbal abuse in his deep Scottish accent. A language that is, shall we say, industrial. The accusations and insults being aimed at Sutty were severe, Jock's verbally machine gunning him, battering Sutty with every expletive and every insult he could think of, as well as managing to invent a few new ones. And I was stood there watching it.

After about ten minutes, Jock ceased his tirade and just stood there, glowering at Sutty, waiting for a reaction, an explanation, an apology. He had spent hours sorting out that dressing room, hours of effort, hard work and preparation and this is what happened. His cheeks were red raw with rage and no wonder. Sutty's stood there taking it all in. Then he broke into a big grin and just said 'Jock, settle down son' before walking off. That was a bit out of order really, he should have showed Jock a bit of respect.

That tipped Jock over the edge. He flew for Sutty, grabbing him and nearly dragging him down to the spotless floor of that once immaculate dressing room. The screams and shouts from Jock were loud as Sutty held him back, laughing. But this was now a serious fight, it was amazing. We were about to play the biggest game in the club's history and our kit man was trying to throttle our player in a classic bar type brawl on the floor. In the end, a few boys came into the changing room to separate them, quite literally dragging a still protesting Jock away so Mike could give his team talk, with Sutty sat there in a ripped shirt and with his hair all over the place.

Mike didn't need to say very much. We knew what needed to be done. We were prepared, ready and confident. We hadn't spent much time worrying about what they might do to us, our focus was on what we could do to them. Yes, Mike hadn't been able to significantly add to the squad as I have already outlined. The players we still had were good ones, playing at their peak, both in terms of ability and confidence. We had a small squad. But we worked well together, fought for each other (or with Jock!) and believed in one another. Underdogs? If you want. We didn't think so.

The tie itself, and the trip out to Germany, had generated a lot of media attention. It was great to get this but, at the same time, we knew that the neutrals thought we had little to no chance of winning the game. But that didn't matter to us, we were feeling confident and very positive about it. The club looked after us, making sure that the hotel we stayed at in Munich was class, and as usual, I was rooming with my good mate Rob Newman, someone who I roomed with for a few seasons and who was always a top man. I'm so pleased that many of my best times, in and out of the game, were shared with Rob. He was always a tower of strength for me, and I couldn't help but thrive on his confidence and cheerfulness. He was like a brother to me and I was delighted that we were side by side again for the Munich trip and the game to come.

And it wasn't a 'normal' game. It was the biggest game in Norwich City's history for a start. The whole club had travelled out to Munich and as many fans as possible, thousands in fact, got there. We players were relaxed throughout, focused on really enjoying the experience. That is, until we arrived at the stadium and were getting changed for the match itself. That's when the enormity of the occasion really sank in. I found myself getting increasingly nervous and sweating for no reason, focusing on some nice deep breaths to calm myself down, chatting and joining in with the normal pre-match banter as it started to build up. It might have looked the same, but it didn't feel it, there was an intensity in the air, players looked more focused, more determined and more confident, a real belief in their eyes. As the minutes ticked by and the music blared out, Mike gave us a 'Don't give them any respect' speech before sending us out to the sound of a loud changing-room bell.

Out we walked, clapping our hands and geeing ourselves up for that walk onto the pitch, quite a long one as it happens. What a sight that greeted us. This was it, matchday at the Munich Olympic Stadium. The floodlights were on, the pitch was perfect, and the freshly painted white lines stood out bright and loud. The Norwich fans packed into the stand to our left were in good voice, in what was an amazing atmosphere, even if the stadium wasn't full, that didn't matter. And this was it, this was one of my dreams coming true. I'm lining up against the great Bayern Munich, playing against Germany's captain, Lothar Matthaus, and in one of the world's greatest stadiums. I remember stopping at one point and staring up at one of the giant scoreboards positioned high above one of the goals, displaying, in huge letters, 'Bayern 0 Norwich City 0'. This started off a tingling sensation that ran down my spine for a full five minutes until the ref blew his whistle to start the game. I was pumped up, full of excitement and adrenaline, just loving it, absolutely loving it.

When the game started, we closed down, gave chase to and got tight to the red-shirted Bayern players as soon as possible, stopping them playing, not giving them any time or space. Get at them and get into them. That was the plan, that, and stay tight as a unit, don't get isolated, close down in twos and threes and get back behind the ball quickly with the wingers tucked in and the strikers able to drop off. And we did all that, we started well and we were solid. But I wanted a touch of the ball, I needed that touch to get into the game. Just a header, a tackle or a simple pass to another yellow shirt. Once I'd done that, I would feel I was in the game and, sure enough, it came and all was well, I was part of the match and up to speed with the pace of it all.

As for my goal, well, it was right place and right time. Mike was always telling me to get forward to support our attacking play, to make that part of my game. It paid off that season, I ended it with nine goals, the most well known of which came in the 13th minute of this game. It was all down to my mate and room partner, Rob Newman, who got forward down the left and chipped a ball into the box, aiming for Mark Robins. That pass was met, awkwardly, by Matthaus, who was probably focusing on Robbo; lurking in between him and another one of their defenders. His defensive header came out to where I'd been making my supporting run from, dropping down nicely so I could meet it in my stride, where I made the spontaneous decision to volley it first time. I had no time to bring the ball down, I just had to hit it. Nine times out of ten, that shot would have flown over the bar and into the stand, but, on this special night, I got lucky. I got my body shape and balance right and focused on making a clean strike. Timing was everything, as it's so important to hit the target, to at least give the 'keeper a save to make. I caught it very sweetly, perfectly almost, not so much with power but using the pace of the ball coming at me to steer it back at their goal. It was a good connection and I knew, as soon as I hit it, that it was going in. Aumann, their goalkeeper, didn't even move, which made it look so much better.

Wow, what a moment. I headed off in celebration. It's a big place and a big pitch, Foxy caught up with me first, grabbing me around the waist and nearly sending me flying. Luckily, I kept on my feet as Chippy and Sutty swept into share that moment with me. I could hear the Norwich fans going mad with celebration as the lads now all swarmed around me, all shouting, 'Gossy! Gossy! Brilliant son, brilliant!' It was such a euphoric moment for me, I was almost in a frenzy, injected with more adrenaline that I even needed, as it was already spilling out over the top of the glass. I also realised that our taking the lead would make us all the more resilient and difficult for Bayern to break down. I also thought, with a little smile on my face, just how good that must have looked on the TV back home.

But of course, you can't live off that, you can't walk on air for the rest of the game day dreaming about what you've just done. You've got to get the focus back, bang, immediately, no messing around. Before you know it, in this or any other game, you're back in position for the kick-off, concentrating on the job in hand. I've scored, great. But now, move on, we've a game to win and ten lads out here with me who won't appreciate it if I switch off and Bayern get back in the game. But here's the thing. We've gone 1-0 up against them in their own backyard. No British club has ever beaten them at the Olympic Stadium. I expected them to wake up, to raise their game and to really get at us now with their pace and power, that we'd now be on the receiving end of a real backlash.

We awaited the onslaught but it never came. They didn't up the tempo, didn't push forward or try to get in behind us. It was almost as if the problems we initially had against Vitesse were being repeated here, only they were having them with us. They kept possession well but played lots of square balls across the pitch and never really put us under any pressure. And that was fine. We were 1-0 up, we didn't need to chase the game, the pressure was on them. But then, just as we thought things couldn't possibly get any better, we scored again to go two up. Chippy's cross into their penalty area was missed by every player apart from Mark Bowen, who was not picked up as he made a far-post run. His accurate header was perfect and nestled perfectly into the far corner of the Bayern net, Aumann beaten for a second time. By now, their fans were in a state of shock. We were in a strong position and with half-time approaching, we looked to keep it tight and compact until the break.

But they're a good team. They won a corner, one that saw Nerlinger rise above everyone else to head the ball past Gunny and into our goal. Bollocks! It's a blow but not a terminal one, half-time is now here and we can used that time to recover, take some fluids in and listen to the gaffer.

And that changing room at half-time was buzzing, despite their late goal. And by that I mean some serious high fives and slaps on backs. But, as Mike Walker reminded us, we were only halfway there. So we settled down, regained our composure and listened to Mike and John Deehan as they reminded us all to stay close together, leaving no gaps, to keep behind the ball and stay hard to beat, counter-attacking when we could and always looking to retain possession. We knew that maximum concentration and work rate would help see us out the game as winners and we ran out for the second half feeling reenergised and inspired by each other's presence on the pitch. That second period went on to pretty much follow the pattern of the first.

They kept the ball well but we closed them down too. They did have some chances, admittedly, but none of them really frightened us, and we pretty much had things under control for the entire half. Not that I didn't want the game to end! I must have shouted to the ref 'How long to go?' about ten times. His answer to my first enquiry almost killed me off for good when he replied, '15 minutes.' Oh no, ages yet! Come on Gossy, dig in and get this result. I did just that, risking the occasional glance at that electronic scoreboard which was counting down the minutes. Nearly there now, so close, so close...

Then they got a corner. A set piece where they were the most dangerous. The cross comes in and I can see Valencia, their striker, in space on the 6-yard line, he's got a free header. Oh shit, he's going to score, he's only got Gunny to beat. In a flash, Valencia makes contact, his header is good and its goal bound, but Gunny spreads his body and makes one of the most important saves of his life. We scramble the ball away and those that are close to Gunny jump on him: 'Gunny, what a save, different class mate'. And it was.

Minutes later, the final whistle went. We had done it and both players and fans went wild as the Bayern players, heads down, trudged off their pitch and vanished into the night. We, in comparison, maintained that seriously high level of concentration, and why not? The press joined us, as did the TV crews, and the pitch-side madness continued for a good half hour before continuing in the changing rooms where the Gaffer gave an incredible speech, all about how we should be proud of what we have achieved but, at the same time, to remember that we have to stay focused as there was still a second leg to be played in just a fortnight's time. Then the music was back on, full blast, and as we slowly changed and make our way out and back onto the coach, we had a little time with the waiting Norwich fans. It was high fives and hugs all around with complete strangers. We were all family that night.

Back at the hotel, we all gathered around the bar and started sipping a few beers as well as some champagne. The overall feeling now, however, was one of tiredness. We'd all put so much effort into that game and it was catching up with us, we were knackered! I remember taking time out to sit near a piano where the player was just playing some soft stuff, just chilling and taking it all in. If I'm honest with you, I was even close to tears at one point. I looked around at all my mates, including Rob, who was smiling away as usual, who'd had a great game, and I sat there and thought that it can't get any better than this.

We had a special team with a special team spirit, a good group of lads who also just happened to be bloody good footballers, a team that had just beaten Germany's best, along with, the icing on my cake, a goal from me. It felt so special. But it wasn't just about me or Taff. The whole club beat Bayern that night – every player, Mike Walker, John Deehan, our physio Tim Sheppard, Jock the kit man, and the fans. Thinking of what we'd achieved together, and, aided by both the alcohol and the fatigue, the emotion finally caught up with me. There were no obvious tears running down my cheeks, but there were some watery eyes that told their own story. My time had come.

How powerful is sport? I find it hard to explain all the sensations and feelings I had at that time. The game, the goal, those few hours afterwards of wild celebration and quiet reflection. The game and the goal will stay with me forever. As will Taff's goal and Gunny's great save right at the end, plus, of course, all of the lads who were there and who played their hearts out. I wanted that night to last forever and would do anything to relive it again, alongside that same group of lads who I would have willingly died for at that time.

We flew home the next morning to be greeted by Norwich fans at the city's airport. We then had to contend with all the national press being there, many of whom wanted to talk to me or take my photo. I thought that was a bit over the top and that everyone should be receiving the same amount of attention, after all, it had been a team effort – but then someone shoved a copy of that morning's paper under my nose and, for the first time, I saw that photo of me in midair, in the process of scoring that goal, and I have to say, I stared at it for ages. What a great photo! But then, everything that followed took me by surprise. We were big news, dominating the back pages of every local and national newspaper, as we got all the credit that we finally deserved for what we had achieved and for what we had become. Then, for the next two weeks, my phone never stopped ringing, as I got constant requests and invitations to chat through the game and 'that' goal. At one point, it even felt as if I was getting more media attention and newspaper space than either Mark Hughes or Ian Rush. It was crazy. Even fans from clubs all across the country were taking time out to write to me and say congratulations. It was amazing stuff and I loved it. I had to make the most of it because we had a return game to play against them at Carrow Road, and that would be an opportunity for someone else to score and be the hero, a chance for them to bask in the sunlight rather than me.

Boy, was I in for a big surprise. After that first game, Bayern Munich began to have a pop at us. Matthaus was the worse culprit, he started mouthing off about how Norwich was a nothing, little city where the people just ate mustard. Not a good idea son, it's that sort of thing that does a manager's team talk for him, he should have known that. But, like it or not, the pressure was on us now more than ever. We'd won that first leg and now had to show that the result wasn't a fluke, something which Matthaus was strongly alluding to prior to the second leg. As always, our preparation was excellent, and we didn't go into the game feeling overconfident or that we had won the tie already, far from it. Mike's last words in the changing rooms before we ran out for the second leg were particularly important: 'Just make sure you don't concede an early goal.'

So what did we do? We conceded an early goal courtesy of Valencia, who bundled the ball in from close range after less than 5 minutes. Oh no, the last thing we wanted. I wouldn't have liked to see the gaffer's face after that. The very last and most important thing he told us to remember and we let it slip. But this wasn't a time for panic or self doubt, even though they've got the momentum. Just as we did in the first leg, we expected them to really come at us. Except they didn't. In fact, if anything, they seemed to go back to how they'd been in the first leg, lots of square balls again. We started to get back into it, to take the game back to them. And it paid off. Late in the second half, Foxy sprinted down the left wing, checked back onto his right foot and crossed into the box, the ball heading towards Sutty just as I was making a run into the box myself. I carried on, reading the headed-on flick from Sutty that landed right in my path, leaving me time to adjust my body shape and side foot the ball into the goal from 6 yards out.

I've never heard a crowd make as much noise as they did after that goal. I ran off, right arm in the air, screaming and screaming in joy. Because I knew, we knew, that Bayern wouldn't score again because we were defensively too strong for them. Fantastic stuff. The noise in the ground was unbelievable. I just soaked it all in as I went off on that happy sprint, finding, astonishingly, as I went to celebrate with some of our fans, my mum, beaming all over her face and looking to give me a hug! I couldn't believe it. I hadn't even known she was there. It was pure chance that took my run to her. An amazing moment for me, and, of course, made all the more special as I was able to share it with her briefly. She, who had, along with my dad, given so much to help me follow my career and chase my dreams. Fantastic.

The final whistle blew soon afterwards and we'd won the tie 3-2 on aggregate. What a beautiful moment to savour that was. Naturally, the fans went nuts. They have always been special to me and so supportive of the club – and that night, they'd played a big, big part in our famous victory. I got Matthaus's shirt at the end, which was a result for me, and I had it signed and framed. He took my shirt off me but I'm told he threw it onto the floor some seconds later. Maybe he didn't want an '11 Goss' shirt hanging up with his World Cup winners' medal and Ballon d'Or award?

Suffice to say, my life went just a little bit crazy after that game. The tabloids were linking me with a big money move. Chelsea were supposed to be preparing a bid of £400,000 for me. Then there was talk of Portuguese giants, Benfica, being interested. That would have been one to think about had there been anything to it. But it was all paper talk. Besides, I wasn't exactly desperate to get away. I still thought I could achieve things with Norwich, and that included winning trophies. We showed how serious and professional we were in our next Premier League game, after the Bayern tie, by going to Sheffield United and winning 2-1. I got the opener with a header (a rarity for me) from a Foxy cross. So it was into the next round of the UEFA Cup and still in second place in the Premier League. There was no reason to think, therefore, that even though Mike still hadn't been given the money to strengthen the squad, that we couldn't keep the momentum going.

After the Sheffield United match, we went on a disappointing little run of just two points from a possible nine. We certainly should have beaten Manchester City at home; that ended 1-1, with a sucker-punch equaliser from them only a minute or so after we'd gone ahead. The sort of thing that causes raised voices in a dressing room at the end. By then we'd heard that Inter Milan were the club we'd drawn in the next round of the UEFA Cup. I think it came through as we were heading off to Sheffield for the league game there, cruising up the M1 when the news came through on the radio. Pandemonium? Just a little. I'm surprised the resultant cheer and excitement didn't result in Barry having to pull the coach over and join in with us.

Maybe we all still had the San Siro on our minds a week after that Manchester City game. We travelled up to Oldham, who were struggling, and lost 2-1, our first away defeat of the season. Hardly the best preparation for another trip to that part of the country, a week later, at Manchester United. Our Premier League record against them was played three and lost three and we desperately wanted to get something that showed we were still, as the saying goes, contenders. And we did. It was an excellent performance that saw us get a 2-2 draw, one of our goals being that hitherto unknown thing, a penalty at Old Trafford. Wins over Leeds and Tottenham followed, and, after the game at White Hart Lane, we'd retained our position of sixth in the Premier League and were looking forward to pushing onwards and upwards in the new year.

By then, we were out of the UEFA Cup. Milan had come to Norwich and played a typically disciplined, cautious game against us. I guess we should have been honoured to have been held in such high regard by them. We'd certainly been positive throughout the first half without really creating any serious chances, and near the end, I rattled the crossbar down at the River End. What if that had gone in? In hindsight, I suppose 0-0 would have been a good result. You only need to score once at their place and then they've got to get two, but we only knew one way to play and we were going for it until the bitter end. And it was the bitter end. Reuben Sosa got free on goal, with Rob Newman's challenge resulting in the referee awarding them a penalty. Denis Bergkamp duly stepped up and stuck it away. So now they had an away goal and we were going to be up against it at the San Siro.

We certainly had our chances and played well, despite missing the three Ians (Culverhouse, Butterworth and Crook), as well as John Polston. All of them key players. I really think things would have been very different if they had played. They had a lot of possession, but Gunny had a good game, keeping them at bay. In the end, it all came to nothing, as Bergkamp showed some class at the end and stuck it away from their left-hand side. Game over, run over, dream over. I was devastated. I honestly believed we were going to win the UEFA Cup that season. I truly thought we were capable of beating Milan and going all the way, with this defeat, although hard to take, being a good example of what we could achieve and what we felt we could have gone on to do. We had quality players throughout the squad and I could see us competing at this level every season. We'd become, for a few seasons in that wonderful era, a group of lads that started out with a determination to be the best team of our time. By the end of that European campaign, we'd had dreams of being one of the best teams of all time. I'm so proud to have been part of it all.

Sadly, my thoughts turned out to be very wrong, as Mike Walker, now more than ever, became a very wanted man. He was there, as large as life and twice as suntanned (the gaffer liked to catch the rays, whether on a beach or a sunbed) at the Tottenham game, chuffed to bits with our performance and result, one which was up there with our best performances of that season in the league. Yet, as we headed back to Norwich and started to prepare for what would have been our second game in three days in a home clash against Aston Villa, little rumours and talk started to fly about the place. Rumours that suggested the gaffer and Mr Chase, the chairman, were slightly at odds over a few things and that their relationship was not exactly as good as it might have been.

I'm sure that following our exit from the UEFA Cup, Mike would have gone to see the chairman, in good faith, and asked him about his long-term plans, both for the club and, not surprisingly, himself. Mike was probably still on the contract the club had given him when he took over. To coin a phrase made at the time, he was 'not even a household name in his own household'. Things were different now. Everyone knew who Mike Walker was, everyone wanted a bit of him. He was seen in the audience at the BBC 'Sports Personality of the Year' ceremony just before Christmas, and was always a wanted man for sound bites from the BBC, Sky and the daily papers. He'd put together a bloody good football side as well, so he knew his stock in the game was high. He would have been hoping that the club might have acknowledged that and rewarded him accordingly.

Plus, he would have wanted some assurances that he would finally be able to spend some serious money on some new players. We had been struggling to get a fit and available squad ready to play in Milan for goodness sake, with four lads out suspended, plus Mark Robins who was injured. Who was left? Lads like Darren Eadie, who was then just nineteen, and David Smith, a bit older but hardly any games for us under his belt, and finally Andy Johnson, another youngster. You can't just throw them in at somewhere like the San Siro, romantic a notion as it sounds. It was not really acceptable for a club that had the same sort of aspirations as ours to find themselves in that sort of situation. And Mike would have said so, I'm sure.

The rumours didn't go away. There wasn't the online presence back then, no Facebook or Twitter, no internet forums and fan sites. Had there been, they would have gone into overload. But you heard them, nevertheless. They wouldn't go away, you heard them and you discussed them with your mates. The Villa game came and went, as did one against Southampton on New Year's Day, and a home game against Newcastle on 4 January. By then, Everton had declared that they were interested in talking to Mike and it was all everyone else wanted to talk about among the players and fans. Yet he gave away nothing, we prepared for that game as normal and played it. We should have won it too, we were 1-0 up after only a few minutes thanks to Taff (Bowen) but they hit back and won 2-1. Peter Beardsley was in sensational form that day, what a player he was.

As a professional, you should not allow yourself to get distracted by gossip and rumour. You get on with your job and whatever happens, happens. But come on, we'd all been on this ride together, the lads and Mike. How could we not be distracted by what was going on? We were at the training ground getting ready to depart for an FA Cup tie down at Wycombe. I had just left the main changing room, having originally gone in to change my boots. The rest of the lads were all up on the main pitch at Trowse. As I walked down the corridor and headed out, I noticed Mike walk out of the staffroom there, he came past me, and, as he did, I said, 'Gaffer, you alright?'

Mike's answer was the last thing I was expecting, even despite all the gossip that had been doing the rounds over the last few weeks. 'Look, Gossy. I'm pleased I've bumped into you. I'm leaving the football club. I'm going to be the new manager of Everton.' It was just the two of us stood there in the corridor. I was beyond shocked. I said the first words that came into my mind, spilling out of my mouth like a runaway train. 'Well it's brilliant for you Gaffer. But, I tell you what, you're going to leave a big, big hole here. We'll miss you bad, really bad. And this club isn't going to be the same without you.'

I can still recall the moment so clearly. Was I trying to convince him not to go? I don't know. I didn't want him to and I knew that things would change overnight. But then it was a great opportunity for him, you couldn't deny that. He gave me a half smile and made to carry on, saying, 'Come on, it's time for me to tell the rest of the lads.'

From that moment onwards, Norwich City became a different club. And mainly because most of the people there who had contributed to the success we'd had were now focused on how they might be able to continue their careers elsewhere. On leaving Norwich. Whatever Mike had created, had put together, was gone. In truth, it had probably already been fading a little, as he hadn't been able to substantially improve the squad and the cracks were showing; look at the team we had to put out in Milan for example. From a personal point of view, I was desperate for everything to be as it had been. But deep down I knew it wasn't going to happen. I also had the thought in my mind that, if Mike was off to Everton, wouldn't there be a more than reasonable chance that he'd take me with him? He trusted me, knew what I could do. Plus, I knew Barry Horne, who was then playing for them, as well as Neville Southall, both lads I'd teamed up with in Welsh squads.

It wasn't just me thinking along those lines. I think most of the lads were hoping that Mike might give them a call and ask if they wanted to join him there. And, probably, me most of all. But, for whatever reason, it didn't happen. Indeed, he didn't take anyone at all from Norwich, not even (and this surprised a few people), John Deehan, the two of them having proved what a brilliant team they were at Norwich. John, therefore, took over from Mike, initially on a caretaker basis and you could tell, straight away, he wanted to have success, but he wanted it with his team, not Mike's. So he was prepared for change.

He appointed Meggy as his assistant and got to work. We started well, that FA Cup game we'd been preparing for before Mike left was a potential slip-up if ever there was one, but we won 2-0, Sutty scoring both goals. Their manager at the time was Martin O'Neill. I remember him coming up to me after the game and telling me how well I'd played, covering every inch of grass and giving it my best as usual. 'I'd have you in any of my teams Gossy,' he said, adding, 'Well played today. Top class.' Words that I never forgot when he eventually turned up at Norwich as our new manager, but I'm coming to that.

Dixie saw players go and players come in. He signed a group of lads who soon became known around the club as the 'Northern players'. Neil Adams, Ashley Ward, Mike Milligan and Carl Bradshaw. Five-a-sides in training between the northern- and southern-born players were, as you can imagine, quite heated at times. They came in and some big players left. Chris Sutton went to Blackburn for big money, Ruel Fox to Newcastle. I'd known things would never be the same after Mike had left and they weren't and they couldn't be. It was all part of the new beginnings that were taking place in and around the club, changes that saw the chairman, Mr Chase, choose to invest heavily in the ground and a new training facility at Colney. Decisions, of course, he got a lot of criticism for at the time, but look at the Colney training complex now, it's one of the best in the country. I felt for Dixie, I really did. He'd taken over at a really difficult time but he coped with it well. He appointed Meggy as his assistant and training, to their credit, was still fun and enjoyable. We all, new lads and old, still got on well. But there was that certain something missing, the feel around the place, the charisma that Mike had which seemed to go wherever he went. I was still waiting for the phone to ring, for that familiar deep voice on the other end to say 'Gossy, I'm settled in at Goodison now, I've evaluated the squad. I'd like you to come and join us.' Would I have gone had he made that call? What do you think? I'd played the best football of my life under him, and with him as my manager, had now got myself a reputation in the game. Even lads like Mark Hughes and Ryan Giggs were complementing me at Wales get-togethers, shaking my hand and saying things like, 'You're doing really well Gossy, top class. You should come and play alongside us at Manchester United.' I think they were only half joking with that one!

But the call from Mike never came. And I eventually accepted I was going to have to keep pushing on at Norwich to make things as good as they could possibly be with the new manager and players. It wasn't a hardship. I loved the club, the city and Norfolk in general. But it would have been nice to have seen if I could have made the grade at Everton. It would have been even nicer if Mike had stayed put and been given a chance, a real chance, to see what we could have achieved together. How Mr Chase didn't see what we could have done I'll never know. Maybe he did, maybe he thought it was possible but the money involved would have been too much for Norwich to sustain in terms of investment, and that it would, just as it did for Leeds United later on, seen the desire for short term success muted by long-term financial hardship.

If I'd been in charge, I would have given Mike whatever he wanted in terms of his own contract and a transfer budget. He'd have been realistic. He wouldn't have been demanding the sort of figures that only the top clubs could afford, he might even have accepted the £5 million Blackburn paid for Sutty, which was too good a deal to turn down for most clubs, let alone Norwich. He would have wanted the bulk of it back as funds for new players.

You never know, he might even have tried to bring Duncan Ferguson to Norwich, the player who he signed for Everton from Rangers. 'Big Dunc' was a formidable player and a great centre-forward, no one messed with him. Ask him today what he thinks about Mike Walker, how he rates him as a manager, he'll say some very good things about Mike. He was clearly a player Mike had always admired. I wonder how we'd have got on with someone like him in our team, had that chance ever transpired?

Dixie kept us going until the end of the season, although it was tough at the end. Results-wise, he didn't have the best start as our manager. His first seven games all ended in draws, followed by two defeats, one of which saw us let in four at home against QPR. Come again? We were a team that had finished third in the Premier League, played in Europe, done well, been into the top two of that same league this season, and we were letting QPR put four past us at Carrow Road?

The week before that Wimbledon had done us 3-1. We were all over the place. There were now rumours going around that Sutty had been the subject of a big bid from Tottenham. He was probably thinking of where he was going to be next season. Fair play to him, he gave it his all for us, as he always did, but he must have felt distracted. Mike brought Everton to Carrow Road in March and, on an emotional night, his old team put on one last good performance for him, winning 3-0. He got some stick from the fans which was sad, considering all he'd done for the club. Plus, deep down, I'm as sure as I was then, that had he been given the slightest encouragement from Mr Chase, he would have stayed. Yet there he was in an Everton tracksuit, sat in the away team dugout and giving instructions and encouragement to lads like John Ebbrell and Ian Snodin. I was glad when that game was over. In fact, I was looking forward to the whole season coming to an end, a chance to get away from it, have a break and get ready for whatever the hell was going to lay in wait for us from the following August.

There was one final high spot for me before the end of the season. Our penultimate match at Liverpool, the last game ever to be played in front of the old standing Kop at Anfield. What an occasion! It was a bit of a party atmosphere at Anfield that afternoon, a celebration of all the great and good of Liverpool, famous faces everywhere and a little walk on tribute before kickoff; the Kop, as usual, was an ocean of red, full of noise and life.

It was one of those games where you could get swept up in the emotion of it all and maybe even get hammered as a result, but we were professional, focused and out to win. This was still Mike's side at the time, as Dixie brought in Neil Adams (a future Norwich manager) at that point, and we played as we had under him, with great passing, movement and confidence. Maybe it was an epitaph, a final great game and result from us before it all fell apart. A last hurrah? We scored after just over half an hour, a cross was knocked into their box from our right, which they only partially cleared. I was following up, and just as it had done in Munich, the ball fell just right for me to take one touch to control it before volleying past David James. Plus, oh, about seven Liverpool players who were in front of me! I'd caught it just right and it flew in, a great feeling and one that felt all the better as it had been scored in front of that famous stand and all the noisy, yet appreciative, masses that stood in it.

They applauded me at the end, chanted my name and gave both teams a great reception. I'm sure all of Liverpool, maybe even all of English football (other than the Norwich supporters, of course) were disappointed that they hadn't won, or even scored at that end on its last day. As it stands though, I'm down in history as the last ever player to score in front of the old Kop, and it's a record that I am very proud to be the holder of. How typical of us to follow up an impressive win at Anfield by drawing at home against Oldham on the last day of the season. They were fighting to avoid relegation and, as you'd expect, came from us right from the start.

A large following of their fans had come to support them on the day, so any thoughts from Carrow Road regulars that it would be a comfortable last-day win in the spring sunshine were swiftly dashed! They went a goal up fairly early on, but we hit back through Rob Ullathorne and the game ended 1-1. Oldham went down, just as they would have done if they'd won. We finished the season in twelfth place, a major disappointment really, as, at one point, we'd been in second place. Not only that, we'd been in and around the top six from September through to January. As we all knew it would, Mike's departure had hit the club very badly, putting us into a downward spiral that was soon to become a tailspin.

10

A Week in the Life

Tuesdays were tough days, we labelled them 'Terror Tuesdays'! A mixture of timed runs would be the order of the day flavoured up with hard keep-ball and one-on-one sessions. Bags of lung-busting stuff that could 'mess you up' quickly, making your legs feel like jelly, pumping your heart rate up and reducing your energy levels to zero!

So why did I put myself through all the tough training every day and push my body close to the edge of near physical breakdown, even injury? What was the end product? Was there a method to the madness? Yes, I got a massive kick out of just training. I was addicted to the adrenalin buzz and the sweat. But was there an overriding motive? Well yes, there was – my love for the game of football.

Everything I did, all that hard work, had one objective in mind – matchday. That wonderful moment when I ran onto a pitch to represent my club, to fight for my teammates and the fans. A day to be immersed in those familiar feelings of stress and anxiety, a chance to reacquaint myself with that my old mate pressure. Every time, that whole experience made me feel like a little boy on Christmas Eve, 90 minutes to be embraced and treasured, it was what I lived for. But dealing with all the pre-match stuff? That was different. My inner demons would cause me to constantly doubt myself and my capabilities. If we lost a game or I played poorly, it would confirm that post-match self doubt, and chisel away at me for all of the following week, shredding my confidence even further. Yet, if I played well and we won, those unbearable feelings would be immediately extinguished, until the next game of course!

As a player, matchdays are your opportunity to become either a hero or a villain. It's theatre. Footballers are athletes but they are also entertainers, expected to perform on their stage in front of a demanding audience who want nothing but entertainment and victory. Win at all costs. You put your reputation on the line in as harsh and exposed a working environment as there could ever be – a football stadium. There's no hiding place, you sink or swim. That stark reality is why I pushed my body so hard every single day in training. I wasn't the best player but I wanted to be the best-prepared player, the most committed. I wanted to be ready for matchdays. I wanted to stay afloat and swim, swim fast.

So, when did our countdown start for that all-important matchday? When did the Norwich City squad start its build-up for the next big game? For us, it began the moment the final whistle blew to end the previous match. Let's take a Norwich City match played away from home on Saturday, to be followed by a home game the following weekend during the Mike Walker era. This is my interpretation of what we went through from one game to the next, starting from the final whistle of the previous match.

As you trudged off the pitch knackered and exhausted, you immediately started the physical recovery process. Whatever the result. you got back into the changing rooms and started taking on board the fluids that rehydrated you as swiftly as possible. As a box-to-box midfielder, I would have run anything from 10 to 12 miles in that preceding 90 minutes, and that was without the jumping, sprinting, tackling, twisting, heading and other anaerobic match actions.

That all takes it out of you and by at the end of the game your body is completely empty of energy and fluids. Dehydration takes control and, with another game in seven days time, we would be drinking water, high-energy glucose drinks, tea, coffee, even a few beers if that's what you wanted.

We would sit there in a typical away Premier League changing room. The gaffer has started to dissect the match and is already giving us either the old 'you were great' or 'you were crap' speech. As we listen, our bodies have already started to recover, simply because we've stopped running! Any knocks or strains meanwhile, have been instantly iced up and treated by Tim Sheppard, our excellent physio. There's still an air of seriousness, an intensity among us all as the game only finished a few moments ago, so we're still very much in the mental zone with adrenalin coursing through our bodies. Emotions are still running high and anyone can erupt, shouting and screaming at any time. Because of that, you quickly learn to shut up and say nothing because you're not in control under these circumstances, so any ranting and raging would only add to the post-match tension and quite possibly make you look stupid. It was always best to recover totally before airing your thoughts, whatever they might have been.

That dressing room is usually an amazing sight. Up to twenty-five players and officials all squeezed into very cramped surroundings, all listening to whatever the gaffer has to say. Steam is pouring off the lads' bodies, steam and sweat, mud, assorted cuts and bruises. The room is, by now, in a right old state, it'll be stinking of *Deep Heat* and liniment, the stench bouncing off the walls big time. The floor is coated in socks, muddied boots and assorted bits of kit the lads have discarded already. Empty water and Lucozade bottles strewn all over the place, some tangled up with bits of tape, plaster and shin pads. It's a hot, humid and humming atmosphere that now has the steam from the freshly-run communal bath, mixing with it all to cause a thick miasma, once smelt never forgotten! And the silence is overpowering at times, it often used to amaze me how a dressing room could be such a quiet place post-match as we either waited to hear the gaffer say his piece, that or we sat there, taking in what he'd said.

I always used to look around and clock the lads who, like me, were shattered and looked like they'd barely be able to walk, let alone run. That was always brilliant to see, albeit in a sadistic way. Why? Because it showed that they'd worked hard until they'd almost dropped, they'd cheated no one. I wanted to play alongside people with that honesty and endeavour. If I didn't see that in players I would take an instant dislike to them. Players who cruised and cleverly cheated their way through a game did my head in. Big timers who would never take the blame and always pointed the finger of blame at others. Dave Stringer always said that if you needed to be carried off the pitch through exhaustion then you'd be in his team for the next match. The principle was simple, if you're having a good game, work your nuts off, and if you're having a bad game, then work your nuts off anyway. That high level of work rate was your starter for ten, the minimum criteria required by the manager to make his team. The fans expected no less.

And neither did I. After each game I played I was gone, fatigued to the extreme. Stomach cramps would kick in very quickly, something that I and many other players experienced after a match. This type of pain often occurs after vigorous exercise sessions and can trigger vomiting or cramping. Chronic stomach pain would be a sign of overtraining, exercising too intensely while not hydrating sufficiently. Hydrating and stomach pain after exercise are closely linked. When you train hard, especially in hot temperatures, you lose fluids through your sweat, including sodium that is needed to maintain chemical balance within your cells. If you lose too much water, without replacing it during exercise, you might experience stomach pain, lethargy, a dry mouth or even diarrhoea.

On top of this, my chest would be on fire due to my overworked lungs, especially if it was a freezing cold day, and for a few minutes I wouldn't be able to think straight. My body had been physically battered and it was if my mind couldn't cope with it. When I spoke I could never get my words out, or they would come out but never in the right order. I'd just have to sit still and quiet for a while and wait to get myself back together, sat there in that minging dressing room, body drained and mind numb, my muscles now starting to slowly stiffen up due to the build up of lactic acid.

Once the gaffer has finished talking, the atmosphere in the room begins to change. If we'd won the match, a loud and boisterous jolly-up would begin. The banter would start and the volume button on the CD player would be turned up to the maximum – and what a feeling that would be, every time. For me, experiencing the atmosphere of a winning changing room was exceptional. Incomparable to anything else I've ever encountered in life. The shared feeling of satisfaction and pleasure that comes from victory was enormous. If we had lost the silence would continue – and for a long time. I hated losing! With my disillusioned face on, I would quietly amble about getting showered and changed, blaming myself for everything that had gone wrong. I'd be devastated, even distraught at times. All that work for nothing. Letting your teammates and the fans down. Obviously, I knew there were worse things in life to experience and 'distraught' is a strong word to use. After all, it's only a game isn't it? Maybe. But to me, it wasn't just a game, it was something I lived and breathed, something I battered both mind and body for. I was part of a team that shared the same desire to win, so when you failed, when you lost – it hurt!

Eventually, we'd start to chit-chat among ourselves and get our trainers on, ready to get back on the pitch to go through a cool down with the sports scientist. Stretching helped massively in aiding the recovery process and it was something I did a lot of all day, that ready and easy flexibility always helping my game.

It's still a big part of my life today, and needs to be because, as the years go by, I'm seizing up a lot more than I used to. So, after that and either a hot bath or shower, it was into the dreaded ice bath. This constricts the blood vessels and flushes out the lactic acid from your muscles. It also reduces swelling and tissue breakdown. Re-warming straight after would increase blood flow and improve the healing process – or so we were told! I think the staff threw us into this just for the fun of it, having a giggle at our screwed up and pained facial expressions as we slid in.

After this was all done, it was time to change back into the club suit and get back onto the coach, ready for the trip home. But, given that constantly steamy environment of the changing room, you could never get dry after a bath or shower. As much as you tried to dry yourself, your body just stayed wet, the heat and moisture clinging onto you until you hit the outside air, you'd be getting on the coach with your clothes already damp, the sweat still dripping down your face. Horrible. Getting back onto that coach was good as well, a time to get into your normal seat and rest. We all had, believe it or not, the same seat on the coach every time. Yes, we'd all move around and chat among ourselves but, more often than not, you'd just want to chill in your own place. Plus, almost as soon as we took our seats, food was being handed out. And not just any old food but food loaded heavily with carbohydrates and proteins, all with the purpose of getting us energised again. We were expected to eat within one hour of finishing the match because the sooner you ate, the sooner the recovery.

The additional protein intake was crucial in helping to build and repair muscles that were broken down, as a result of our pushing them to their limits. Now, I'm no sports scientist but I've trained hard so regularly throughout my life that I have got to know a little bit about the dietary side of things, and certainly by that stage, I knew what I needed and when (although I was never a big eater and probably under-ate throughout my career).

Getting off the coach after some long and horrendous trip home was always a good feeling because I was just a short drive away from my own home and bed! And I found every coach trip a horrible experience, not, I hasten to add, because of the lads I was with, but because of the boredom. It was unbearable. I was never part of the back-of-the-coach card school, or interested in cards, but a lot of the lads were and those little schools could get a bit heated at times, with a few rows and disputes boiling over through the years. The lads would be good mates before the card games began, but after some severe controversy and a lot of money lost, some would leave the game as big enemies, something we all hoped would soon be sorted out.

As for the coach we travelled on, well, it was half decent with all the basic facilities, but we never had all the gadgets that today's lads have to hand. Hence the easy boredom. At least if we'd won the match, we could have a few beers and get the banter flying. But if we lost? Hell, it was worse than a morgue.

It would have been easier for me if I could have just switched off and had a sleep. But I could never do that. My 'preference' was to sit quietly in my seat and mentally beat myself up, running through all the crap things I'd done in the game. It's a form of demoralisation I wouldn't recommend to anyone, but it's what I did and I couldn't help it. If we got back in good time then a few of us might slip out for some more beers before finally heading home. It was a sort of easy togetherness, working and playing together was crucial in getting things out of our systems. The game was, even then, so serious and full of pressure. For me, having the chance to let off steam with a few drinks and a lot of laughs often did the trick. Plus, I was being a good lad and rehydrating my body, as instructed! In any case, I could never sleep after a match. The adrenalin stayed with me for a long time, I'd be all hyped up, still soaring high. I'd put my head on the pillow and lay there, wide-eyed and wide awake, going over every minute of the game. Switching off was impossible.

Eventually, Sunday would greet me. Just six days to the next game – time to start preparing! It was, in theory, a rest day, but I would spend my day of rest having a gentle jog somewhere before going through some stretching exercises in order to keep the muscle stiffness at bay. If I had any serious or niggling knocks, I'd go to meet Tim Sheppard at the Colney training centre so he could give it a working over for a few hours. However, if we'd played really badly, then we'd all be in at Colney to hear what the gaffer had to say about things. I had more Sunday's like that then I would care to remember. But, if the session was constructive, then great, no problem. If, on the other hand, it was more of a 'we'll make you pay for losing by making you run' session then that was crap and didn't go down well, it was old school punishment and a waste of our time and energy, as well as a good way for the manager to lose some of the respect he had with the players. Sunday would usually be a day off and one when you could chill out and put your feet up.

On to Monday then and the start of the working week. It would start with the gaffer holding his pitch-side meetings alongside his coaching staff, before training started with warm up and stretching exercises. These would have been followed by five-a-sides, 'keep-ball' possession work and crossing and finishing drills. I'd hit the gym in the afternoon, pumping weights for an hour or so, always feeling better prepared knowing I was physically strong. That's what the gym was for. It bettered my strength, my agility, my power. They were all important aspects of my game, crucial when you had to battle and exchange punches against menacing, hard-as-nails players like Wimbledon's Vinnie Jones and Mick Harford. Vinnie was hard, tough, intimidating and to be honest, frightening! Other players would often join me in the gym, but for entirely different reasons. They were there to get summertime 'beach body', the look that all the girls loved. These lads were more in love with themselves and the mirrors on the walls than they were the football. Footballing-fancy-Dan's who would pump up their egos and their bodies.

Tuesdays were tough days, we labelled them 'Terror Tuesdays'! A mixture of timed runs would be the order of the day flavoured up with hard keep-ball and one-on-one sessions. Bags of lung-busting stuff that could 'mess you up' quickly, making your legs feel like jelly, pumping your heart rate up and reducing your energy levels to zero! I'd still find some strength to bang out some weights after lunch mind you. Tuesday's were tough days for a reason, for Wednesday was our day off, one when we could do what we liked. Relax, recover and eat. I'd probably take it easy by going for a run somewhere.

Thursdays and Fridays were spent planning how we were going to go against the team we'd be facing on Saturday. Sometimes we'd play a full match against the youth team; the gaffer regularly stopping and starting the game to go over team shape, formation, and set pieces. We'd follow up with short, sharp five-a-sides, plus crossing and finishing drills, all topped off with shooting practice. My focus on the match started seriously at this point, but among the lads there would always be the constant banter and piss-taking. This was great and very much welcomed, after all, you (and especially me) can get too intense about the situation. After all, if you're playing against Manchester United at Carrow Road, in front of a packed house, it's only natural to get a bit anxious in the days leading up to the game, we all did. So we coped with it in our own different ways. Having a laugh at each other's expense was a great way of taking your mind off things and staying relaxed and happy. A happy, relaxed player will usually be an effective one. Having a smile on your face was one thing the staff insisted on at Norwich City during that time. And I'm no different to most players in missing all of that banter now.

On the Friday morning, the Gaffer would jot down on a sheet of paper the names that were in the squad for Saturday's game, and pin it on a board in the changing rooms. The lads would swarm round the list and, as they walked away, you would know by their facial expressions if they had been selected or not. If your name was on the sheet then you knew you would be in for a physically easy morning of training, but your maximum concentration and focus was needed to take on board the important set pieces and planned team organisation. Being excluded from the squad was always painful and made you feel isolated, ignored and forgotten about!

The flip side of that was seeing my name on the team sheet. It'd secretly have me clenching my fist and punching the air in delight – my time had come again! A chance of glory, to score great goals and make the back-page headlines. This is what I'd been working hard for. Seeing my name on that team sheet was another opportunity for me to prove to people I was a decent player, not that lad stuck in the reserves, but one essential to the first team and the club. But then, the positive emotions would mix right in with that familiar anxiety to start rushing around my body. For, in just twenty-four hours time, I'd have to put my reputation back on the line, a case of 'here we go again'.

Once official training was finished on the Friday, I might have pushed out a few light weights in the gym. There was no real need but I just felt better prepared if I did them. The remainder of the day was then my own. Food-wise, I'd indulge in a big pasta dish, with spaghetti Bolognese with loads of bread a big favourite. The week's training was now complete so it was time to overdose on the carbs! I'd also drink all day to hydrate my body ready for the match as well. Then, feet up, watch some TV, get to bed. But sleep? Not a chance. I'd lie there for ages thinking about the game ahead, the set pieces, where to stand, who to pick up, positional play, the lot. All the time trying to squeeze in thoughts of scoring great goals and making great passes and tackles. Visualising moments like these made me feel better, but not sleepy! Forty-five minutes of lying there covering every moment of the match I was about to play in was enough to send the anxious feeling racing through my body yet again. My heart would pound through the duvet and that would be that, no sleep for me, not for a few hours anyway. I'd occasionally revert to sleeping tablets but preferred not to as they were a bad habit to get into. I found the best way to deal with the insomnia was to do some breathing exercises to help calm myself down. In fact, so frequent was all this, that I got sick to death of Friday nights meaning not sleeping, wondering, as I woke up on a Saturday morning, how I'd get through the match having just had a few hours sleep.

I greeted matchday by taking the first looks at the clock. I was obsessed with knowing what the time was on matchdays, planning my whole day around certain times and the rituals that filled them. When to eat breakfast; how long to relax in front of the telly; what time to have a pre-match beans on toast; when to drink a little, and when to drink a lot to get hydrated; what time to get changed into my match suit; what time to leave. It went on and on. Those six hours or so before kickoff were vital in terms of preparation, and the crucial time I'd work backwards from was 1.30 p.m. That's the time when the whole squad would have to report to the home changing rooms at Carrow Road. If you were late getting through those doors, it would result in a big fine, or, if the gaffer was in a foul mood, you could be dropped from the team. So it was important for me that everything fell into place leading up to that time, and I'd normally want to arrive at the stadium at around 12.45 p.m.

Weather-wise I wasn't too bothered, unless it was windy as I hated playing in a strong wind. The weather would dictate what type of studs I'd have on my boots. They'd be with me all the time, always close and ready – another little superstition. By late morning, the old matchday nerves would already be upon me, but I could normally contain them and keep them at bay, although I'd sometimes be a bit sharp while talking to my parents on the phone hours before a game. I must have been very rude on some occasions but I couldn't help it. All they wanted to say to me was good luck for the game and find out where to pick up their match tickets.

I loved the drive to Carrow Road on matchday. I'd get my favourite music on and drive, slowly and calmly, towards the stadium, constantly checking my watch as well as constantly sipping water. This was the start of my matchday mental preparation, my visualisation time. Great tackles, passes and goals and all to the backdrop of some quality music – maybe some Springsteen, Bon Jovi or Boston. On some days, it'd be a bit of fifties rock and roll, or even, if the mood was right, Metallica's 'Nothing Else Matters', a song that made sense because on a matchday nothing else did matter to me, other than this team, this stadium, these fans and this match.

Everything else in my life simply didn't exist. I didn't know it then but it was, and is today, a huge part of sport psychology, a technique used by all athletes to heighten confidence, increase focus and improve performance. Visual imagery was my method of mental training. My way of switching on and getting up for it. It relaxed me and it worked, just as it does today's Premier League players as they arrive at the stadium, all wearing their oversized headphones and doing exactly the same thing.

After I'd parked my car in the usual place reserved for players and officials outside of Carrow road, I'd walk past a small gathering of Norwich fans and autograph hunters who were always lining up to greet the lads as they arrived. I would always stop and sign my name on some action pictures of myself that the fans had tore out of match programmes or football magazines, and don't think I ever refused anyone an autograph. After all, how privileged I was that someone thought so highly of me that they wanted my signature on a photograph. I could never understand it as I wasn't anyone special, just a footballer doing his job. Five minutes later, I was inside the ground and walking around the outside of the pitch, making my way to the tunnel that led into the main stand and the players' changing rooms. The stadium would be empty at this time of the day and it was always such a strange feeling – quiet and peaceful now, but within two hours transformed into a cauldron of colour and vociferous noise. I'd carry on walking, taking it all in before entering the players' tunnel, walking along a short corridor and pushing open the home changing room door on my left where I would always be met with a glorious sight. That huge, square-shaped changing room was prepared by the ever-meticulous Jock that morning, long before the arrival of all the players. Everything was immaculate, tidy and ready for use, with a full set of pristine yellow shirts hung up all around the room with the front of the shirt always facing outwards. Stacked together below each shirt was the rest of the kit for each player, a towel, slip, socks, T-shirt, shorts and warm-up top. The way that kit was laid out in the changing room and where you, as a player, changed, never altered in all my time as a professional at Norwich City and I can remember it to this day.

Starting from the far left were spaces for the manager and his assistant. Next to them hung the green shirt of the goalkeeper, usually Gunny, followed by the full-backs, centre-halves, midfield players and, finally, the wingers. The substitutes, of which there could be up to five at the time, would all sit and change on the right-hand side of the room. The rest of the space in the room was occupied by a physio's bench, a wall table containing cups for hot and cold drinks, a case of isotonic bottled drink, two more cases of water and the all-important music player. Next to this table was the tactics boards, and high in the middle of the room was an oversized wall clock.

One of the first things I would do was pour myself a cup of tea complete with a spoonful of sugar for the energy boost, before grabbing a copy of the matchday programme, casually flicking through the pages while waiting for the other lads to appear. When everyone had arrived, most of us would walk onto the pitch and test the ground to see how hard or soft it was, another moment I always looked forward to because the pitch always looked and felt so magnificent just before a game. With no divots, the surface would be beautifully flat and smooth, the white lines standing out gloriously against its freshly-mown lines. The goal nets would already be in place, pinned back. I'd look at them and would picture myself bending a shot in from 25 yards, seeing the ball hitting the top corner of that net. More visualisation, more dreaming. Sometimes I would stand there in the middle of the pitch with my NCFC club suit on, looking around the whole stadium and thinking back to all the crap and muddied up pitches I had played on, even, at times, going back to me and my brothers messing about playing headers and volleys in the rain, using our coats as goal posts. At that point, it would hit me really hard just how far I'd come. From all those local recks to this tremendous Premier League stadium. There was no better place in the whole world to be.

But no time to dally. A few minutes later, we'd be back inside the changing rooms waiting for the kick-off. I'd like to say that, because we all had a big game ahead of us, things would be dead serious in the room with everyone quiet and focused on their responsibilities, slowly mentally preparing for the match coming up. No chance! It was like training days, banter and piss-taking for fun all the way until the gaffer came in at 1.30 p.m. This was all good stuff because it was the perfect way to get relaxed and settle down. We would feel nervous and we would all handle it in our own way. Some would be quiet, some fidgety and some would be larking around, joking and having a laugh. I've seen some players be sick in the toilets because they were so nervous. Thankfully, I never got to that stage. My way of coping was to listen and laugh with the funny lads in the team. I was never the instigator or teller of jokes, but I loved hearing the funny stories and getting involved, just being together, all in the same boat, sharing the same type of anxiety relaxed me and chilled me out. It was good knowing that I wasn't on my own going through this.

At this stage, it's important to mention that we had strict rules and regulations in our changing room on matchdays, similar sorts of rules, I'm guessing, that a lot of the other football clubs in the English leagues all share to this day. So pay attention, because you never know, it might apply to you one day!

The first rule was *never* assume or take for granted that you will be starting the match. No matter what happened the day before in training, never go to your seat where you normally change and start acting like you're in the starting eleven before the gaffer has arrived. That means taking off your rings and getting some tape ready for your tie-ups, sorting out your shin pads and using the towel on the bench under your shirt. This would be a big mistake as you would instantly be labelled as 'Billy Big Time', the man who thinks he knows the team for the day, who's good enough to be in it without the manager's confirmation. Secondly, never actually start getting changed before the gaffer arrives at 1.30 p.m., that was even worse. Taking off your jacket and tie and hanging it on your peg, or taking off your shoes and putting your match socks on. This would be bang out of order and simply not the done thing. If you did this, the lads would give you a huge amount of stick, and the manager, on his arrival would verbally batter you, guaranteed.

The done thing when arriving in the changing rooms was actually to sit anywhere but your normal place. Even if you knew you were in the team because you'd started the last ten games, or because the manager had had a quiet word with you beforehand, to confirm that you were playing. Only when the manager came in and turned the music off, only after he named the starting eleven and only after he'd finished his initial team talk, did you make your way to your place and start getting changed. Got that?

The variety of pre-match speeches by different managers has always amazed me. A pre-match team talk to the squad, at 1.30 p.m., was always similar in its content, but delivered differently depending on the style of the manager. Each manager has a different voice and a different tone. Some are loud, quick and enthusiastic speakers who go on very quickly from one point to another with very few pauses. Others speak more quietly and take their time to deliver crucial messages. Others choose to say very little and keep their instructions short and precise, with strong emotion in their look and voice. I think how you look as a manager and how you deliver your speech is a big part of winning the respect of the players. However, more importantly than this, and even more crucial to winning over the changing room, was *what* you said. Managers are obviously in charge. They are the ones that make the rules, develop the strategy and style of play. They have the responsibility of selecting eleven players to win a match, are credited for the team winning and criticised for a team losing.

The players have to believe in, buy into, and accept the manager's philosophy, and he will only be accepted and respected by the players if he knows what he's talking about, speaks football sense and is knowledgeable of the game. All this becomes apparent during team talks. A manager's speech has to be 'spot on' and delivered with confidence and self-belief. He has to be convincing, positive and speak with an air of authority and experience. A football manager's job is not an easy one, irrespective of personal profile and lucrative salary; a tough business to be involved with and carries with it a strenuous and daunting set of challenges and responsibility. Get it all right and the team will work hard for you and win games, resulting in you keeping your job, but get it all wrong and team lose with lacklustre performances, then the P45 will be waiting for you just round the corner. So, the manager, at 1.30 p.m. on a matchday, in the home changing room, has one main objective and that is to motivate and inspire a squad of players to go and win a game of football. This, I can assure you, is not an easy task.

This motivational speech, an hour and half before kick-off, in front of all the players and coaching staff, physiotherapist, kit man and other members of staff, would invariably focus on praise and encouragement. I know it sounds simple, but to inspire someone you need to tell them how good they are. First of all, Mike would name his starting side and substitutes. He'd then go around the room, one by one, arbitrarily directing his quotes at all of the first starting eleven players, saying things like, 'Sutty (Chris Sutton), you were brilliant last week. You held it up well, brought players into the game and were in the box for every cross. Today, let the centre-half know he's in a game, make it hard for him, drop off and show for it more, when you get it turn and run at them. You're a great player son, so go on, get me a goal today.'

He would then move onto another player and give more praise. 'Gunny (Bryan Gunn) top man last week and you made some great saves, your distribution was good, you commanded the 18-yard box and dictated you back four. You were different class so same again today big-man!' All around the room he went, lifting the spirit and mood of all of the lads, giving them confidence by reminding them what good players they were, such a simple technique but so effective. That done, he'd move into tactical stuff like team shape, high-tempo play, counter-attacking, keeping a high line of defence. Organisation is key to any team's success and he would go into this in detail, speaking about the opposition and their strengths and weaknesses, who their 'danger' players were, who to mark close, who makes what runs, how they play. Even so, he'd still focus on us and how good we were, let the opposition worry about us, not the other way around. If we'd won the previous game, he'd conclude by saying something like 'you were all brilliant last week lads, so just go out and repeat that performance. Today, give me the same work rate and the same attitude. Don't let the fans down, go out and win this game.'

Immediately after, the first-team coach would then go through all set pieces on the tactics board, including where each player stands on corners, free kicks and throw-ins. This was crucial to us all. We would have worked on it during the last two days, but it was important to be reminded. Before the match started, you had to know where you needed to be in relation to where the ball is in any given situation. Also, knowing where you need to position yourself on defensive and offensive set pieces is vital. Where you stand and who you mark. Then there's no mix-up or confusion. Your responsibility is clear and you are expected to be aware of it and carry it out. There are no excuses. Cock something up and you will get a battering from all of the lads, and that's before the gaffer will have started on you, and he's a big bloke who could give you a hefty clomp if he wanted to!

That would be the first set of speeches over with. We'd now start getting changed with the music on. Many of us would go through stretching exercises while slowly slipping into our shorts, socks and warm-up tops. I never put my match top on until we ran out to start the match. The feeling in the room would be good and the air would be full of excitement with the banter still flying around. The time now would be around 1.50 p.m. and our team warm up on the pitch would start at 2.25 p.m. In between this time, players would be doing their own thing. Whatever you needed to do to get you ready and up for the game, you did it. Some lads, the comics in the team, would be joking about anything and everything. Telling all sorts of stories to get a reaction from the boys changing around them. Others would be just sat, quietly getting ready in their own space and their own time. But most of us would be chatting about various mundane topics while we stretched, that's if we could hear each other over the loud music blasting out. The music was good though. The beat and bass of whatever song really got us all moving in our own way and relaxed us too, taking our minds off the match for a short while. By 2.25 p.m. we were all out and ready to start our team warm up, with the ground starting to fill up nicely. By 2.45 p.m. we'd be back in the changing rooms getting out of our warm-up tops and into the match shirts. Final preparations were very much on the go at this time. Match boots on, shin pads on and tied up, rings taped up, shirts tucked in and we were ready to go. The loud music would then be turned off and the gaffer would give his final 'be positive, be confident, stick together' speech, followed by another, 'Go out and win this game' shout.

The bell would then ring very loudly, indicating the referee was ready to lead the teams out onto the pitch. That would be the signal for all the boys to start instantly revving other up, shaking hands wishing each other a great game, the mood, by now, suddenly very serious and intense. Players' facial expressions would change from a laughing, relaxed look to one of deep focus.

This was a crucial time for us all, preparing mentally for what was about to happen. Seb Coe came up with a fantastic quote in his autobiography. He said, 'It's not in the four years of training and preparation that the race is won or lost, but in the moments leading up to the sound of the gun'.[1] In other words, as he lined up across the track, did he actually believe he was ready enough, fit enough and good enough to win the race? Did he believe in himself? Any self-doubt at this time would be disastrous for him. You can be the fittest athlete and best runner but if you're not right in your mind, if you can't deal with the big occasion and self-doubt creeps in, then you could lose the race before it has begun. In my case, the sound of that bell in the changing rooms at Carrow Road was my pivotal time. Was I ready? Did I feel good and confident? Was I positive enough in my approach to this game? Had I worked hard enough this last week and was I fit enough for today? All these questions and doubts would be in my head on the sound of that bell.

Playing at the highest level, against the very best players, was always my objective, and to get to that position I had to test myself and deal with moments outside my comfort zone. That last five minutes before running out and playing was certainly one of those moments. A big mental test of self-belief. To think positive thoughts, and remain supremely confident. As we all marched out of the changing rooms, the gaffer would pat each of the starting eleven on the back and give us all a loud 'Come on!', while the very last thing he would say to me was 'Look forward, pass forward', an indication of how he wanted me to play. We'd then wait in one straight line in the corridor leading to the tunnel with the opposition lined up right next to us. This was the big moment to control yourself because you could now see the players you would be playing against. They'd be so close, you could smell them! This sight could intimidate some and scare many others. And, on top of all that, you could hear the stadium music and the crowd waiting in anticipation of the arrival of their team, ready to roar you onto the pitch! What a moment it was as the referee gestured to us all before leading us onto the pitch. The run out of the tunnel and onto that pitch was exhilarating, even magical, with the noise hitting you first. It was loud, momentous and scary but so vital to the team, that and the sight of the fans all packed in to see you play and perform, the Yellow and Green Army jam-packed into Carrow Road.

This sight was, to me, both beautiful and motivating. The buzz and lift it gave me was a mighty one, overwhelming sometimes but always truly captivating. I was back on the pitch, with my teammates, my best mates, revved up and ready to do battle. The best stadium, the best players and the very best league in the world. Another moment to savour forever. This was what I worked so hard for. This was what I wanted to do all my life. Another chance to relax and simply play a game of football. And, for me, so much more than even all of that.

---

1   Sebastian Coe, Running My Life:-The Autobiography (Hodder, 2013).

11

Flying the Nest

I looked over at Rob. 'Mate, what's going on? I can't believe how things have gone from being so good to so bad in such a short time.'

Scoring the last ever goal in front of the standing Kop at Anfield means that the ground, city and the fans of that special football club will always have a place in my heart. It also, however, resonates within for another reason, one that isn't connected with professional pride at all, but was of a moment that, when it happened, made me realise that, as far as Norwich City were concerned, our time in the nation's footballing spotlight was swiftly coming to an end.

We were just over halfway through the 1994/95 season of Dixie's first full campaign in charge. Dixie's new boys, those Northern lads, were all settling into the team nicely, Jon Newsome, the club's first ever £1 million signing, came from Leeds and fitted in particularly well. Dixie had also given a few of the lads their debuts, boys who, like me, had come through the ranks at the club. Johnny Wright, Keith O'Neill and Jamie Cureton, who was, at the time of writing, still knocking them in today for Cheltenham Town, a big surprise to me as he never looked the type to still be playing when he was over thirty. But, seriously, nice one Curo, keep it going mate. We also saw the first appearance of Andy Marshall in the first team, our teenage 'keeper who'd been busy keeping the bench warm for the immovable Gunny. Immovable, that is, until we went to play Nottingham Forest two days after Christmas. We were seventh at the time and not doing at all badly, Ashley Ward had come in and got two goals on his debut against Chelsea, Curo scoring the first of his many career goals in the game in that fixture as well. All things considered, therefore, we weren't doing too badly. I'd missed a few games and had a few more on the bench, but I was as fit as ever and determined to make a go of it as Dixie gradually built his own side.

Maybe if Gunny hadn't been injured at Forest, things would have turned out differently? As it was, he was in the action early as usual, blocking a shot from Ian Woan before collapsing into the ground in some pain. Gunny was like the Terminator, he only stayed down if it was really bad and, believe me, this did look bad. He'd broken his leg, which meant the end of his season and a debut for Andy, one he could hardly have dared to expect, even though, as a professional, he would have been prepared for it to happen at any time. Which it now had. He had a nervous start however and a little indecision at a corner kick cost us, a kick, from Lars Bohinen, going straight in. Not a good way to concede in any circumstances. It was enough to give Forest the points and give us a raw 'keeper to bed in with half our league fixtures to play.

To be fair, Marsh had a blinder in our next game, a 2-1 win over Newcastle at Carrow Road, which had Kevin Keegan, their charismatic manager, singing his praises post-match. Little were we to know, in our post-match haze of sweat, steam and joyful banter, that we would only win one more league game that season. Such celebrations were to become an endangered species within the Canary family.

Anfield was up next – cue my little epiphany about how things were going. It was our first fixture of the year (1995), played around seven months after the game, the goal and, most importantly of all, the great overall team performance that had seen us act as the party poopers in the Merseyside sunshine at the end of the previous season. Sublime moments. The ridiculous inevitably followed.

Liverpool were at us from the start. It was like trying to hold back a fierce, red tide. Honestly, they were everywhere, hungry for the ball, for space, for the early tackle and telling pass. We were at sixes, sevens and probably eights. They were 2-0 up at half-time and we were lucky it was only that many. Dixie wasn't a happy man, he waited for us to sit down and have a little bicker among ourselves before he spoke. 'You,' he motioned to Rob Newman. 'Off.' Rob's face fell a mile and I felt for him. But Dixie wasn't finished. 'And you,' he continued, looking at me straight in the eye. 'You're off as well. Get in the bath, get changed. You two, get on, make a difference.'

That was Neil Adams and Darren Eadie. A brave move by the still new gaffer, putting on two wingers at the expense of a couple of more, shall we say it, 'solid' players. Rob and I brought many good things to the side, but lightning-fast runs and searching crosses weren't among them. We started to tear off our kit as Dixie went through his plans for the second half, before making for the big communal baths that were in the away team dressing rooms at Anfield, the scenes of some celebration among us all, Dixie included, the previous season. They were now the setting for big Rob and I to hold a little wake between the two of us.

We'd hardly immersed our aching bodies into the hot water before we heard a huge roar from within the ground. Norwich fans make a lot of noise at the best of times, home and away, but that wasn't our lot, that was 30,000 Liverpool fans celebrating as one as they went 3-0 up. I looked over at Rob: 'Mate, what's going on? I can't believe how things have gone from being so good to so bad in such a short time.'

There was nothing much more to be said after that. We sat in silence while the ebb and flow of a delighted Anfield crowd sounded outside, no doubt enjoying their side's total dominance and, ultimately, easy 4-0 win. It was a crushing blow and the start of a terrible sequence of games that saw us win only one of our next fourteen league games, a 3-0 defeat at Newcastle on 8 April sealing Dixie's fate as manager.

He'd previously said that Carrow Road was not the nicest of environments to be playing football and he was right, although the hostility in the crowd was very much directed at the chairman, rather than him. He'd had enough by the end of that Newcastle game, however, and resigned, paving the way for Gary Megson to be appointed as temporary manager until the end of the season.

Meggy only got four games to win his case and stand any chance of becoming the manager on a permanent basis. By the end of the third game, we were down, a 2-1 defeat at Leeds sealing our fate, a game that I played really well in. Unbelievable. Down with a game still to play, we hadn't even managed to take it to the last day of the season. That was a home game against Aston Villa that we drew, scant consolation of course, but I got our goal early in the second half, a far-post header. But it was much too little and far too late.

I was really down at this point, in fact that game, and the relegation that followed, was the worst moment of my career. But regardless of that, as a footballer, you have the first part of the summer to recharge your mental batteries and get away from it all, to try and forget football and everything that goes with it as you do. Not so easy, but I went away with my wife for a couple of weeks. It was while we were away enjoying ourselves in the sun somewhere that the news filtered through to me that Martin O'Neill had agreed to leave Wycombe Wanderers and become our new manager.

Well this was fantastic news and it gave me a real buzz. A brilliant appointment for the football club, no question. I'd trained alongside Martin when I was a young player just starting out in the game, his class was there for all to see. A great player, a big name, someone who'd gone to a World Cup, won a European Cup. He was a man who I knew, through experience, was good with young players and wanted to work with them, to encourage them, improve them. We got back from holiday and I was out running the miles and doing the gym work straight away, I wanted to be fit and ready for pre-season, my philosophy had always been that you get fit for pre-season so that you are ready to go, you hit the ground running. That's somewhat different to Chippy Crook, his was that you used pre-season to get fit, but there you go. He was a maverick. Chippy could stroll in, have a puff on a ciggie, eat a Mars Bar and then go and spray the ball about like he was another Maradona. Besides, he didn't need to be as fit as me, because I did all his running for him!

It was while I was out on one of my pre-, pre-season training runs that I felt something go in my leg. If you want to be technical, it was my soleus muscle, which is at the back of the calf. Ping, gone. Not good. I arranged to meet up with Tim Sheppard at the club's new training complex at Colney, and before long, I was laid out on one of the physio's benches with Tim working away on that muscle for me. We were chatting away and the subject of the new manager came up. 'As a matter of fact,' said Tim as we talked, 'I think Martin's in here today.' Right on cue,

Martin O'Neill walked into the room. Were his ears burning? I don't know. But I was pleased to see him and offer him my hand, awkward as it was to do so, as I was laying, face down, on this bench. But I was sure he'd appreciate the gesture.

'Gaffer, congratulations. Welcome to the football club. What a fantastic appointment, I'm sure you're going to do some really great things with us. It's good to see you here.' All this time I was laying there, arm outstretched, waiting for him to shake my hand. He knows who I am after all, it wasn't that long ago that he'd praised me after we'd beaten his Wycombe side in the FA Cup. But he didn't shake my hand, he just stood there, looking at me and shaking his head. I could swear he might even have been tutting as he was doing so. 'Gossy, Gossy, Gossy. What the f*** have you done, why are you here, before pre-season, getting treatment?' 'Gaffer, I was out on a run, I always train throughout the summer, just felt a little tightness in my calf so Tim's just giving it a once over, nothing serious.'

Martin replied, 'You train throughout the summer? Well now, that's a nightmare isn't it? Anyway. We'll have to wait and see what happens with you Gossy, we'll have to wait and see.' I'm a bit shocked at all this. There's no hello back, no handshake, no banter. And it got worse. He walked over to where the front of the couch is and puts his hands on my head before rubbing and roughing up my hair, making a right mess of it. And I have to say, I have always been sensitive to people touching me around my head, my face and hair. I don't like it. Yet here he was, standing there, playing with my curly barnet as I was laying there on the couch. And it was a big old curly mop back then! The fans were great with it, they used to get curly wigs and wear them at games, a wonderful, even humbling, thing to do. I loved that. But I don't love being prone here while the new gaffer plays with it. It's embarrassing for a start. Tim is there. I also think there was a young lad nearby getting treatment as well.

And then the new gaffer walked out. Not another word. I was trying to put all my hair back in place because it looked like a force 10 gale had blown through it, talking to Tim as I do so. 'Bloody hell Tim, that was a strange thing to do. What was all that about?' Tim, a lovely bloke, couldn't answer that. So he carried on treating my calf. In silence. It wasn't the best first meeting I'd ever had with a new manager. He had a pop at me because I wanted to be fit, something that I at least thought he might respect me for. I just hoped he would give me a fair chance at training, playing me to show him the sort of player I am, the player who impressed him when he was at Wycombe and said, 'I'd have you in any of my teams Gossy'. But would he have me in this one?

One good thing that came from Martin's appointment was the arrival of Steve Walford as his assistant. Steve was another ex-Norwich player, and someone else I'd immensely respected during my first spell at the club. He was a different class from the off. A funny man who wanted us to work hard and achieve great things, someone who, like me, wore his heart on his sleeve. I respected him for that. Martin also brought along Paul Franklin as first-team coach, he'd played a few games for various clubs in the lower leagues but had nowhere near the top flight experience of Martin or Paul, which you could see in how he handled some of his sessions with us.

I'm going to have to go off on a tangent here while we're on the subject, and mention another coach we had at Norwich, Mick Wadsworth, who worked with Meggy during his second spell at the club. He was an intense guy, and very what you would call 'FA' in his approach. The badges, the cones, the drills, exercises, square yardages, the lot. A coach's coach. He was really enthusiastic as well, loved what he was doing, loved the game. He did a session with us one morning, and it was, believe me, a really complicated one. It was based on circle work, the sort of thing that a lot of clubs do as part of a warm up, two lads in the middle, passing around them from the outside, that sort of thing. Quick, easy and warms you up nicely. Now, Mick had other ideas. He got us in the circle and was all, 'Right lads, when you get it, run it in, run around, pass to second man on your left as you go in, then run round his opposite and get the ball back in time to circle the other second man, before passing square across the third' – that sort of thing. Hugely difficult for all of us to remember, much less to carry out. And we didn't have a clue. Not. A. Clue. Mick, needless to say, couldn't believe it.

'For God's sake, I do this with kids all the time. Look, when you get it, run it in, run around ... oh forget it, let's do something else. Eleven-a-side on the main pitch, First team against the Ressies.' Now this we can do. Or we thought we could. We start the game. but every few seconds, Mick's blowing his whistle.

'Stop. Right, you there, and No. 20. Do this, this, this, this and this.' He's going through all the motions as he says so. But all he gets in return is a sea of blank faces. It's no good, we don't have a clue. Again.

Mick had crossed his patience threshold. He picked up a large stack of cones and threw them onto the pitch before laying down, on his belly, banging his arms and legs into the pitch in sheer frustration, venting his frustration as he does so. 'I can't cope with you lot, you lot are making me sick. I do all of these drills with kids and they get it, why can't you all get it? You're all making me look stupid.' This was not our intention at all. But we just look on, watching him, a few of the lads stifling the odd giggle. He's winding us up isn't he, having a laugh? Apparently not. Because he then gets up and storms off and away from the training pitches, back to the changing rooms, passing Gary Megson, who is all kitted up and ready to join training with us, rubbing his hands in happy expectation. 'Alright lads, what are we doing today? Let's get started eh? Alright Mick?' Mick carried on, walking back to get changed. He didn't even offer Meggy a backward glance. 'Fook 'em, Meggy.'

Mick really was a crazy guy. Likeable. But crazy. On another occasion, he came into the dressing rooms at Colney, wired and fired you might say. 'Right lads, who wants to punch me? Anyone?' He pulls up his training top to reveal a pretty well-racked stomach and upper body. 'Come on, hit me, anyone? Gossy, you'll hit me. Get over here and give it yer best shot.' The lads all stepped in at this point. 'No, no need for that Mick. Gossy. Don't hit him.'

Most of the lads had seen me punch, and be punched, before. Mike Walker, Gunny and me used to have punching competitions, usually on away trips, each of us taking turns to give the other a punch in the six pack area. We were all pretty well built up at the time so no one got hurt, and it was more for show than anything, but, even so, I could still pack a wallop if I needed to, and I'm sure the lads were worried that if I hit Mick he'd go flying into a wall or something. Mick wasn't at the club for very long but he certainly left some memories.

Martin O'Neill held his first meeting with all the lads on the first day back of pre-season training. He had us all in the main room at Colney and we sat waiting. He walked in, as did Steve Walford and Paul Franklin. He's had a stopwatch on a cord in his hand and he was playing with it, not looking at us, not talking, just stood there in front of the group, playing with this stopwatch. Then, after a while, he started to talk. 'Right. I'm the gaffer and what I say goes. Everything revolves around me.'

He then started playing with the stopwatch again before carrying on. 'What I expect from you is...' Stopping, mid-sentence, looking across at Rob Ullathorne, one of our full-backs. Rob was negotiating a new contract at the time, with John Deehan and then, after his first brief stay, Gary Megson. It still hadn't been sorted out and all the details remained with the club secretary. Now we all knew Rob was negotiating a new contract. It was common knowledge. But what we didn't know is what he was on or what he had asked for. We didn't talk money. But Martin O'Neill clearly did know what Rob had asked for, so he switched tack and suddenly started having a pop at Rob: '...and you, if you think you're going to get what you've asked for, you've got another thing coming son. Because you ain't getting that, you ain't getting that by a long way.'

Rob is completely embarrassed by this and we all feel for him. It's the new gaffer's first day and he's opened it by embarrassing one of our mates in front of everyone. Rob's now in tatters. Job done for Martin, who gets back to the subject in hand and a spot of training. 'Right. We're going to run.'

And off we'd go. All the time he was at Norwich, he had us running. We never stopped running from the day he arrived until the day he left. He ran our nuts off. Now, I could cope. I loved to run, you know that by now. But some of the other lads? It was killing them. And it got me thinking. This wasn't the Martin O'Neill I'd known as a player here, or the one I'd spoken to at Wycombe that time. This was a different man, a different personality. I didn't know this Martin O'Neill at all.

If we weren't running, we were playing little jelly and ice cream games. By that, I mean, the sort of group games that children play when they're doing a little sport or something. Two lines of ten players, passing the ball back down the line, in between our legs and then over, that sort of thing. We all did it when we were at school. Well, we became reacquainted with it when I was a professional footballer. But these little games, they were competitive. You bet your life they were. If you lost, you had to go on a monster run as a punishment. And if you didn't do that monster run in the target time that Martin set, then you did another run, another punishment. 'Right,' he'd say, 'you didn't do that in time so now you've got to do this. Run up to that cone, then to that tree, twice around the tree and then back via the goalposts up there. You've got 10 seconds. Go.'

Ten seconds? It couldn't be done. You'd get back, there'd be Martin, stood with his stopwatch. 'Didn't make the time lads, do it again.' And off we'd go again. How we longed to kick a ball. But when we did, well, what was that all about? It'd either be one-on-one in the 18-yard box, which is bloody knackering. That, or twenty-five pros all stood in an area about the size of two pitches, watching Paul Franklin kick a ball as high as he can into the sky before saying, 'Okay lads, keep-ball.' And that was that.

During the whole of Martin's brief time at the club I found the training dismal. In fact, it was the worse training routine and exercises I have known in my time as a professional footballer. He didn't even come out and join us until about midday. Then, whatever else we'd been doing, or working on, with Steve and Paul, he'd have us running. He loved players who could run, players who were quick. Two of our quickest were Darren Eadie and Spencer Prior, both players who, eventually, joined Martin at Leicester when he went there.

He was a hard, hard man to please. He'd inherited a good squad, a lot of players who'd done well, played in Europe. But he battered us, day by day by day. Embarrassed us and belittled us. I could deal with that but I couldn't deal with being ignored. We went on a pre-season training trip to Ireland that summer where I cracked a rib. I couldn't therefore train. So he totally disregarded me. I was nothing. I was beginning to think it was personal, that he didn't like me. When we travelled down to Luton for the first game of that (1995/96) season, he took a full party of twenty-five professionals. We all went, all travelled to Kenilworth Road, all changed, all took part in the pre-match warm up on the pitch. Then we all went back in at 2.50 and he'd name the team. No one had a clue what it would be up until that moment. Neither Chippy nor I made the team or subs. So we got changed and had to sit in the stands, watching the game, where, at one point, we just exchanged glances, you would have been able to tell exactly what those looks meant if you had seen them. Looks that said things had changed and we didn't know if it was going to involve us or not.

Anyway, we won 3-1. Played well, good performance. Couple of goals for Jon Newsome with Neil Adams getting the other. Everyone got changed, we all get on the coach ready to go, we're just waiting for the manager. And keep on waiting. One hour passes. No manager. Two hours pass. Still no manager. Two and a half hours now – and guess what, still no sign of the manager. We're all climbing the walls by now, bored stiff, desperate to get off home. It must have beeen getting on for eight o'clock. Eventually, we delegate Jon Newsome to go and look for him, Captain's responsibility and all that. Jon goes into the stadium, finds the managers room and knocks on the door. The door opens, Jon sees Martin. 'Just to let you know Gaffer, the lads are on the coach, we're ready to go.' Martin's reply is succinct. 'F**k off.' Which is what Jon does. He got back on the coach and said, 'He told me to f**k off!'

There is a collective sigh. Oh God! If this is what he is going to be like after a win, after a good performance, what's he going to be like when we lose, when we play badly? Eventually, Martin climbs onto the coach. He goes around it, hugging each of the eleven players who started the game, telling them, as he does, how much he loves them. When he's been around those players, he addresses Jon Newsome. 'Don't you ever come looking for me again. If you do, I will sack you. I say when you go. I say when we arrive. I say when we leave. I'm the manager. Anyway. Great result lads, great performance. The eleven players who started today, see you on Thursday morning. The rest of you, subs who came on included. I'll see you at Colney tomorrow. Now, let's get home'

I'll never question Martin's desire, his passion and how he always wanted to win games. He'd be there at matches, tracksuit on, running up and down the touchline, kicking every ball. He desperately wanted success. But I couldn't handle his methods or the way he'd treat people. I think I know why he did it, there was some Brian Clough in there. A sort of, if I wind them up then, they'll react to prove me wrong. It works with some players but it didn't for me or some of the other lads. Take Mike Sheron. He battered Mike at training once. He liked these little exercises where we all stood on the edge of the 18-yard box, two players would get called inside and they'd play one-on-one. As soon as Mike got in there, off Martin would go. 'Shez, you're going to fall over son.' 'My mum's better than you, Shez.' It knocks the stuffing out of you straight away. Mike probably did fall over but you can't blame him, he'd been conditioned to!

On another occasion, Martin had a pop at Mike Milligan, a strong and hard-working midfielder and a brilliant lad, I thought it then and still do today, I think the world of Millie. Dixie had brought him in from Oldham, one of his famous Northerners. 'Milly,' queried Martin. 'Do you go to Church?' 'Yes gaffer, I do, every Sunday. Why?' 'Next time you go son, get on your knees and pray to God for some ability.' Milly wasn't having that. 'I will gaffer. But do you go to Church?' 'I do indeed, Milly.' 'Well when you go next time, you pray to God for some personality.'

A fabulous response and one of the best comeback quotes I've ever heard in football, one that would have had us busting a gut not to laugh. Martin, naturally enough, busted Milly the next day, making him run all over the place.

There are so many other little stories like that. Martin O'Neill was there because of his character, his way of thinking, the way he liked to motivate people. Some liked it, most didn't. I hated it, but true to this motives maybe, I wanted to prove him wrong. And I thought I had the chance, a few days after that Luton game, when I was named in the reserves team to play Millwall, at what was then their new ground, the New Den. And it was ... well, new. Sparkling, pristine, smart, the works. With a beautiful, immaculate pitch. Right, I thought, the gaffers watching,

I'll show him what he's missing. I'll cover every inch of that turf, make every pass, win every tackle. I'll win him over. And I played as good a game as I had ever done at that level, doing all the things I'd set out to. I came off that pitch feeling a million dollars and was pleased, as I did, to see Martin walking towards me, though not so pleased with his reaction. 'You were crap.'

I knew then that it was never going to happen for me at Norwich under Martin O'Neill. I gave it one last go, another reserve game, this time at Carrow Road. I'd arranged for Margaret to come and watch, as well as her parents, Robbie and Janet Scott, two lovely people who have provided wonderful support and friendship to me since I met Margaret. As they were proving that day, them and about 500 other people watching me play for the Ressies again, it felt as if things were going full cycle. But we were all getting together and going out for a meal afterwards, so I was looking forward to that.

It didn't help that some chap, I guess he was one of the ball boys' parents or something, came into the dressing room before the game and started having a go at me. I think it was partially banter, rather than outright malice, but I still didn't appreciate it. 'Gossy,' he goes, 'you've lost it son, it's all gone. You're not the same player you were.' Bear in mind that this is the dressing room before a game. It doesn't matter that it's a reserve-team game, that area is sacrosanct. I would love to see what Mel Machin might have said or done to him, had he been around. It was a disgrace, I wanted to hit him, but, of course, I didn't. I sat and took it then went out and played the game. A little while later, Ade Akinbiyi came up to me and said 'I can't believe you let him get away with that.' Ade knew, as did all the lads, that I could look after myself and would if I had to. But it wouldn't have been worth anywhere near the aggro it would have caused.

There were also problems for me during the match itself. I went to tackle a lad who pushed the ball ahead of me, just a little bit too far for me to realistically win it. In fact, it was probably 60:40 in his favour. But I went in and, as I did, I felt my right ankle go over. And shit, did that hurt!

I never stayed down if I didn't have to. In fact, I hate it when players today go down and make something of half a challenge when there was nothing in it. It's a disgrace when they do, they don't need to, they've all the talent and ability in the world and some of them are trying to win games in this manner, by getting an advantage, trying to fool the referee. Rugby players laugh at professional footballers because of this reputation some of them have, and rightly so.

Everyone knew this about me and, because I hadn't sprung straight to my feet, Tim Sheppard was on the pitch and by my side like a hare. He knew something must be up. But that's all I wanted to do – get up. Still in a lot of pain, I managed to do so and to see the game out. My ankle has swollen up and, by the end of the game, it was twice its normal size. I was stupid to carry on but I wanted, somehow, to impress the gaffer. Now I had hurt myself. I went to hospital, had an MRI scan and it was bad news, the ligaments were badly torn. It would have been better had I broken it. But there you go, another battle, this time to get fit again. My confidence was at an all-time low and I decide to go and see Martin O'Neill, to have a proper one-to-one with him in his office.

'Gaffer, I can't stand this. You constantly belittle me, you embarrass me, you're sarcastic and, worst of all, you're arrogant. It's obvious you and me don't get on. I can't play for you, so I'm off, I'm handing it a transfer request.'

'Gossy son, you're not the first to come and see me in my office to say that and you won't be the last. Listen. My job is simple. I'm here to win games, get points. That keeps me in a job. I'm not here to make friends. You can do what you want. I couldn't give a toss.' And that was that.

Not long after that, Martin O'Neill quit the club. I won't go into the reasons here for why he felt he had to go. The fact is that we were third in the table and looking good for a real push for promotion when he did, and we'd have gone top of the table if we'd won a home game against Stoke, one of his last in charge. So he was doing well and the club was progressing. No one can deny that and no one can say he wouldn't have got us up again had he stayed. In fact, he very likely would have done. I'll never argue against his track record and the success he had, he is a very good football manager and one who would, I stress again, have done very well at Norwich. The problems I had with him were about personality and the sort of person I was. We were never going to get on, no matter what.

And that's a pity because, when he was appointed, I thought it was the best thing that had happened to the club for years and couldn't wait to play for him. He went onto join Leicester City as Manager and he took them up at the end of that season via the play-offs. If he'd have remained at Norwich, he would probably have done that with us.

Gary Megson returned to the club as Martin's successor. That cheered me up a little bit. I liked Meggy, we got on well and understood each other. He'd been bombed out of the club, a little unfairly perhaps, after we'd gone down, but he'd forgotten all that and carried on playing, as well as having a spell helping out Chris Kamara at Bradford when Kammy was the gaffer there. So he'd done some coaching and had a little more managerial nous about him. But I was still struggling. I was working as hard as I'd ever done, staying back after training on most days, trying to get the momentum going again, something that is so hard to do after you've had a bad injury and missed games.

I eventually got back into the team for a home game against Southend on Boxing Day 1995 before starting at Derby on New Year's Day. Meggy had me coming off the bench in six out of eight league games at that point, preferring, at one point, Jan Molby (in from Liverpool on loan) rather than start me. Then, from March, I got a run of games as a starter, but now everything was reversed. Rrather than coming on from the bench, as I had been, I found myself coming off and not finishing the matches, something which all came to a head in an away game up at Barnsley in April. I was still struggling. There was nothing wrong with my fitness – I was making the runs, covering the whole pitch, going from box to box and back again.

In short, to use that Alan Ball story I mentioned earlier, I was busy being 'the dog'. But, as far as Meggy was concerned, that was part of the problem. He told me I was coming off at half-time at Oakwell and, as he did so, he patted me on the head and said, 'It's just not happening for you Gossy.' The way he looked at me, the look in his eyes as he did, that was enough for me. I realised he didn't mean it wasn't happening for me in that game, he meant it wasn't happening for me as a footballer, that it was all over, certainly as far as Norwich City were concerned. He'd said as much without needing to say anything. I knew.

The lads all went out for the second half, leaving me alone in the dressing room. Well, I thought, 'That's it. I've got to move, got to find another club.' Meggy had told me that my game was all wrong, that I needed to stand still, to stop running about, in essence, he was telling me to, as I read it, cheat. But I couldn't do that. Giving my all was my game, and I was still fit enough to do that, I didn't *need* to slow down. Maybe the great days at Norwich were coming to an end, but I didn't think that meant I would have to bring my career to a halt. No way. I was fit, I was still ambitious and wanted to be part of a team of winners. Stand still? Not for anyone.

I started just one more league game for Norwich that season, the one that turned out to be my last ever for the club. It was at Selhurst Park where we beat Crystal Palace 1-0. The mood in the camp was good and the travelling fans were in a state of high excitement as Robert Chase had, a few days earlier, resigned as chairman. It was as if, with his departure, a brand new era was about to start at Carrow Road, but I wasn't going to be part of it.

12

Running Around Arthur's Seat

Eventually, after some more screaming and shouting, mostly from me, I advised them that they had best stick their football club up their respective backsides.

In the end, it didn't make any difference as to whether I wanted to leave Norwich City, or not, because I ended up with no choice in the matter. The summer of 1996 saw the club's finances reach a worryingly parlous state that they had to address as swiftly and effectively as possible, implementing a very tough and hard-hitting cost-saving programme as a result.

One of the best ways they could immediately save money was by drastically reducing the wage bill, one of the consequences of that meaning any players who were out of contract were not offered new terms. In other words, they could go. The trio who subsequently faced the axe in this manner were Mark Bowen, Ian Crook and I. It was very hard for me to leave Carrow Road for the last time but, as I did so, I at least had the consolation of knowing that two clubs were chasing my signature as a free agent. Charlton Athletic, then, like Norwich, were in the old First Division and, intriguingly, Hearts were up in the Scottish Premier League.

The Charlton manager, Alan Curbishley, certainly did all the early running, constantly ringing me and letting me know how much he and his club wanted me, saying things like, 'Come and join us Gossy, this is a good club with some good players' and 'Look at the quality players we've already got here, you'll fit in straight away.' And he was right. They did have some good players, some of whom I'd played against. Richard Rufus was one, Mark Robson and John Robinson a couple of others. Curbs was looking to put a squad together that would push on to the Premier League in the 1996/97 season, something which, with the greatest of respect, Norwich didn't quite seem ready to do at that stage and, with that in mind, Charlton looked like a step up for me. It was tempting. It wouldn't have meant much upheaval for Maggie and myself or Mum and Dad, as they wouldn't have had to travel far to see us. Charlton was almost a local side for people living in Kent. I'd end up playing against Norwich that season of course, but I didn't have a problem with that as it would have been a good opportunity to show the Norwich fans that the club should have offered me a new contract. To be honest with you, I'd been surprised that I hadn't had a call from the club since Mike Walker had returned for his second spell at Carrow Road. He'd already reversed the Canaries' decision not to renew Ian Crook's contract by getting him to re-sign, snatching him away from Ipswich in the process. But my call never happened and it sank in, irrevocably, that my career at Norwich now really was over, something I found hard to accept for a while.

There was no time to feel sorry for myself because I had Curbs on the phone again. He was very upbeat and I was beginning to like the fella, a great manager and a gentleman. 'Gossy, I've had a chat with the chairman and this is what we can pay you.' To be honest, it wasn't great, but it was a small improvement in what I'd been earning at Norwich. There wasn't a car included, which was something that I had eventually 'earnt' at Norwich. But I couldn't really complain. I was thirty-one years old so needed to get something from someone. After all, players were seen as past it when they hit thirty, so the prospect of a two-year deal at Charlton was a brilliant option, car or no car. I needed a club and I needed to be needed. And Curbs was doing his very best to make me feel just that.

Except then, things got a little more complicated. The interest from Scotland became apparent, with another manager on the phone this time, Jim Jefferies at Hearts. He gave me all the spiel on the phone, just as Curbs had done. 'Get up here to Scotland Gossy. This is a massive club. You can push on here, win things with us. We know all about you, what you did at Norwich. You'll play every game for me. Come and have a look around the place.' The wage package on offer was a fraction better than Charlton's. Plus, this time there was a car, so that would save me a bit of money. Plus, they'd be playing in the European Cup Winners' Cup that season, an appealing prospect. I'd never written off the possibility of playing in Europe again and this would have justified that belief. It was, no doubt, an appealing prospect. As was the offer from Charlton. Suddenly, from being without a club, I was left with a big decision to make, which of the two clubs to sign for? I didn't have an agent (I never had one all the time I was in the game) so I got in touch with Mick McGuire, a former Norwich player who was at the PFA as it was all getting to be a bit of a nightmare, strange as that might seem.[1] The truth of it is that I was really letting myself get bothered and over-wrought by the whole thing. I was starting to lose fitness and focus and that wasn't a good thing, as soon, somewhere, I'd be wanting to hit the ground running at pre-season training.

In the end, I opted for Charlton. Curbs had been really persuasive when we'd spoken and made me feel wanted. That was important. It wasn't that far away and plus, I'd have the chance to come back to Carrow Road and play for them there. It just made sense. So I signed for them and, in no time at all, found myself a decent hotel close to the Dartford Tunnel, settled in and got ready for the next stage of my career. And I was a new boy again. Hell, it had been a while! I would have been one of the senior players at the club of course, but I wasn't going to come in and shout the odds.

No. Quiet and respectful, that was my way. I would slowly integrate myself into the group, show them what a good lad I was, that I would fight for them, run myself into the ground if necessary. Players take notice of how a new face performs at training and I didn't hide, didn't shirk, I gave it everything. I'd do my best to quickly win the respect of all the other players so they saw that I would be someone good to have around the place, helping me settle in and, in time, becoming part of a good group, just as I had at Norwich. So, with that positive attitude, I got in my car and headed off for my first day at training at my new club.

Shit. What have I done?

The moment I arrived at Charlton's training ground things didn't feel right. Nothing did. All the lads came up and wished me all the best but I wasn't happy about something. I felt uncertain and uneasy, I wasn't sure what it was but it just felt wrong. After a few days, time in which I'd anticipated it being over, I found myself feeling worse and worse. In fact I wasn't comfortable with anything. The hotel, the drive around the M25 to get to training, the training ground itself. It all just felt wrong. With regards to the Charlton players, well, it was the same as you'd expect at any club, a few little cliques about the place, with some friendly faces and most of the others barely acknowledging the rest. Football as life. This is easy to pick up at training, the players don't have their 'public' faces on and can be whoever they want to be and behave just as they want towards one another, there's no disguise or bluff anywhere. It was all very intense at times and, as an incomer, I felt I didn't really belong in any of the groups. I had come from a very close-knit club at Norwich, part of a group of players that had, in some cases, been together for a good few years, bonding a togetherness and team spirit which was second to none. Now, of course, not everyone was close mates, not even at Norwich, but there certainly weren't any cliques or 'big timers' there either.

But there sure as hell seemed to be a few at Charlton. I tried to put these uncertain feelings to the back of my mind, but they kept on making their way back to the front of it and, try as I might, I became ever more convinced that Charlton wasn't the right club for me. This realisation, naturally enough, made me feel sick to my stomach with worry about the situation. I'd signed a two-year contract at the club so I couldn't just walk away. They'd retain my registration and could, if they wished, stop me from playing for anyone else. I didn't want to hang around going through the motions either, I'd get found out too easily. My unhappiness would show in my performances, which would mean my reputation, one I'd worked so hard to build, would go up in smoke. And, more importantly than that, I'd be letting the club down. So, with all those thoughts racing around in my head, I took a deep breath and went to see Curbs.

'Gaffer, look, I'm sorry to mess you about, but I think I've made a mistake here, I don't think this move is right for me.' Alan Curbishley is sat at his desk in his office. He listens, pauses, and then looks me straight in the eye. 'Well then Gossy, we've got a problem haven't we?' There was a pause and, for a moment, I thought he was going to say it was too bad, I was to get a grip and he expected me to honour my contract. He would have every right to do so and I would have knuckled down. 'Well I can see there's no point trying to get you to change your mind. I can see in your eyes that you want to leave. Go and sort yourself out. Whilst you're doing that, I'll go and see the club secretary and ask them to cancel your contract. It's a shame Gossy, as you're a good player and could have done well with us. But I won't stand in your way.'

And that was it. I was no longer a Charlton Athletic player. None of the biographies that I have seen about me list them as one of my clubs, but they were, albeit for only a week or so. It was a pity. Alan Curbishley is a good bloke and a top manager and, to this day, I still feel terrible for letting him down. Having said that, I wasn't the first to make a 'U-turn' on a decision and I certainly won't be the last. But, as from that moment, it meant that I now didn't have a job or club to go to. Luckily for me though, Jim Jefferies had heard what had happened and was back on the phone to me almost straight away. 'Gossy, come on up here, this shows you're meant to be a Hearts player. This is the club for you, a big club playing big games in a great stadium. Come and join us.'

What else could I do? I got myself up to Edinburgh and went to speak to Jim. He sold me the challenge all over again. And listen. They are a big, big club, even despite all that they've been through lately. They're one of the biggest clubs in Scotland after Celtic and Rangers. They had won loads of honours and were the club where two of the all-time great Scottish players, Alex Young and Dave Mackay, had started their careers. So shouldn't I feel privileged to perhaps be bringing mine to an end with such a footballing institution? It helped, again, to hear both Jim Jefferies and his assistant, Billy Brown, saying all the right things. Brown emphasising in the press that I was the 'ideal type for us, a great professional with plenty of experience in the game', the sort of thing you want to hear, simple as it might sound. For my part, I had words with two of my ex-Norwich teammates, Bryan Gunn and Colin Woodthorpe, both of whom had spent part of their career in Scotland. Gunny had been at Aberdeen under Alex Ferguson before he joining the Canaries, while Colin had joined Aberdeen from Norwich a couple of years earlier and was, as he admitted, loving it there.

Both were very complimentary about the club, saying they were ambitious and looking to push on. I would have another European campaign to look forward to and Edinburgh was a lovely city, somewhere I knew I'd enjoy living and working in for a while. And remember, with all the moves I'd gone through with Dad when I was a boy, making a new home somewhere was hardly something I wasn't used to. So yes, bit by bit, Hearts were ticking all of the Goss boxes. It had bothered me a bit, moving so far away. I would not just be far from Norwich, but also from my parents who, being based in Folkestone, would now be getting on for 500 miles away. This would be tough for them and for me. I had a word with my dad, as I usually do when I've got a decision to make or something is bothering me, he is honest and gives it straight, nothing changed on this occasion, not that I expected it to.

'Well it'll be a bit further for us to come and watch you play. But we will. You must do what you feel is right, what makes you happy. This sounds like it could be a good move. Take it, get up there, play and enjoy yourself, it's a lovely part of the country and they are a big club' So, on 30 July 1996, after thirteen years with Norwich City and a week with Charlton Athletic, I signed for Hearts.

On the day I signed for the club, they also announced they were bringing in another couple of new players: Neil McCann, a winger from Dundee, as well as David Weir, an imposing centre-half who had played for Jefferies while he was at Falkirk, the club he'd managed before he joined Hearts. Good players with good reputations in the game. It always helps when the club you are either at, or joining, is bringing in good players, as it shows they are ambitious and they want to compete. It also helped that I wasn't going to be the sole new boy, and, with that in mind, I was looking forward to meeting and getting to know Neil and David, as well as the other lads at the club. Hearts held a photo call on our big the day with the press busy taking pictures of the new lads on the pitch at Tynecastle; Neil, David and I looked resplendent in our new Hearts kit, while striking a pose or two. There was also a press conference that featured the three of us sat at a table alongside Jim Jefferies, the questions flying in from all corners of the room, that and more photographs on what was turning out to be a busy and high-profile day for the club.

Neil and David got a lot of questions, as did Jim, who was asked why he'd brought each of them into the club and what he thought they, in turn, would bring to the team. They were then asked the same question. Nice answers, the sort of talk everyone wants to hear. This is a big club. Ambitious. Wants to win things. Jim is a top manager. Hearts have got the basis of a strong squad this season, players like Colin Cameron and, in his second spell at the club, John Robertson. On and on and on it went, except, for whatever reason, no one asked me a single question. I spent the whole of the press conference sat there with my best smile on, missing out, as time and time again, someone asked Neil a question or requested David's opinion on something. Then, Jim would be drawn into proceedings before the process went back to Neil and David again. And that's how it stayed. The whole event, press call, TV, radio, the lot, and I hadn't been asked one single question or asked for my views on anything. And maybe it shouldn't have done and maybe the ego was playing up a little bit with it. But I did think it a bit strange that no one at all wanted to hear anything from me. But then I was never one for being the centre of attention anyway. So maybe that was a good thing? Yes, of course it was, I assured myself, turning to thoughts of training and ingratiating myself with my new team mates instead.

My first competitive game for the club came only a week or so after I had signed. I'd clearly done enough to convince Jim I was fit and ready, so, full of excitement, I joined up with the squad for the trip to what was then still Yugoslavia, for the first leg game in our European Cup Winners Cup qualifying game against Red Star

Belgrade. And I played well in what turned out to be a great team performance. We easily dealt with whatever they threw at us, and, on more than one occasion could have scored ourselves and won the tie. I even went close myself at one point in the game. But we looked good and that was more encouraging for me than my own performance. Solid at the back, quick and first to the ball in midfield and lively in attack, we were no mugs, not even at this level. That valuable draw, an excellent result against perhaps the best team in the competition, at this early stage, meant I came off the pitch with a smile on my face, looking forward to what would be an upbeat dressing room and a good trip home. Admittedly, I hadn't yet got to know most of my new teammates just yet, but it had all been a rush. With the signing, getting into training as well as finding a new place to live, at least there seemed a good chance we could all bond during the post match celebrations which, to my mind, were thoroughly deserved.

Except, to my great surprise, our dressing room after the game was like the scene at a wake. No one talked, let alone let off a bit of steam. No banter, no joking around, no energy, nothing. Everyone just stood or sat around, quietly getting changed and keeping themselves to themselves, the odd murmur perhaps, but that only between two lads stood next to each other and probably someone asking if he could borrow some shampoo or something. Even if we'd been done by three or four goals, I'd have expected some sign of life, some spark, some anger. But we'd just fought our way to one of the most impressive results in the club's recent history, one that any Premier League team in England would have been delighted at. What, 0-0 at Red Star Belgrade? Yes please and where do we sign? If it had happened at Norwich, Mike Walker would have been peeling us down off the ceiling by now after such a performance, but here? Nothing. I simply could not believe it. And yes, I was still one of the new boys but I couldn't let this pass, I had to say something, and I did.

'Hey lads, I reckon we should be delighted with that, what a great performance all round, shouldn't we all be celebrating that a little bit?' Nothing. In fact, most of them didn't even look my way as I said it. I tried again. 'No, great performance. Hey, that's a really good sign, if we can play as well as that, here, and so early into the season. Good work, great effort lads, really top notch.' OK, so I was trying to be like the guy in the movie *Rudy*. But to no avail. They just carried on whatever they were doing, completely oblivious to my presence. So I just thought 'Wow! This is a strange one,' and carried on changing myself. We got out, on the coach, back to the airport and home. It was a weird sort of trip. Not much team spirit flying around and no spark or life among the lads. Was this what it was always going to be like? Of course, I had to remember that I'd come from a Norwich City side where the team spirit had been, arguably, the best in the league. As I looked around that dressing room, I realised that, with our mix of youngsters, new players and senior pros, I might be expecting too much, too soon with regards to the banter. Maybe we all needed a little more time to gel a bit. But, even so, it still worried me. I'd messed a few people around in order to leave Charlton so quickly so I desperately wanted the Hearts move to work out. Right at this moment, however, quiet changing rooms and a quieter trip home had me feeling very concerned about my move and club, again.

It really bothered me. I ended up having a quiet word with Neil Pointon. Neil was our left-back who'd had good top-flight experience in England with Everton and Manchester City, two big clubs where expectations were high, especially after he won a league title with the Toffees in 1987. So he knew all about pressure, expectancy and winning, he knew what it took and he'd know, as well as, or better than anyone else at the club, what the 'vibe' in a good dressing room would be like. I had to mention it to him.

'Neil, that dressing room after Red Star, it was so quiet, no one seemed bothered, and after we'd got a great result. Is it always like that?' Neil paused before answering in his experienced voice, a philosophical reply that seemed to indicate that he'd seen it for himself and, aware that he'd never change anything, accepted it and was just going to get on with playing, keep his head down. 'Mate, it's a different mentality up here but it's a good one. They all want to win and do well, so it's a case of you getting them used them and them getting used to you. We're going to have a good season, so stop worrying and you'll soon get used to the lads.' Reassuring words, but I wasn't so sure it was something I wanted to get 'used to'.

Things didn't get much better. During training in the following week just about the worst thing that could have happened to me football-wise did happen, as from nowhere, it turned out that I'd torn my right abductor. I knew straight away that it was a bad one that would keep me out for long time, which is exactly what it did. As a result, I missed the return match against Red Star at Tynecastle which we lost, and more than a few league games that followed.

I hated being out with injury, loathed it. Everything becomes routine, predictable, it does my head in. Two or three treatment sessions every day with the physio in his treatment room is the very worst position that any player can be in, especially a player who has only just signed for that club, as was the case with me. The daily routine that you are getting used to going through is affected, which means that, just as you're getting used to your new teammates and they're getting used to you, you're suddenly not part of the picture, a case of 'out of sight, out of mind'. These were circumstances that meant I wasn't in the best frame of mind and my wife, Maggie, had to cope with my bad moods. Inevitably, I took my frustration home with me, stupid I know, but hardly a new situation for Maggie who had seen it all before and, who was, as always, brilliant with me, lifting my spirits daily. I worked hard to recover my fitness but never really won a regular place in the side during that first season.By the summer, all I had to look forward to was getting myself fit and ready to finally make an impression on my new club, teammates and the fans from the start of the following season.

And I did get fit. The injury was behind me and I was more than ready to play and make an impression. But, once again, I found myself playing more games for the reserves than I was for the first team. Talk about déjà vu. It was like that press conference all over again, like I was there but wasn't. One game would see me in the team, then I'd be sub, and then I wouldn't even make the matchday squad. It really got to me so, in a state of near despair at where my career was going, I went to have a few words with Jim. 'Gaffer, I want to play. I'm fit and I can do a good job for you, that's why you brought me in, that's why you signed me, you said so yourself. I haven't come all the way up here to be a regular in the reserves so why aren't I in the team?'

Now Jim was normally a bit of a scary character. He wouldn't hold back from being loud and aggressive, or from having a right go at his players if he felt they deserved it. I saw footballers at Hearts reduced to tears at times after a heated confrontation with Jim. Off the pitch and away from the heat of battle, however, Jim was a gentleman, one who was brilliant with me. He'd helped in all manner of ways with mine and Maggie's move to Scotland, knowing that it was a massive move and personal upheaval for us both, and, with me, he was always there for a friendly chat, more than willing to offer a wise word or two and be straight with me, no matter what the situation. And he was straight with me regarding this one. 'We've eased you in Gossy. It was a difficult first season up here but you'll get your chance, your time will come again, don't worry.'

Oh my God. Not those words again, I'd heard them so many times in the past. 'Gossy, you can still be a big player for us and the next game will prove it. We've got Rangers coming up and I'll tell you this now, you'll be starting, you're in my team. It's a game that's made for you. Keep training hard, keep your head up and boss that midfield against them.' This was all I wanted to hear. Maybe my luck was starting to change. This was a great opportunity, a huge fixture against one of the biggest sides in world football. I was, for once, elated. It hadn't been easy settling into the club or the group but this looked as if it would be the turning point. Jim had made a statement, he clearly wanted to put his best side out against Rangers and I was in it. Brilliant.

Naturally enough, I wanted my parents to be there. So I arranged for them to have tickets, I also did the same for my brothers, Mike and Tim. I wanted them there. It had been a while since they'd been to watch me at a big game. I didn't need anything more than the fact we were playing Rangers to raise my game, but the fact they were all going to be there certainly helped! I couldn't wait for that Rangers game to come around, and yes, so what if I was still having a few communication issues with my teammates(as in they didn't communicate), I was there to play football, and a good performance might make all the difference and convince everyone at the club that the lad from Norwich had come good.

I got to the ground in good time for the Rangers game, making sure that my mum and dad had got their tickets. Then, as ready and prepared for a game as I had ever been, I got to the ground and started to psyche myself up for what was certain to be a footballing experience unlike any I had ever had before. Except I wasn't in the team.

I couldn't believe it. Had I misheard Jim? He had said I'd be playing. Well, hadn't he? Okay, so maybe I was on the bench. But no, not there either. And, as I wasn't involved, that meant I couldn't even go into the dressing room before the match to wish the lads good luck. Or, as it turned out, even watch it from the tunnel, having been curtly informed that I wasn't allowed to be in that part of the ground at any time during the game, even though I was one of the club's players! Crazy.

In the end, I got a ticket and went to watch the game from the stands but I couldn't even do that, as, when I got to my seat, someone else was already sitting there. Was I going to argue? No, I couldn't be bothered at that point. Instead, I walked out of the ground and sat in my car, alone in the car park with the commentary on the radio, hoping Mum, Dad, Mike and Tim were enjoying it, even though they'd be wondering and worrying where the hell I was. That just happened to be the car that the club had given me as part of my signing on agreement. A Ford Mondeo that I'd almost knackered driving to Norwich and back on a regular basis, as knackered, it would seem, as my career with Hearts.

I didn't last much longer there as a result. My morale dropped ever lower as I could not, in all honesty, work out why Jim would not give me a run of games in the first team, especially given all the effort he had made to get me up there. As I had originally rebuked him in order to sign for Charlton, you might have thought at that point he'd have wanted nothing more to do with me. Yet he'd sold me the club and the league, assuring me that he had big plans for the club and that I was to play a major part in it. Had he been lying all along, did he actually not mean anything of the sort? Of course not. He would have meant every word. Jim is as honest as they come. Maybe there were issues about me joining the club that he couldn't affect? Maybe some of the senior players didn't feel comfortable with me coming in? Perhaps they thought I'd be on a massive wage and would put it about a bit, wanting this and that and acting like the superstar that I wasn't and never had been? Maybe there was a bit of Scotland and England in it. Who knows. I certainly don't. A case of wrong move, wrong time, wrong club.

I ended up leaving the club by mutual agreement, having spent one and a half seasons with Hearts. It's a shame it never worked out as I desperately wanted it to. The fans were good to me and always patient, but they never got the chance to see the best of me and neither did my teammates. Maybe a lot of expectation came with me? Perhaps they all thought I'd be drilling home 25-yard volleys in every game, Leeds and Munich style? Of course, that never happened. But I did all that I could, and that included running myself into the ground at every training session. I was also, aside from that one injury, as fit as I'd ever been. In fact, I was breaking club records at one point. One of the club's favourite places to go during pre-season training would be Arthur's Seat, the 251-metre-high dormant volcano that's situated within Holyrood Park in Edinburgh, I set the club record for running around it, and maybe it still stands today! But look. I'd have happily swapped that 'record' for fifty first-team appearances and twenty goals to look back on from my time at the club. I'd arrived there determined to make it work and play a part in helping the club towards some success, something that I believed that squad was more than capable of doing. The fact that it didn't happen for me was certainly not for the want of trying or a lack of desire. I was mature enough to know that, sometimes, things just don't work out and that it was time to move on again. The problem was, I wasn't getting any younger.

One constant during the whole of my Scottish footballing experience was Maggie. She was always there for me by my side, always supporting me and lifting me through all of my frustrations. We'd hadn't long been married when I joined the club and Maggie gave up working in her dad's family hotel business to be by my side, and enjoy what was meant to be a happy extension to our honeymoon period.

On one day in particular, just as I was finding it more and more difficult to keep all of my professional frustrations at bay, Maggie told me something that well and truly put all of my worries into perspective, when she happily announced that she was pregnant. Wow, big shock but two very happy faces! However, an even bigger shock was to follow when, a short time afterwards, she had a miscarriage and lost the baby. Oh dear God. This, of course, hit me hard, but forget about me, my thoughts were now with Maggie. Naturally, she was deeply upset, which hurt me even more to see her so sad and distraught. It was a dark and horrible time in our lives and I hated myself for all the pain and hurt that she was going through. It was just not meant to have been like this, we had headed up to Edinburgh, full of excitement, looking forward to what was going be an adventure for a couple of years that was something new and different. Instead of that, we found ourselves dealing with real difficulty and some serious issues that convinced me that me and my obsession with football was the cause of.

Yet out of all of the hurt, Maggie came through it, all that distress and pain were, in time, swept away and she found her strength again, shining through it brighter than any star. She insisted that we carried on with our lives there and enjoy every day of what was still, she insisted, our adventure in Edinburgh. She could, at any time, have returned to Gorleston to be close to her family but no, she chose to smile everyday and stay by my side. This positive reaction to all the anguish that she had just gone through was astonishing, and one of the most impressive things that I have ever experienced in my life. I'm so proud of her and so very lucky to be with her.

During this terrible time, Jim Jeffries, along with Billy Brown and the reserve-team manager, Paul Hegarty, were all wonderfully supportive, showing great compassion and sympathy, something we very much appreciated. So, with that support from the club and Maggie's determination for us to still enjoy ourselves, we did get out and about and enjoy exploring the countryside surrounding the city. I was, however, about to be without a club to play for and I needed to put that right as we needed the regular wage coming in. I made a few phone calls to various people who I knew in the game, one of whom was Terry Yorath, who'd been my manager when I'd been playing for Wales and the person to whom I will be forever grateful, for providing me with the opportunity to become an international footballer. He invited me down to Huddersfield Town where he was the first-team coach under Peter Jackson, their manager. I was lucky enough to know Barry Horne, an old midfield teammate from the Welsh squad who was also at the club then, and was their Captain. Off I went and, after spending some time training with them and playing in a few reserve-team games, the club chairman took me to one side and asked me to come to the ground the next day in order to sign a one-year contract, news which I was delighted to hear.

I duly turned up at Peter Jackson's office the next day to put pen to paper, only to discover that he knew absolutely nothing about the chairman's offer and, in addition, that he didn't want me at the club and that I should to get a deal somewhere else. Well, to say that I went nuts at hearing this news would be an understatement. I had a right go at both Jackson and Terry Yorath, demanding to see the chairman, but they refused to contact him no matter what I said or argued. Eventually, after some more screaming and shouting, mostly from me, I advised them that they had best stick their football club up their respective backsides before storming my way out of the office, ground and Huddersfield. I thought their attitude and behaviour was a disgrace, there had been a complete lack of communication between everyone and, as a result, they completely messed me about. They showed that they really couldn't give a toss about me, their arrogance clear, as they saw me as just a name, a number on a piece of paper somewhere, and one they'd decided that they didn't want after all. But that sort of thing happens in football. Players are seen as commodities rather than people by many, and you just have to take such setbacks on the chin and get on with it.

Early 1998 saw Maggie and I based at her parents' house in Gorleston while I did all that I could to get back into football. I spent a short time training at Colchester United just to keep my fitness up but that's all it was, nothing serious was ever going to come from it. Not long after that, Tony Pulis, who was then manager at Gillingham, asked me to go down there to do a bit of training with them, play some matches and see how things went from there. Naturally, I jumped at the chance, and threw myself into training with them, playing in a few practice matches, but unfortunately, nothing serious came from that either.

Tony Pulis was an interesting character. He was renowned, even then, for absolutely battering his players physically, for getting them as fit as possible. They basically ran all day. His style of play wasn't particularly elaborate either. His game plan was to get the ball into the opponents last third as quickly as possible, to achieve those ends, the full-backs and centre-halves would be ordered to hit 40-yard balls up towards the corner flags before the whole team pushed up to chase the ball or win the knock-downs. It wasn't the prettiest type of football you'll ever see and it can't have been that entertaining for their fans, but it was effective as they won more games than they lost that season. Unfortunately for me, there was nothing going there either, with Pulis telling me that the club wouldn't be offering me any sort of contract. So, once again, I was looking for a new club and someone willing to take a chance on me.

By now, I was beginning to realise that I was in trouble. I'd even had a spell out in China with a short trial at a club called Guangzhou Apollo, while my old Swedish mates at IFK Luleå got in touch with the prospect of me going over there to be their player-coach, something I would have been more than happy to do. The package on offer was nowhere near what I was looking for, however, or even close to something I could reasonably have expected to live on, so, again, that and the opportunity to play in China, swiftly fell by the wayside.

By now, I was thirty-three going on thirty-four, and needed to start asking myself a few serious questions about what I wanted to do in life and the game over the next few years. Was I now past my best and in a situation where it was unlikely that I would ever find another club or, put another way, no club wanted to take a chance on me? Despite the odds now seemingly stacking up against me in that regard, I was still determined to carry on as a player, I remained very fit and was convinced I could impress and do well at a club with no fitness problems, by playing a forty-six-game league season if necessary, no problem.

As I mulled all these thoughts over, Maggie gave me the amazing news that she was pregnant again and not just expecting one baby but two, as we were due to become the very proud mum and dad of identical twins! Fantastic news, although, I was a little bit scared as well. It shouldn't have been that much of a surprise really, as Maggie is a twin, as is my dad, so the odds of the two of us having twins must have been quite high. The news obviously made me even more aware that I needed to get my career up and running again, to find a new club, a new role, anything in the game that would keep me involved, as well as help my fast growing family. What I didn't know at the time was that I would never again sign a contract with any professional football club and that, much more importantly, there would be more personal suffering, agony and misfortune coming our way surrounding Maggie's pregnancy and the subsequent birth as we were both about to be thrown a swerve ball and put through more tribulation and torment.

---

1 Professional Footballers Association – the trade union for professional footballers in England and Wales.

13

Wales

What a player he was. I should also add, one of the smelliest players I have ever played against. In fact, he stank! But one of the best of all time, without a doubt.

The call I got from Terry Yorath to be part of the Welsh international squad was as unexpected to me as much as it was a delight and a pleasure to accept. I jumped at the chance and being English didn't come into it. Terry had been watching me play for Norwich and had clearly liked what he had seen, asking me to join my Norwich teammates Mark Bowen and David Phillips in the squad, and giving me the chance to not only train, but play alongside some of the greatest players in the world at that time, players who would never have been plying their trade alongside me at Norwich, people like Neville Southall, Ian Rush, Mark Hughes, Ryan Giggs and Dean Saunders. What an opportunity! In my first few training sessions, it felt that I was training at somewhere like Liverpool or Manchester United, such were the high standards being applied and the intensity of the training, it was fantastic stuff from beginning to end and I loved every minute.

The biggest difference I noted at international level was the commitment to keeping the ball, retaining possession. Eastern European international sides particularly excelled at this at the time, and they could have hung onto the ball for 5 minutes had they wanted to. Away from home they'd play a sweeper and just knock that ball about between them, making their opponents waste energy and space by chasing after it, before, bang, they'd hit you on the break and, more often than not with the quality of striker they had available to them, they'd score.

Mind you, we had our own superstar striker in Rushie. I'd actually come out of one game that I'd played in feeling sorry for him. Mind you, it was that one at Anfield in 1994, when I scored the last ever goal in front of the old Kop at Anfield. When the game ended and, to my delight, I could hear parts of the crowd chanting my name, I looked across at Rushie and he was trudging off the pitch, head down and looking desperate. And no wonder. That game was all set up for him to score that last ever goal, not me. I thought at the time that he'd give me some stick at the next Welsh squad get-together and he probably did!

There were some great characters in that Welsh squad, really fantastic. The way the really well-known players dealt with stardom, they were so down to earth, so nonplussed about it. We'd be out and about and Ian Rush and Mark Hughes would be surrounded by autograph hunters, so many that they'd need bodyguards. If I hadn't got a Wales tracksuit on, no one would have even known I was a player! They were all a joy to be around, let me give a few a mention.

Neville Southall. Big Nev. I think at the time I was first called up and playing for Wales, in the early 1990s, that he was the best goalkeeper in Britain, no question. I've no doubt Gunny would agree with me on that. He had these incredibly strong arms. He'd stretch them out to the side of his body and we would hit these old Tango balls at him. Whenever one struck his arm or wrist, it wouldn't move, it remained in place and the ball would shoot off at an angle somewhere, that, or he'd punch it miles away. And intimidating? Just a bit. If you were coming in on big Nev, on a one-to-one, you had to be pretty confident about what you were doing as he would rush out of his goal and he would take you out. He intimidated penalty-takers as well. His massive presence would put them off just by being there. I've seen it happen! Amazing. I recall him once not coming in at half-time for a league match against Leeds United, he just sat against his post for all of half-time rather than back to the dressing rooms. Magical stuff. And only Nev could have got away with doing that.

Barry Horne was a special guy. He had a touch of class about him, the way he carried himself, treated other people, looked out for them, including, at the time, the young Giggsy. And he was a good player, one who everyone, even the big names, looked up to. Terry Yorath marked him out as a leader early on and that's exactly what Barry was. So, mind you, was Mark Hughes. For me, he was the ultimate leader in football. He just led by what he did and however he went about it. And what a player – again! You can work your way through his ten best ever goals and they make my few efforts look quite ordinary.

David Williams was one of the coaches I played under at both Norwich and Wales, although I had seen him as more of a player at Carrow Road. He was different class. The way he put the sessions together, the ease with which they ran, the way he explained everything so we knew what was expected of us was a bit different to Mick Wadsworth and his over complicated routines at Norwich. No wonder Dave ended up coaching at Manchester United, I bet he had the respect of each and every one of their players, no question. It didn't matter to Dave who was in his group of lads when he took the national side for training, he could have had the superstars of Rush, Hughes and Giggs, or he might have had the less glamorous players, the other lads like me, shall we say. It didn't matter, the training was always first class, he treated everyone with respect and he got it back.

I was proudly wearing the red shirt of Wales when I played against the best player I have ever faced on a football field without a doubt. Gheorghe Hagi. What a player he was. I should also add, one of the smelliest players I have ever played against.

In fact, he stank! But one of the best of all time, without a doubt. He ran the show in one of the most important games I have ever been involved with, the match between Wales and Romania at Cardiff Arms Park.

It was one of the biggest games in the history of the Welsh international side, for the simple fact that, if Wales won the game, we'd have qualified for the following year's World Cup Finals in the USA. Easier said than done. The Romanians were a class side, they'd beaten us 5-1 in Bucharest where Hagi had us chasing his shadow all night long. But they were far from a one-man team – if only. They also had players like Dan Petrescu, Gica Popescu and Florin Raducioiu, all of them quality individuals.

But we were confident. We also had some great players in our side, those I've already spoken about. Plus some real strength in depth, lads like Andy Melville and Paul Bodin that wouldn't let us down. Added to that were my Norwich teammates, Mark Bowen and David Phillips, both regular starters then. Taff (Bowen) was of a different class and one of the big leaders in the Welsh set up. So yes, it would be tough, but we were confident of winning.

I occasionally replay the match to myself. Rushie was unlucky not to put us ahead early on. That got the crowd going, and what a crowd, 40,000 Welsh fans in full voice was the best thing I've ever experienced. That crowd got going even more when Hagi scored for Romania, his shot squirming in under Neville Southall. Nev has since said he gets fed up with hearing about how Wales' ultimate loss in that game was down to Paul Bodin's penalty miss, saying he should have saved the shot from Hagi. A consumate professional is Nev, taking some of the flack off a teammate even to this day. Dean Saunders equalised for us, and from that moment there was only going to be one team winning and that was us. I came on for Kit Symons early in the second half and got busy, eventually making the run and pass to Gary Speed that saw us get the penalty. Paul Bodin was our designated penalty taker, it wasn't a case of someone like Mark Hughes or Rushie stepping up, Paul was the penalty taker and had something like three out of three for us in previous games. So he was the best bet. Unfortunately, Paul struck it well, too well almost, it thundered off the crossbar and that was a glorious chance gone. We still could have won but it wasn't meant to be, the Romanians started to play a little bit more offensively and could have scored themselves on more than one occasion, before Raducioiu made it safe for them near the end.

Remember how I described what a dreadful, desolate, depressing place the Norwich dressing room was after our FA Cup semi-final defeat to Sunderland? The Wales one after this game was a lot worse. Everyone was silent, heads were down, tears were being shed. Players like Sparky and Ian Rush, who had achieved so much in the game, were inconsolable. They've won and celebrated so much in their careers, but their grief after this game was very clear and very painful. Only a game? Maybe. But people are proud to play for their countries, they love to represent them and they cherish being able to do something for them, even if it is 'only' through sport. Taking Wales to the World Cup finals would have been so special, not just for us, but for football in Wales as a whole, especially as England hadn't managed to qualify. What a chance for a bit of banter that would have been! Indeed, we'd have been the only home nation at the finals, you'd like to think there would have been massive support for us from all around the county, England included. It would have been fantastic.

I made nine appearances for Wales from 1991 through to 1996, five of them (this fact nicely mirrors my early career at Norwich) coming from the substitutes bench. That Romania game is the most memorable one for me. Another good game was one I started, a European Championships qualifying game against Albania in September 1994 that we won 2-0, and during which Ryan Giggs was absolutely outstanding, unplayable.

I'll always look back on my international career with another load of fond memories. I know I only played nine games but I was as proud as everyone whenever I was called up, and always happy to be part of the squad. You couldn't help but learn in the company of such great players and we shared a great team spirit in that squad, superstar and artisans alike. One thing I particularly remember is driving home after squad get-togethers, heading back down the M4 in my car, music on, grinning all over my face and just having to stop so I could phone my dad to say something like 'Hi Dad, just wanted to let you know I shook hands with Mark Hughes this morning and he wished me all the best'.

Lining up on the pitch at Cardiff Arms Park before kick-off, listening to the passionate fans thunder out the Welsh national anthem was one of the most amazing experiences of my life, and certainly one of the proudest. Unforgettable. Being part of that Welsh squad was a magical, unforgettable time and I will always be grateful to Terry Yorath for giving me the opportunity to experience life as an international footballer.

14

Life After Football

I really do class myself as a lucky man to have captured, even if it was for only a few brief moments while whizzing past on my bike, the stunning views of the Austrian mountain ranges and idyllic Bavarian towns and villages. Although, I must admit, I had to put myself through an extreme endurance test to savour such sights.

Football? I'd had enough. I had given my all to earn a contract at Huddersfield only to be mucked about right at the last minute and for all of that to fall through. After the subsequently disappointing experiences I had with Colchester and Gillingham, I was ready to pack it all in. I'd been getting a strong feeling inside me that the time to move on was approaching and, when I took stock of things, I knew that time had arrived. I was more than ready for it. I'd had enough of driving all over the country in order to get a game or the chance of a contract. That lack of motivation meant that my desire had gone and, without any further fuss or bother, and certainly no announcement, I quietly faded away and out of the game I loved.

The possibility of playing in China had been an intriguing prospect and one I couldn't really turn down. A friend of mine had been playing in Hong Kong and mentioned in conversation that they were looking for good players to come to China, and that it might be a very good experience for me. Certainly, there were opportunities to be had out there, even at that time. So I flew out there to have a look, with the intention of fully exploring all of the options surrounding playing professional football in Asia, as well as experiencing what the new lifestyle and culture would have been like. Sadly, it was not to be, as I found the set-up at Guangzhou a little unwelcoming, but it was an interesting life experience and I'd at least given it a go.

Not long after I'd got back from my Asian trip, I was contacted by my ex-Norwich City teammate Tony Spearing. He was playing for non-league Kings Lynn at the time and was wondering if I might like to come and do some training with them, with a view to playing some games. Tony had always been a good friend to me so I didn't really feel as if I could let him down. I agreed to come along for a while and see how things worked out. Gary Mills was their manager at the time and, to be fair, for a semi-professional club, they had a really good set-up, with some decent players in their squad. I certainly coped with the training and running that was involved, and eventually signed a match-by-match deal, something I don't regret doing in the slightest. The harsh truth of it was, however, that I simply wasn't enjoying myself and soon realised it wasn't something that I wanted to be doing at that stage of my life. It ended up being a very short-lived deal and I prepared, once again, to move on, now more certain than ever that my career as a footballer had come to an end.

Matters relating to the game suddenly didn't matter anymore. We'd still not long returned from Scotland and had temporarily settled in temporarily with Maggie's mum and dad, Janet and Rodney Scott. Both had been really supportive to us over those difficult times, and this was another great example of their caring nature. I had no job, no house and no car at that time. It really was a case of 'welcome to the real world Gossy'. Janet and Rodney were, once again, fantastic, by letting us stay with them and providing a roof over our heads while I sorted my life out. What a new life it ultimately turned out to be, for, almost immediately Maggie announced that she was pregnant. Brilliant news, obviously, but what a shock it was to hear that, after her first scan, we would soon be parents to identical twin boys! Excitement, apprehension and fear, all in one. Any Dad would agree to feelings like this.

On Friday 16 October 1998, Maggie, who was twenty-seven weeks pregnant, phoned the local hospital to report that she didn't feel very well. Maggie's pregnancy had gone really well up until this point. Her obstetrician was excellent throughout, making sure her check-ups and examinations were on time and providing an excellent level of personal service throughout. During these examinations, we were always told that everything was fine and normal, which was always a relief to hear. From a very early stage, we knew Maggie was carrying identical twin boys. The expectation of becoming parents was exciting and slightly daunting but very thrilling. Maggie was working at her dad's family business throughout this period but during the last week she had felt slightly uncomfortable, sometimes verging on the side of unwell. She was, and still is, not the type to moan and groan about things, rarely complaining and always saying that she felt fine, no matter what the situation might be. But on this particular night, things were not fine. In fact, they were seriously bad.

During her conversation with the hospital, she was told not to worry, as feeling uncomfortable was considered normal in a twin pregnancy. So, off she went to work, feeling reassured that all was well. However, after work and while she was in bed, her waters broke, even though Maggie was only twenty-seven weeks into her pregnancy. We immediately got her to the James Paget Hospital, which was fortunately a short journey away. The A&E staff quickly admitted her onto the ward and started to run some tests. Maggie was given steroid injections to help the babies' lungs, as well as drugs to slow the contractions.

It all seemed to progress very slowly from here as we stayed on the ward overnight on the Friday and all of the Saturday. It wasn't until the Sunday, when Maggie was scanned, that we were told things were not good and, due to a complication called

Twin to Twin Transfusion Syndrome, the babies had to be delivered as soon as possible. TTTS, as it's more commonly known, only affects identical twin pregnancies.

The boys were sharing the same placenta that contained the blood vessels linking them together. Both should have received an equal share of this placenta enabling them to grow, but in this case, one was receiving insufficient nutrients to grow normally, while the other was gaining too much and being overloaded with blood, something that could cause heart failure. So things were not right at all and were very quickly going to become even more stressful.

Our local hospital, the James Paget Hospital in Gorleston told us that they could not deliver the boys because they had a policy in place that stated that the hospital could not accept premature babies born under twenty-eight weeks gestation. Basically, our sons would be too small and too young for the hospital to be in a position to keep them alive, so another specialist hospital had to be found that had both the facilities and the availability. We were now in a nightmare situation. The longer we waited, the more chance there was of losing one, or even both of our boys.

Eventually, after trying and having no success at either the Norfolk and Norwich Hospital, or Addenbrooke's in Cambridge, we were told that Hinchingbrook hospital in Huntingdon had availability to take us. So, with no time to waste, Maggie and I took our seats in the back of an ambulance and were quickly transported the 100-mile distance from Gorleston to Huntingdon, accompanied by the midwife and paediatrician, in case the twins arrived en route, our journey's urgency emphasised by the ambulance's blue lights flashing and screaming sirens. On arrival at Hinchingbrook, and after a quick consultation with the obstetrician, Maggie was immediately rushed to the operating theatre to undergo an emergency caesarean. There was no way I would let her go through this on her own so I stayed by her side, to comfort her and watch my sons arrive into this world. We were warned by the specialists that the end result may not be good, and that there may well be complications, but at that moment all I could think about was Maggie. I so desperately wanted her to be free from pain and I prayed that she would be OK.

Now, I'm not queasy when it comes to stuff like this, but I have to admit there was a lot going on around Maggie and the operation itself made me swallow quite deeply at times. At one point, the anaesthetist insisted on giving Maggie some oxygen, which she didn't feel she needed, but its function on that occasion was to conceal the smell of burning flesh as the surgeon lasered through her skin. That surgeon certainly didn't hang about and before I knew it, at 6.32 p.m. on Sunday 18 October 1998, Joseph had arrived and was quickly held up, very pink and very small, for both myself and Maggie to see.

Within seconds, the umbilical cord had been cut and he was taken away to be treated and put on oxygen. Two minutes later, at 6.34 p.m., Jacob arrived. Unlike Joseph, he was very blue and very quiet and was immediately taken to the far side of the room where I saw several members of staff quickly surround and treat him, a very worrying sight. It was the culmination of a sudden birth that was over and done with in fifteen minutes; it had all happened so fast. Maggie was then wheeled out of the theatre and placed back on the ward. One minute we had arrived in the hospital and, a quarter of an hour later, we found ourselves the very proud parents of identical twin boys. But nothing in the last forty-eight hours had been natural or normal, and this was not how it should have been. The emergency was a shock to us both, that shock continuing as we didn't get to see the boys until many hours later. Something that immediately gave us obvious reason to be concerned. It wasn't a good time. We had sons but didn't know how they were, or even if they were still alive.

Eventually, after what seemed an eternity, the specialist came into our room and announced that the boys were settled in separate incubators and both were receiving oxygen. He made it quite clear that the boys were in a serious but stable condition, and that we would have to prepare ourselves for 'difficulties' and 'complications' and a long stay in the Special Care Baby Unit. When babies are delivered this early, no one can predict the problems that may suddenly arise, or predict a short-term or long-term outcome. We were just told a worst-case scenario and a best case scenario, and I can assure you that someone telling you a list of problems that may arise is horrible to hear. To hear that your sons, who were just hours old, could develop mental and physical disabilities is a tragic thing to have to listen to. We didn't ask many questions at that point. We just listened, quietly taking in what we were being told, what had happened and what would be happening in the coming hours and days. We were both shocked and upset, but choose to keep all our emotions inside, taking each hour as it came.

A paediatrician talking you through issues was one thing, but to see the boys for the very first time was something else. Absolutely shocking. They were both in separate incubators in the SCBU, both smothered in wires and tubes and both being kept alive by a machine. Nothing could have prepared us for this sight. It was dreadful. Maggie, who had just had a major operation, peered over her sons for the first time with a look of huge concern and worry. She was, as always, trying to stay strong while hiding her upset but I could see in her eyes that she was being emotionally ripped apart by the whole sight. The urgency and seriousness of the situation was obvious to see, and really stamped home the fact that our boys were in a bad way. What made it worse was the fact that a risk of infection meant Maggie wasn't allowed to touch the boys, let alone hold them. All she could do, like me, was to look and stare in amazement at our newborn sons, hoping that they would be strong enough to pull through and praying that they would stay alive. We made a promise to ourselves at that point that no matter what problems the boys developed, we would always be there to care for them and to love them. They were our sons and no matter what the outcome we would always cherish them. And football? That stupid game had completely evaporated from my mind.

One small piece of comfort we had was knowing the boys were in the very best place. The SCBU was equipped with specialist staff, monitoring alarm systems, respiratory and resuscitation equipment and access to physicians in every paediatric speciality, twenty-four hours a day. The sight of this sophisticated equipment was overwhelming and scary. We were thrust into an unknown medical world of specialist equipment and phrases such as bili lights, incubators, central intravenous, oxygen hood, continuous positive airway pressure (C-Cap) and endotracheal tubes. We could do nothing else but put our faith and trust in the staff. Our sons' lives were in their hands.

A six-week stay in Hinchingbrook Hospital followed. We never left the boys for one moment and we slept in a room adjoining the SCBU. Brain scans and blood tests were done on a daily, then weekly basis, and eventually they came off ventilation and began breathing for themselves. Joseph and Jacob weighed in at 2lb 2oz and 2lb 4oz. That, I can tell you, is small. Maggie was eventually allowed to wash the boys with cotton wool and her first experience of feeding them was to press fluids out of a syringe, down a lead and into their bodies. Oral and nasal feeding as it's called. Incredible! But that's how it was done and it got Maggie involved in the care of them both, starting the bond between Mother and sons that she so desperately craved for. This bond was strengthened when the boys were taken out of their incubators, still attached to wires and tubes, and placed on Maggie's bare chest. Now she could hold them, hug them and get close to her boys. The nurses called it 'skin to skin' or 'kangaroo care'. It was emotional to see but a sign of good progress. We got into daily routines and the lads became stronger. Chronic lung disease was the big immediate problem but slowly they were improving. One day, Albert Cadmore, the vicar who conducted the marriage service between Maggie and me, unexpectedly arrived at the hospital. He sat us down and chatted for a while, before spending some time with the boys by the side of their incubators. It was lovely thing for Albert to have done. He had travelled a long way to come and see us, and no doubt he said a few prayers fpr the boys that day. As did Rodney and Janet, Maggie's mum and dad, who made continued trips up to see us from Gorleston. My parents also made the long trip up from Folkestone. Their support and comfort was effective and very much needed.

Joseph and Jacob grew strong enough to be transferred back to the SCBU in the James Paget Hospital, Gorleston, and after a three-week stay, we were eventually allowed to take them both home. The whole experience had been traumatic, distressing and very upsetting, but with all the love, care and attention given to them by so many different people, the boys found the strength to pull through. I firmly believe that they could feel the love that Maggie and I were giving them. I believe it helped and made a huge difference. They wanted to live and they wanted to be with us.

Maggie and I and are so very grateful to the staff of both Hinchingbrook Hospital and the James Paget in Gorleston. They, through their dedication and expertise, helped our sons recover from a life-threatening situation. We, and the boys, will be eternally thankful.

Football now became irrelevant, and for the next year and half I devoted all my time and energy, along with Maggie, to being with our boys. To this day, we have not missed a moment of their lives. We love them dearly and our whole life's objective is to guide them, support them and be there for them as they grow up in this fascinating world of ours. The overwhelming love I have for my family is so strong, so binding, it's sometimes indescribable. I am so proud to say that at the time of writing this book, both Joseph and Jacob are very strong and healthy young men of fifteen who have already achieved so much in their young lives, including, on a sporting front, reaching a Norfolk County standard of table tennis. What proud parents we are.

Margaret was so strong during that time, there for the boys just as she is now, as she always has been. She completes my life and means everything to me. She rarely moans or grumbles about anything, and has always supported me no matter what I have been doing with my life. I can honestly say that getting married was the best thing I ever did in my life and, despite all that has happened in my life, all those wonderful moments and occasions, there is nothing better than spending a Saturday together. They are days, memories past and moments to come that I want to ring fence forever. And to think, I might easily not have gone out for a few beers with the lads after that game at Highbury a few years previously.

It's certainly no surprise to me that the best and most successful time of my sporting career coincided with the time I first met Maggie, at Chicago's, in Norwich that evening. She was an inspiration to me, and the joy she gave me, coupled with the love and admiration I felt for her, transformed me, both as a person and as a player. Thus, 20 November 1994 will be a day I remember forever, as that was the day Maggie and I got married at St Mary's church in Sisland, which is around 10 miles south-east of Norwich and only a mile or so away from Loddon, where we lived at the time. Our marriage was a big surprise to everyone who knew us as we made it a very private occasion with only our immediate family members attending. No best man, no flamboyant ceremony and certainly no over-the-top reception. That sort of thing just isn't me, and it's certainly not Maggie.

All that mattered to us was being married. We loved each other and just wanted to celebrate quietly with no fuss or bother. And it was everything we'd hoped, a meaningful, momentous and special day. And our feelings for each other are as strong now as they were then. Yes, the last twenty years have, like all marriages, been a roller coaster with lots of ups and downs, and we've had to work hard together to cope with some of the issues that life throws at you, its myriad problems and difficulties, but we've stood strong together throughout. For the last fifteen years, we have had the wonderful experience of being Mum and Dad to our beautiful sons, Jacob and Joseph, providing a loving, happy and stable family home for them.

Naturally, I couldn't not tell the lads we'd got married. So, on the Monday after the wedding, I took twenty-four bottles of champagne into training, calling everyone together to inform them of our marriage the day before. Both teammates and coaching staff were shocked. In fact, I think they might have been less shocked if I'd announced that I'd won the lottery! We all drank some champagne together, toasted our marriage and then went off to be put through one of the hardest running sessions I have ever known – there were never any excuses for not training hard!

Great days. Playing for the club I loved at the peak of form and fitness. Having ended my arrangement with Kings Lynn, I took stock of things and wondered what on earth I was going to do next. Because, from a working point of view, now I'd decided to pack up playing, I needed a job. Football hadn't made me a wealthy man by any stretch of the imagination. Yes, it had meant a few years of earning an 'all right' wage but, even so, I was nowhere near the highest-paid player at Norwich. We would have had one of the lowest wage bills in the top division when I was there, with much of the money we earned coming through a bonus scheme that was, to be fair, one of the better ones in football at the time. This meant your monthly wage could be boosted up a bit if you won matches. It was an incentive scheme that did exactly what it was meant to do. It motivated everyone that little bit more to get the win. If we won one game, we'd get £250, win the next, £500, then £1,000, and so on and so forth.

I remember going to sign a new contract with Norwich not long into our first Premier League season and, after I had done so, the chairman, Robert Chase told me, 'Congratulations, Jeremy, you are now the best-paid player at this football club.' The best paid player at the football club with the initials JG maybe, and I told him so. 'With respect Mr Chairman, I'm not the best-paid player at this football club. You know it and I know it.' But he would never have it! As I've already said, you never talked the cold hard facts about money and your salary with your mates, but, one way and another, you get to know what people are on, and I knew I was miles away from what some of the lads were earning. It didn't make me resentful or jealous. That was just the way it was at the time and I accepted it. Like my dad always said, if I'd been a bit nastier, a bit more self-assured, maybe I would have earned more, either at Norwich or elsewhere. Even so, I didn't regret anything and that remains the case to this day.

In the end, I got an invitation from Norwich City to come and work at the club. I really needed a job so I will always be grateful to my mate Bryan Gunn for giving me the opportunity to work at Carrow Road. Gunny was, at the time, the club's sponsorship salesman, and together with Andrew Cullen, agreed that it would be good to have me join the commercial team. This was a great opportunity for me to earn again and provide for my family. However, after a short time, I began to hate the role. For a start, I found the transition from professional sport to an office-based job very difficult to take and often felt like a schoolboy, having to learn and relearn things all over again. It was my first experience of using PCs, laptops, emails, faxes and making and taking business phone calls, all things I really struggled to get my head around.

After all, I'd been used to my working days being spent outside, that had been all I had known for almost all of my life. Yet here I was now, trapped in an open-plan office from 9 a.m. till 5 p.m. with a suit and tie on. I couldn't get to grips with that, nor the heat, the inactivity, or, indeed, the job description! Now I know that what I am describing has got you thinking 'hey tough, Gossy, welcome to the real world', and I realise that is exactly how millions of people spend their daily lives, but please, just try putting yourself into my (nice, new, shiny, black) shoes, mine and the thousands of other former professional sportspeople who have had to adjust and adapt overnight in a similar fashion. I'm telling you now; it's very tough mentally to do that.

I felt as if I had started a brand new life and that football had never happened.

Now, my attitude with the job at the club was always professional and I always gave my absolute all, doing my very best and with a smile on my face. After all, it was Norwich City FC, the club I loved dearly, but underneath it all, I hated it. So I swallowed my pride and thought only of the wage I'd receive at the end of every month, as I still needed the work to pay the mortgage.

Gunny, on the other hand, was magnificent. He'd made that adjustment brilliantly. He is a very strong man, who was incredibly successful working behind the scenes at the club, a great man-manager and motivator who inspired those around him with his confidence and assurance in the role. He was always positive, always optimistic and, most of all, was always encouraging, just as he was as a player. Gunny is someone I respect and admire greatly.

Not long after I left my commercial role at the club, my old midfield playing partner Ian Crook, the club's reserve-team coach at the time, rang me to ask if I wanted to join him to help coach the reserves. I immediately agreed. It was a great opportunity to get back to Colney training centre and get involved with the football side of things again. I knew that would never lead to anything permanent but it was nice of Chippy and the manager at the time, Paul Lambert, to invite me to join the coaching staff, even if it was just for a short time. I got to know Paul Lambert fairly well during my time back at the club and have to say that he was an excellent man manager who had a stack full of passion for the game and the club. It's certainly come as no surprise to me that he was as successful at Norwich as he was. As for my old mate Chippy, well, as a footballer, he was brilliant, one of the very best-and as a coach, he was the same. I thought he was magnificent as a coach and manager and really enjoyed working alongside him and the reserves. But as I have already said, a permanent job was never going to come out of the role and, with Chippy moving back to Australia at the end of that 2009/10 season, I moved on again, searching for another new role for myself.

On 1 October 2010, I was fortunate enough to meet Julie Lythgoe, the assistant director of a local Norfolk charity called the Norfolk and Norwich Association for the Blind (NNAB). She, in turn, introduced me to their director, John Child, who offered me a role as the charity's chief fundraiser. I was amazed at the genuine sincerity of both these people and their staff, and the charity's utter dedication to helping local adults and children who were either blind or visually impaired. I was also introduced to an excellent fundraiser, and now good friend, Donna Minito, and I soon realised that what I saw around me amazed and inspired me, so I took up their offer. Sport seemed nothing compared to this charity and the work it was doing, work that was so real and made a difference to people's lives. I immediately knew that any help that I could give would be both meaningful and rewarding. It made me think differently about people and what direction I wanted to take in my life. The NNAB, which is based in Norwich, was founded in 1805, and is dedicated to providing high quality accommodation and care for blind and partially-sighted people throughout Norwich and Norfolk as a whole, as well as offering educational and recreational facilities plus community visiting services throughout the county. My role was simple. I was entrusted with raising money for the charity but also raising its public profile, making people more aware of what it did, how it did it, and how it might be able to help a family member or friend who could be suffering from sight-related issues.

The first big project that I created, managed and participated in was called 'Gossy's Back to Bayern', a sponsored cycle challenge, which took place on 3 August 2011. The premise was simple. I'd 'get on my bike' and cycle from Norwich, via Arnhem in Holland, through to Munich and the Olympic Stadium where I scored 'that goal', against Bayern Munich in 1993, before cycling down into Italy, finishing the ride off at the San Siro stadium in Italy, the scene of Norwich's last game in our UEFA Cup journey that year, a 1,500-mile solo ride for which I would seek both individual and corporate sponsorship, with every penny raised going to NNAB funds.

It was a colossal project to organise, never mind to undertake, and was a challenge that was as hard as any I've faced in my life, but which I absolutely loved. I really do class myself as a lucky man to have captured, even if it was for only a few brief moments while whizzing past on my bike, the stunning views of the Austrian mountain ranges and idyllic Bavarian towns and villages; although I must admit, I had to put myself through an extreme endurance test to savour such sights.

It took me eleven days to complete the journey, covering, on average, 110 miles per day. The challenge took me through five countries, as well as some particularly gruelling mountain passes. As I went over the Alps, I did wonder if I'd make it in one piece! The very last leg of my journey was a spectacular run from the shores of Lake Garda to Milan, taking place in temperatures that peaked at 34°C!

Accompanying me every painful inch of the way was my really good mate and former Norwich goalkeeper Mark Walton, who drove our back-up motor home as well as acting as navigator, masseuse, chef and a whole host of other responsibilities. He was magnificent, providing wonderful support, looking after me throughout the journey and keeping my morale up whenever the going got tough – which it frequently did! Together we completed a very special challenge and the end result made a real difference to other people's lives. It was all worth it, as in total we managed to raise £34,000 for the NNAB, a remarkable total and a testimony to the generosity and support of all the individuals, organisations and businesses that supported me and the charity throughout. I also take my hat off to the ten local people who cycled with me for a short while on day one, including local MP Normal Lamb, as well as those who turned up and gave me such a great send off from Norwich Cathedral.

Naturally enough, once that had all finished and my legs had stopped aching, I wanted to do something else. I wanted to do something that maybe surpassed the bike ride in its scale, and got other people involved, something that they could do alongside me and, in doing so, get their own sponsorship and interest. The answer to that particular question laid in the opening credits of the James Bond film, *GoldenEye,* when 007 leaps from its towering heights in a bungee-assisted plunge of 220 metres (that's around 720 feet, or more than twice the height of the spire of Norwich Cathedral). And it was while travelling back from Milan, having completed the Back to Bayern event, along with Maggie, Joseph and Jacob, that we happened to drive quite close to Locarno in Switzerland where the dam was built. I wanted to do the jump there and then, but Maggie suggested that I wait and use the jump as a fundraising event, which was a great idea. I then planned to invite other thrill-seeking individuals to join me on what would be the plummet of a lifetime. This is how 'Gossy's Leap of Faith' came to be born!

The statistics of the jump from the top of Verzasca are mind blowing. You freefall for 8 seconds at speeds that peak at 75 mph, with the first recoil (the bit that snatches you straight back up again as you reach the limit of your fall) taking you straight back up again for 100 metres. What an experience and what an opportunity to maybe 'top' the Back to Bayern bike ride, by not only jumping off myself but finding nineteen people to do it with me – though not all at the same time! I had little trouble in getting a party together and we all headed out to Switzerland to do just that. And you know what? I absolutely loved it.

Twenty of us went and twenty people jumped, despite the fact there were some serious nerves on display at breakfast. The first view you get of the dam, as you travel up the narrow roads to get there, was probably enough for a few people to want to lose whatever breakfast they'd had, even before they stood on the edge and looked down for the first time. It was exhilarating and magnificent.

I was so proud of everyone who travelled with me. In total, we raised a staggering £35,000, all of which helped improve the quality of other people's lives. It doesn't get much better than that. I do feel very fortunate to have met and befriended twenty-five genuine, sincere and passionate people who were willing to confront indisputable personal fears for the sake of the NNAB. The wonderful memories created during our time together, the awe-inspiring sight of the Verzasca dam and the feeling of peace, silence and tranquillity that accompanied the jump will remain with me forever.

It is a wonderful and very personal experience with such commendable local charity. My focus and drive is always centered around raising money to aid and assist Norfolk's visually impaired, and blind adults and children. My time spent there is always exceptionally rewarding. Each day gives me the opportunity to experience something so very real and special in my life.

I look back at my life now and I'm amazed at what I've experienced. I've played professional football against, and alongside, some of the very best players in the world at both club and international level, and in some of the very best stadiums in the world as well. During that UEFA Cup run of 1993/94, I was arguably part of the best squad in the history of Norwich City. I scored great goals for the club and, compared to many other players, had a little taste of life in the football spotlight, the big time. To have represented Norwich City and Hearts was really something, but on top of that, to have won England Under-19 and senior Welsh international caps was a huge personal triumph. The football banter has been a joy to have experienced. Players need to be happy, to be playing well, and many lads, the comics in the side have produced some hilarious moments. Step forward Mark Bowen, Ian Crook, Trevor Putney and Andy Linighan, great players but also great comics. Thank you lads for making me chuckle and giggle so much during your brilliant storytelling and one-liners. I so badly miss that type of changing room humour.

I've pushed my body to its limits physically and mentally, in an attempt to reach my full potential. While this was something I believe I never achieved, my natural passion and enthusiasm for football, sport and life itself still carried me a long way. I've made stupid mistakes, wrong decisions and, at times, tried too hard, but it's all been part of a learning curve in my quest to be the very best I can.

Yes, I have been, on occasion, too much of a nice guy for my own good, but you can't change who you are, and I'm proud and content to be just me, all the character traits included. I haven't got a million pounds stashed away in the bank like many people believe I have, but I have got memories and achievements that money will never buy. I've always wanted to be regarded as someone who made a difference, someone who you could trust and have faith in, someone who wouldn't let you down, and I hope that the brilliant fans of Norwich City have that opinion of me. In this book, I've mentioned that I was not the best or the most talented of players, but I was the one who tried the hardest and ran the furthest for the Canary cause. I had heart and determination because I knew the true meaning of wearing that yellow and green shirt, the history, culture and heritage of the club, and what the fans expect and demand of the players, for them to see fight and passion and a huge desire want to win. Those fans have helped give me so many memorable and special times, and I thank each and every one of them.

In my life so far, I've made some unbreakable friendships with both teammates and work colleagues but, most of all, I delight in the fact that I am sat here, writing this now, surrounded by the best family anyone could ever wish for and a wife and two sons who I idolise. Wow, how lucky am I?

The running theme of this book was 'your time will come'. Eventually, after a lot of hard work, my time did come. and you know what, it's still at my doorstep now. Wow, I am enjoying every second, it's so good to be alive! But what of the future? Well, I'm sure it will take on many more twists and turns, but one thing I am certain of is that the biggest priority in my life will always be Maggie, Joseph and Jacob. I'm so very proud of my boys who had such a terrible and traumatic start in life. It's been a joy to have loved and cared for them and an incredible experience to have watched them grow into big, strong young men who excel at table tennis, their own chosen sport. I will be there for them, alongside Maggie, every day.

I sleep well at night because when I look back I know I gave my all in everything I've tried to achieve. I've never cheated anyone. I'm a family man who appreciated the little things in life. Yes, I've been stupid at times and crazy at others, but I've approached life with honesty and endeavour and done the very best I could. I only hope it was enough.

EPILOGUE 1

My Mate Gossy

by Mark Walton, Norwich City FC, 1989–93

This scene became hilarious, as Dave Stringer was being calm and professional while Jeremy was vigorously putting his case forward, clad in only a pair of Speedos.

Jeremy Goss introduced himself to me in the summer of 1989 at Norwich City's former training ground at Trowse. True to his character, it was simple and full of warmth, a godsend. I was the new boy, having just joined the club from Colchester United and now reporting, as instructed, for pre-season training. The first-team squad had departed for a tour of Scandinavia, which meant the training ground was inhabited by an assortment of apprentice professionals, reserve-team players and those in the process of returning from injury.

My insecurities and lack of confidence had stopped me entering the senior changing room, which was situated on the right-hand side of the changing complex. I opted to change with the apprentices, primarily because I was racked with self-doubt, but also because I felt safer in there and wanted to feel my way into the club gently rather than going in with a bang.

As it stands, there was never a bang, but things still happened quite quickly. I opted to do some weight training and was just beginning to work out on my own until a fit looking blond lad entered the room, shook my hand vigorously and introduced himself. We chatted briefly before getting on with what we were there to do. Through our conversation, it transpired that he was recovering from a hernia operation and was on the road to rehabilitation. He then informed me that my changing spot was next to his in the senior changing room, our bench labelled, from left to right, Colin Woodthorpe, John Polston, Ian Culverhouse, Jeremy, myself and Ian Crook.

Thus, my integration into the room and group was made a lot easier by Jeremy's offering of the hand of friendship, which blossomed then and is still strong to this very day. A multitude of events have passed in both our professional and personal lives, but one of the pleasing aspects throughout is that Jeremy's boyish nature burns as brightly as ever. I feel genuinely lucky to have a met such a good man, one who is upstanding, self-effacing, family-orientated, respectful of others, honest and full of integrity while, at times, being ever so slightly off the wall.

Our friendship revolved around the game that we loved, the game that we were committed to intensely and passionately. Football consumes you like nothing else imaginable, there is a slogan that proclaims 'live it, eat it, breathe it'. Multiply this by ten and you will have some idea of the intensity that being involved in professional sport is all about. It is so intense that there has to be a release valve option to this pressure-cooker life, and I freely admit that the lid came off my own on more than one occasion, times when I actively encouraged others to join me. Jeremy was one of those who willingly did just that.

I remember a long trip that the club took to the Cayman Islands where, to relieve the boredom, we all settled down for some liquid intake while watching a few films. One film that struck a note was *The Field*, which starred Richard Harris and John Hurt, their characters known as 'Bull' and 'Bird' respectively. Gary Megson decided, at that point, that Jeremy and I should also be known by those names, which were very apt at the time. Hence I became 'Bull' and Jeremy was 'Bird', names which our close friends still call us today.

Jeremy's love of running is legendary. One story that nicely reflects this happened one wintry night when the two of us decided to take a trip from his cottage on the outskirts of Norwich into the city. Wednesdays were a popular night among the players as the city tended to be quite busy on those occasion. It was also our last opportunity in the week to be able to go out, so we'd make the most of it. Into the city we went, calling first at the preferred watering hole of the time ,which was Hector's House. We followed this by visiting a jazz bar in Tombland, before spending an hour or so in a nightclub. As the evening wore on, it started to snow rather heavily, leading us to decide that we had better head off home, as we didn't want to be stranded in the city overnight. Thus, with our trusted friend and non-drinking chauffeur Rusty at the wheel of Jeremy's club car, we set off through the countryside. Unfortunately for us, the snow had made the roads somewhat slippery and, after one skid too many, we ended up in a ditch on a country lane near Beighton, at least 3 feet in the ditch to be precise. We all got out and decided to manhandle it back onto the road, which we were unable to come even close to achieving.

So there we were, 4 or so miles away from Jeremy's home and stuck in a blizzard. It was not a problem for him, he happily suggest that we run back, not a problem at all for him, in fact it was an unexpected treat if anything. For me, however, it wasn't such a good idea as I was rather a pedestrianised mover. Jeremy, of course, was in his element, a chance to display his fitness in challenging conditions while at the same time, helping somebody else finish. With his help we eventually got back to his place. He was invigorated while I was exhausted! Meanwhile, the car had to be attended to, so we decided to wake early and walk back with a shovel each to free his club Peugeot 309. We eventually got there and diligently went about our work, but had no luck as it was going to need some mechanical manoeuvring to get the car free. We eventually had some good fortune when a local farmer passed by in his tractor who was more than willing to pull the car free. We duly offered grateful thanks before clearing the car of any remaining snow and driving off to training to present ourselves in our usual timely and professional manner!

As for Rusty, well, we didn't see him again for a few days and never worked out how he got home! I often get asked by close friends if I am jealous of today's footballers and their earning power? In response, I can honestly say that I have not one dot of envy regarding their lifestyle and salaries. And good luck to them. Players were, for so long, grossly underpaid so I now hope they fill their boots with the sort of financial reward that secures their families' future. I had the good fortune to play in a time when media coverage was non-intrusive, mobile phones were in their infancy and social media was non-existent. Players had room to enjoy themselves without any repercussions or follow-ups, opportunities that gave us a lot of time and scope to have a good time together

Following one final game of a long season, we all flew off to Marbella with prominent liquid refuelling being taken by all and sundry on the bus. This led to Jeremy and I deciding, as roommates, that we wouldn't wash for the entire trip other than going into the pool for a swim, our challenge now to combine a fun-filled week with an odour-filled one. Needless to say, Jeremy decided to take this a step further by not brushing his teeth for the entire week!

But this was tame stuff – the icing on the cake was to come. So, after more well-deserved end of season liquid refreshments, we all broke into Rob Ullathorne's room, Jeremy proceeding to tip out the contents of Rob's brand new golf bag all over the floor. He then selected a four iron and began to hit ball after ball, as perfectly as you like, from Rob's bed out of the opened patio windows, an impressive enough feat in itself, until you add the fact that Rob's clubs were for a left hander and Jeremy is a right-handed player! Ball after ball shot into the distance and onto, we thought, a bare hillside covered in rocks. Hours later, we'd all changed and got ready for a night on the town, calling a cab to take us there from the hotel. As we left, one of the lads asked if the driver could close his window, his answer was that he couldn't as it was broken, due to the fact that a golf ball had appeared 'out of nowhere' earlier in the day and smashed that window, his story ending with an accompaniment of hoots and giggles galore.

Another club trip involved a tour to Sweden. And, as was the habit of the club, they'd found us all another hot spot to stay in. A beautiful hotel with a nightclub and casino, lots of live music and lively bars for us to visit, as well as a garden of delights for the average jaded footballer. With such a feast of delights on offer, it was a trip that has yielded up many stories, one of which was the tale of the infamous sauna seven.

After training or playing in Scandinavia, it was commonplace not to shower but to have a dip in a lake before retreating to a sauna. A few of us decided that we would do just that, except we'd have the regime in the hotel and swap the lake for the shower in the sauna room. Now, I have had some genuinely great times with various teammates but this was one to behold. Joining Jeremy and myself were Robert Fleck, Rob Newman, Colin Woodthorpe, Ian Butterworth, Ruel Fox and David Phillips, all of us there from the start with other members of the team intermittently joining us.

Anyway, the old chestnut of 'fancy a beer?' became prevalent in the conversations. As we had a game the next day, as well as dinner to make at the designated time that evening, it wasn't the best of ideas to get started immediately. So, of course, we did, and around 3 hours later there was pandemonium in the sauna area, the lads well and truly hitting the straps, building memories which, even now, bring tears to my eyes! The orders were going out fast now and not only for beer, but wine, vodka and Bacardi, the sauna was now the location of a full-blown jolly boys outing.

There soon ensued a discussion that became both heated and passionate. Each player in the sauna had to pick his team for the first game of the season. As he did, that individual was questioned, sometimes aggressively, about the reasons why he hadn't picked certain people in the room. It all started to get quite noisy and we could now apparently be heard by the rest of the players, who were further down the corridor, and we were getting louder! We've missed the aforementioned team dinner, hence a visit by Dave Stringer, who asked us if we had been drinking? We all state our guilt before Jeremy decides to give the gaffer a good talking to, suggesting to him that it was a disgrace that other players were being picked before him and that he should be starting the season. This scene became hilarious as Dave Stringer was being calm and professional, while Jeremy was vigorously putting his case forward, clad in only a pair of Speedos! Dave had managed to work out that we were all in that sauna because, as he sat at the bar relaxing with other club officials, he observed a waitress load up a tray with ten pints of beer and head off out of the room to an unknown destination. Dave never thought for one moment all of those beers would be for his players, but, after watching the waitress depart for the sixth or seventh time with the beers, decided to follow her just to ensure all was as it should have been and we players were all settled in our rooms. Dave subsequently entered the sauna behind the waitress only, to his horror, to be greeted by the sight of most of his team entering a state of severe chaos, madness and confusion.

Jeremy and I played in lots of reserve-team games for Norwich, most of which took place on a Friday night. We would play the game, then, along with another couple of players, be provided with a car so we could all make our way to the hotel where the first team would be playing the following day. People will be surprised at this arrangement today but it was standard practice for us and we just got on with it. As you may have guessed, however, these journeys were never straight forward and occasionally turned out to be great fun.

One particular journey was heading from Carrow Road on the Friday night and down to the first-team hotel in Croydon where they were based, prior to their game against Crystal Palace the next day. Our foursome was Jeremy, Rob Newman, Daryl Sutch and myself, all sorted out and on our way down the A140 towards Ipswich. On the way, we decided to make a quick and convenient pit stop at the

Old Ram in Tivetshall St Mary for some refreshments. As luck would have it, David and Peter Thomas, friends of both Rob and me, were already insitu having a quick half. We all got chatting and, after a few more drinks, David and Peter decided to challenge Jeremy to a quick fitness test, one that incorporated press-ups on the bar floor; triceps dips with the aid of two bar stools and, as a grand finale, some full bodyweight pull-ups using the 200-year-old beams that were conveniently positioned above our heads.

Jeremy, who, as our driver, was not drinking, gladly accepted the challenge. After all, this sort of strength and endurance thing was right up his street. Twenty minutes later, he stepped away from yet another victory, accompanied by loud cheers and applause from the other guests in the bar. This enjoyment inevitably delayed our departure, which eventually saw us arrive at the first-team hotel at around 3 a.m., Jeremy having done a sterling job behind the wheel. This little pit stop turned into a regular occurrence on future trips after this and much fun was always had.

In truth, we didn't need too many excuses as players to have a little celebration or two, and when it came to birthdays, we needed little persuading to do something to mark the occasion. On one of mine, I ended up with Jeremy at Barham Broom Golf Club where, on the spur of the moment, we'd gone to have a game. He'd arranged to hire a buggy as well as some clubs, and a nice relaxing game of golf seemed in order as a birthday celebration for yours truly, with nothing untoward or dramatic likely to happen, for once. Or so we thought. Jeremy had also arranged for the buggy to be filled with associated liquid goodies. Thus, after about eight or nine holes, our games had began to suffer and, under the influence of alcohol and with string sunshine on our backs, we began to invent our own golfing rules, such as running up to the ball for our drives and seeing if we could hit it on the run. Another new rule introduced was throwing the ball around the holes rather than using the clubs. Difficult, different, but fun! By the time we got in, we were both feeling a little under the weather so there was really only one thing left to do ... get a taxi and head off into the city.

One fun day that I shared with Jeremy and Rob Newman involved meeting at Hectors House in Norwich for a long lunch. Our ultimate destination was Jeremy's then girlfriend's (now wife, Margaret) twin sisters' wedding, a big day for her and a huge one for Jeremy, as it meant he'd be meeting her family for the first time.

Having had lunch, we then needed to get to Great Yarmouth for the wedding, this meant calling, once again, upon the reliable services of our good friend and chauffeur Rusty to get us there. He'd promised to acquire his company's limousine for the day, something that greatly excited the three of us as we'd never travelled in one before. Imagine, therefore, our faces when he turned up with a quite magnificent Ford Granada that looked as if it had just come off the set of *The Sweeney*!

This swiftly brought us down to earth but, to be honest, also suited us a lot more than any show of flamboyance would have. Off we went but, after a few miles, a quick break for some bladder relief was in order. This is when things started to get interesting, as Jeremy and Rob started to indulge in a little wrestling, wrestling that was on and down a wet and very steep, grassy bank. It was all playful stuff but their clothes were very much the worse for wear as we got back into the car and headed to the wedding reception. When we eventually arrived, I have to say, the look on people's faces was priceless. Margaret, Jeremy's future wife, came to greet us, and while we were full of confidence, we did look rather shabby. Grass and mud stains adorned our elbows, backs and knees and we were rather more in tune with the celebrations than the rest of the more sober wedding party, so we became its life and soul! And Jeremy obviously made a good impression on Margaret's family anyway, as they were married themselves not long afterwards, so all's well that ends well!

In closing, I think it's important to step away from the fun and games and reflect on our respective lives after football and our friendship. What do I see in this man? Well, unfortunately I do not see enough of him and his family. The distance between us is sizeable and modern life sometimes makes it difficult to catch up in person. What I do see in Jeremy is a man of black and white, things are either right or wrong, maybe a trait that his military upbringing has given him. He does not suffer fools gladly but he will always give everybody the time of day, and happily chat to them about football and life. I also see a fun-loving, life-loving man who loves him family deeply. I think he loves the human condition and the many different personalities that it throws up and is happiest talking to people about their lot and just chewing the fat! We have both matured, and spending a few weeks with Jeremy on his charity bike ride was not only a privilege but actually seems to have heightened our friendship.

There has probably been much written about Jeremy, but the one thing that has stayed a constant with him is his quest for fitness and his desire to push himself physically to the absolute limit. During the bike ride, Jeremy's commitment, mental strength and resilience was astonishing. It was humbling to see a man give so much to the cause and complete 10/11 hours a day in the saddle without moaning or complaining. This was the perfect environment, a challenge that tested him physically and mentally, and with no one to help him. He had to just get on with it, and his strength of character shone through.

And it did shine through, as bright as a beacon. That was, and is, the Jeremy Goss that I admire; no bullshit, no nonsense. Just fight for the cause and battle against the odds.

EPILOGUE 2
by Rob Newman, Norwich City FC, 1991–98

Gossy's incredible, I've never met a character like him in my life. He's 100 per cent devoted to everything that he does, and if he can't get total satisfaction out of that, he's not happy. He's told the story about how he had to move the logs in here, hasn't he? That was extraordinary. They were big, big logs; they would have been very heavy and there were lots of them. He looks at them and says, 'I reckon I can move all of them, it will give me as much pleasure as any football challenge.'

And he did. He just loves a challenge; he loves to test his character and strength – physical or emotional. He likes to do things because they are difficult, rather than because they are easily achievable. And he's still doing the difficult things – the cycle ride to Munich and Milan, jumping off that dam. It's what he does. In training, he would push himself to the absolute limit every time, he wouldn't back off at all. Even on a Friday, when we might be holding back in a little preparation for the match the next day, there he would be, still giving it all – no let up and no rest. Then he would want to do some more!

When he was feeling a little bit disallusioned about his football career, he wasn't content to just go through the motions. He said he wanted to run around the world. And he would have done. Another thing he said he was going to do was grow a massive beard (like the ones on the two lads from ZZ Top) buy a Harley Davidson and ride from one side of the United States to the other.

Character-wise, he is a fantastic person to be around. When I signed for the club in 1991, he had no reason to want to know me. I played the same position as him, and you couldn't have blamed him if he'd disliked me for that. But no, he was friendly and there for me straight away. No animosity at all.

He's done a lot in the game, and in life, but as always, he is very modest. He's become a personality because of his football, and because of that people want to listen to him. I've seen him make presentations and speeches and he is very good at it – but then he excels at whatever he turns his hand to.

He was my roommate at Norwich and we saw a lot of things together! I really enjoyed his company and having him around, both as a valued and respected teammate and friend – then and now. He's a top man.

Acknowledgements
by Edward Couzens-Lake

Jeremy Goss again! Unbelievable stuff. Well, when he scores goals they're either spectacular or important, and that one's both.

Of all the Norwich City related books I've had the tremendous privilege to write, it's fair to say that, from day one, this one has probably been the most enjoyable for me. Much of that is down to the veritable army of people and organisations who have helped and supported Jeremy and myself in turning this book from a much discussed idea into reality.

My deepest and most sincere thanks and appreciation are therefore due to the following:

Tom Furby, Hazel Cochrane and everyone at Amberley Publishing for backing us and the book from the beginning. Mick Dennis for writing the foreword, as well as all of the support he so freely gives. Margaret Goss and everyone at The Pier Hotel in Gorleston, for making it such a splendidly calm 'home from home' for me whenever I was in Norfolk working on the book with Jeremy. Tim Williams, Siofra Connor, Chris Lakey and Diane Townsend at Archant. I am also hugely grateful to Archant for giving us permission to use some of their photographs in the book – including that very famous picture of Gossy on the cover!

Rob Butler, Chris Goreham and Matt Gudgin at BBC Radio Norfolk. Chris Rusby and everyone in the wonderful book department at Jarrold. Gary Gowers at www.myfootballwriter.com. Paul McVeigh at ThinkPRO and Roger Harris for some wonderful photographs, likewise to David McDermott for his own remarkable collection of Canary-related photos.. Mark Walton and Rob Newman for their recollections on a life spent playing alongside Gossy, on and off the pitch. Peter Rogers and Norwich City FC. A whole host of good friends and fellow Canaries, including Karen Buchanan, Mike Carroll, Chris Elliott, Paul King, Mats Lygrell, Simon Moston (even though he's a Coventry City supporter!), Nigel Nudds and Russ Saunders. And, most of all, to Jeremy Goss; a fine player, a decent man and a good friend.

Acknowledgements
by Jeremy Goss

My thanks and appreciation are due to many people. My personal achievements and successes in my last forty-eight years are due to those who have offered me their hand of support and given me a chance in life. People who have trusted me, believed in me and, by doing so, given me the opportunity to excel and experience wonderful and magical moments.

To the twelve football managers and fifteen coaches who believed in me, thank you. In particular, I will be forever indebted to the late Ronnie Brooks for introducing me to NCFC. To Ken Brown for my first professional contract and Dave Stringer for being such a great mentor. Mike Walker, for your ultimate belief in me. Thank you Tim Sheppard for problem sharing, advising and for fixing my body on so many occasions. Alan Curbishley for your understanding, Jim Jeffries for taking a chance on me, and my old pal Bryan Gunn for the memories shared as teammates and opportunity after football.

Thank you to Wally and Shirley Tolliday for taking on this strange lodger some thirty years ago. Roger Harris for your friendship and for capturing so many great photographic memories. Keith Colman, Gill Perks and my testimonial committee of 1994.

To Julie Lythgoe, John Child and Max Marriner at the NNAB for giving me the chance to experience all those humbling and rewarding moments I have felt and lived with the charity.

Thank you to Justin Holmes, the Odeon regional manager for all the movie magic you have created for me and my family; to Gary Cook – thanks mate for all your support and advice, it's has always been much appreciated. Thanks to Rick Waghorn for all the Man of the Match press reports, the '9 out of 10s' and for voting me as Player of the Season a few times. My utmost respect and thanks go to Revd Albert Cadmore for all the love and belief you have given my family over so many. Thank you also to Mick Dennis for writing such a powerful foreword for this book.

I am especially grateful to my biographer, Edward Couzens-Lake, for agreeing to help write my story. You are a wonderful man and gifted author. Without your persuasion, encouragement and expertise, this meaningful book would never have been completed. I'm so proud of you for the personal battle you have won in your own life, and very beholden of our friendship.

Achieving something special together with your teammates and close friends makes the moment extra special and ten times more enjoyable. The camaraderie, the banter has been unforgettable. Mark Walton and Rob Newman. Thank you for your friendship and the hilariously funny times. You are genuine and inspirational people and have been magnificent mates during our time when we were young, fit and living a carefree life within professional sport. We certainly lived the dream together, I look forward to another 'release' in the future when we can, once again, pull up a few old memories of our glory days.

To the fans of NCFC, thank you for the atmosphere, your patience, the Gossy wigs and the prolonged support. Norfolk is my home, yellow and green will always be my colour. I tried my best for you all. It will always be your club. Enjoy its future success.

To the squad of 1993/94 – Gunn, Bowen, Butterworth, Polston, Newman, Culverhouse, Fox, Crook, Sutch, Robins, Sutton, Megson, Ekoku, Woodthorpe et al. – I salute you all and will always cherish the magnificence of our time.

To football, for the exhilarating euphoric rapture, the adrenalin rush and for the love, and at times, loathing of it all.

Maggie's parents, Rodney and Janet Scott, your continued support to our family has been remarkable and always so uplifting. Thank you.

To my parents, Joy and Bob, sisters Jen and Jane, and brothers Mike and Tim for the love, support and guidance you have always given me. Without our close bond and togetherness growing up I would never have progressed and achieved. You all have my deepest thanks, love and gratitude for enabling me to create memories I will treasure forever.

Finally, to my inspirational wife, Maggie. For always being by my side. You are the true reason for my sporting achievements. Thank you for the motivation and for your guidance, encouragement and loving support, but most of all for our incredible sons Jacob and Joseph, who will always remain such a constant source of pride and pleasure to me. Together forever.

I've always tried to be strong, determined and tenacious. I've always tried to be kind, humble and thankful, and I've always resented arrogance and sarcasm. I now really know a lot more about myself, and understand what really matters to me in life. I've done the very best I could. I only hope it was enough.